ON ANGELS AND DEVILS
AND STAGES BETWEEN

Choreography and Dance Studies
A series of books edited by Muriel Topaz and Robert P. Cohan, CBE

Please see the back of this book for other titles in the Choreography and Dance Studies series

ON ANGELS AND DEVILS AND STAGES BETWEEN

CONTEMPORARY LIVES IN CONTEMPORARY DANCE

David Wood

harwood academic publishers
Australia • Canada • China • France • Germany • India
Japan • Luxembourg • Malaysia • The Netherlands
Russia • Singapore • Switzerland

Amsteldijk 166
1st Floor
1079 LH Amsterdam
The Netherlands

British Library Cataloguing in Publication Data

Wood, David
    On angels and devils and stages between: contemporary
    lives in contemporary dance. – (Choreography and dance
    studies; vol. 19)
    1. Modern dance   2. Dancers   3. Dancers – Attitudes
    I. Title
    792.8'09045

    ISBN 90-5755-077-6

Cover illustration: David Wood as the Messenger of Death in Martha Graham's *Clytemnestra*. Photographer: Martha Swope. Wood Collection.

This book is dedicated to the three people who have most affected my life.

My parents, Earl W. Wood and Bliss Kennedy Wood.
They not only created my existence, but in combination they made the selection of dance as my profession almost inevitable. My father bestowed on me a great love for the athletic while my mother gave me an appreciation for the aesthetic.

My wife, Marni Thomas Wood.
For more than thirty years she has provided me with endless support and has enriched all my activities.

CONTENTS

INTRODUCTION TO THE SERIES

Choreography and Dance Studies is a book series of special interest to dancers, dance teachers and choreographers. Focusing on dance composition, its techniques and training, the series will also cover the relationship of choreography to other components of dance performance such as music, lighting and the training of dancers.

In addition, *Choreography and Dance Studies* will seek to publish new works and provide translations of works not previously published in English, as well as to publish reprints of currently unavailable books of outstanding value to the dance community.

Muriel Topaz
Robert P. Cohan

LIST OF PLATES

ACKNOWLEDGMENTS

The acknowledgments which I wish to make for this book exist in two parts. The first section relates to the people who have exerted a strong influence on my career and thus have become an indirect force in the creation of this writing. The second section relates to the people who have participated in the book's development in a more direct manner.

Besides my dance teachers, to whom I will always be extremely grateful and who are all mentioned somewhere within this volume, I am greatly indebted to my major acting teachers, Robert Rees who instructed me at Fresno High School in Fresno, California, and Fred and Mary Harris of the University of California, Berkeley. During my early years, all three helped to direct my footsteps in a straight line toward the theater. In addition Fred and Mary Harris gave me inspirational insight into the integrity of teaching.

My four Kennedy aunts, Edith, Florence, Agnes, and Anne fed my imagination as a child and helped me gain the awareness that within simplicity lies the greatest truth and the greatest beauty.

My aunt Hazel Wood Wright, whose home often provided a haven for me while I was attending the university at Berkeley, listened endlessly to my young troubles and discussed my changing needs when no one else seemed to be interested.

My sisters, Barbara Crockett and Phylis Anne Tidyman represented opposite poles of existence. Barbara was a constant example of a person who dared to attempt the fulfillment of her dreams. Phylis Anne epitomized a person who projected the values of security and love in a close familial relationship. Both of them had a tremendous effect on my adult growth.

My three daughters, Marina, Raegan, and Ellis, by their vitality and individual independence, made me retain, if not my actual youth, at least an easy understanding of it in its many manifestations.

Lastly, every student who has ever studied with me has contributed constantly to my learning process. They have, in truth, been both the angels and the devils of my career, but have always existed with an honesty of intent and an immediacy of the moment.

In a more direct context there are many people who have kindly listened to me read various sections of the book. Particularly they are my wife, Marni, who has been pressed into active duty on many occasions as have my children, Marina, Raegan, and Ellis. From the latter three I felt the need to gain approval on the accuracy of content of several parts of the book which concerned them. It seems that my daughters and I often saw the same events from an entirely different point of view.

Louise Guthman and Helen Nickerson gave me advice concerning the section on Louis Horst. Lois Schlossberg Karatz did the same on Martha Graham.

My sister, Barbara, and Doris Herring read and gave helpful criticism and encouragement on the first chapter, On Classes.

Doris Humphrey's son, Charles Woodford, provided me with an accurate reference concerning who had sculpted the bust of his mother, Doris Humphrey, even though no one can seem to locate it presently.

I would like to thank Mr. and Mrs. Robert Wickstrom for allowing me to include their son's poem in this book.

Carol Egan has given invaluable help in proofreading the copy for this book, correcting my unbelievable mistakes in spelling and punctuation.

Anne Geismar, and Ruth and John Solomon, have helped immensely in providing direction and encouragement.

Most of all I cannot strongly enough express my appreciation to Darleen Bell. She has transformed my badly hand-written manuscript into something which is intelligible. She also never complained about my constant rewriting, but made the changes clearly, perceptively and quietly.

My editor, Muriel Topaz, has worked with me most patiently. She has taught me endless amounts about writing by example.

PREFACE

This book has been written to help inform and elucidate. For those readers who are unfamiliar with the world of dance, it will hopefully provide an insight into a demanding but fascinating art form. For those who are already familiar with the field, it may help to clarify the working personalities of some fascinating and innovative dance artists.

I have not written the book to clear the air or to bare my soul. If at any time during my writing I might have felt vindictive, I would have definitely omitted that subject matter. Such an occasion never arose. To the contrary, my experience with the people included in this volume has been, at the very least, a highly positive one.

There were certainly unpleasant situations, personal difficulties, and emotional upheavals, but I have discovered that the passage of time softens all encounters and heals all wounds. Looking back on the traumas of past years, removed from the immediacy of the occasion, I often found that it was difficult to understand the severity of my previous feelings.

The major dance artists of 1950 through 1970 with whom I worked – Martha Graham, Doris Humphrey, Charles Weidman, José Limón, Hanya Holm, Alwin Nikolais, Helen Tamiris, William Bales, Jane Dudley, Sophie Maslow, and Louis Horst – are presented as individuals encompassing only those years in which I was personally in contact with them. I am not trying to portray these dancers in a total context or to make an overall comment on their lives, but I am trying to present a glimpse of their personalities and professionalism during the three decades of the 1950s, 1960s, and 1970s.

Those thirty years were an exciting period in their lives – and also in mine. Their art was constantly maturing. It was becoming assimilated into the world of dance as an integral part of the total concept. During this time American Contemporary Dance began its sweep through Europe and infiltrated the ethnic dance arts of Asia.

Merce Cunningham and Anna Sokolow are two important personages in modern dance who also came to the fore during these decades. I greatly regret that I did not have the opportunity of working with either of them. As a result they are almost completely missing in this work. By good fortune they became my friends. I was able during several summers when we were both teaching at the American Dance

Festival in Connecticut to take valuable classes with Merce. I taught in Mexico and Israel many times during the same period that Anna was working there, and so could benefit from my observation of this great artist teaching and rehearsing.

In Chapter 9 I have taken the liberty of using Paul Taylor's imaginary Dr. George Tacet. Having become aware of him through Paul, I could not resist the temptation.

In addition I would like to stress that, when the referred to gender is ambiguous, I have used the masculine reference by conscious choice. I find that overuse of the pronoun "one" weighs too heavily in the area of the nebulous, and that the double pronouns "he/she" and "his/her" are too cumbersome to handle. I could have alternated randomly between feminine and masculine but felt that might cause only greater confusion. Being male I elected to use my maleness, and the pronouns "he" and "him" became the words used for general personal reference. I hope readers will understand.

David Wood in Martha Graham's *Acrobats of God*. Photographer: Martha Swope. Photo credit: Wood Collection.

1

ON CLASSES

Every decade creates a unique quality which distinguishes that decade from those immediately surrounding it. In the early 30's life in the United States proceeded from moment to moment at a monotonous pace. Because of the long standing economic depression, few people were motivated to attempt change. Especially in the more rural areas of the country, in contrast to the cities, there was little energy for constructive activity.

The lack of financial means caused much of the population to stagnate. People remained caught, suspended in motion. The country existed stoically, each day an identical reenactment of the previous one. It seemed both inevitable and eternal.

The only discernible movement in the entire country took place on cattle cars, long freight trains which traveled across the country from one end to the other. Along with their authorized cargoes, they carried hordes of migrants, unemployed young men and a few women, struggling merely to keep food in their mouths. Unable to work in one area of the land, they moved on to others.

I remember as a boy standing by the railroad tracks in fascination, watching the endless number of trains go by. As they crossed my vision with monotonous repetition, the shape of each car was hardly perceptible because of the human bodies covering it.

Sometimes, when the cars came to rest in the freight yards, the riders would be scraped off by the local authorities because of the evident danger which riding the freight cars involved. Sometimes the migrants would challenge the authorities even further by secretly and more dangerously riding the rods hidden underneath the moving cars.

Hobo jungles grew up on the outskirts of towns. Here the migrants camped for the night or stopped for a short while to tempt good fortune in a new locale. They built fires to cook their food, or to stave off the cold. The wild stories of the happenings that took place in these jungles lent mystery and magic to their existence.

In 1932, as a seven year old, I could hardly wait to be old enough to join the brotherhood of the road. I absorbed the romance of wanderlust that shone in the reflection of the firelight on the gleaming faces of the jungle's inhabitants, and that was symbolized in the sparks from the fires that pierced the night atmosphere in absolute freedom.

Whether all of this had an effect in later years on my desire for seeing new places and experiencing new things, I don't know. I am sure that the romance and freedom, as well as the danger of the hobo jungles, steered my steps toward imaginative and romantic endeavors. This reaction, however has been tempered by a more conservative point of view, making me seek a consistent direction for the path of my life.

In New York by 1932 Ruth St. Denis and Ted Shawn had reached, and even passed, the peak of their performing powers. Long before the State Department tours of the 50's and 60's, Denishawn had toured Asia with great success. By 1932 Martha Graham had left Denishawn, left the Greenwich Village Follies, and left the Eastman School of Music in Rochester. At Eastman, at the bidding of Rueben Mamoulian, she had isolated herself for two years, making great progress in the long process of developing her unique movement style and her own unique dance company. By 1932 even Doris Humphrey and Charles Weidman, the bastions of the Denishawn school, had left the security of this major dance company. In the same year, Hanya Holm arrived in the United States, after many years of training with the great German and Swiss artists, Mary Wigman and Emile Jaques Dalcroze. In 1932 Helen Tamiris was advocating social reform through dance. She became involved in the government sponsored Works Project Administration, breaking the ground for racial equality with the presentation of her, at the time startling, *Negro Spirituals*.

The artistic world in the depression years was as active and alert as the rest of the country was passive. It was a time for change. While the rest of America, in lethargy and despair, clung to the status quo, artistic America was in foment. Harold Clurman called it the "fervent years" in his book written about the Group Theatre. It was a time when artists could afford to experiment. It was a time when being hungry was a fact of life, and the only way to direct one's energies positively was through a romantic or radical intention.

Costs were as minimal as salaries. Movies were only a dime. Busby Berkeley and the Gold diggers captured the fantasy of the country while Charlie Chaplin with his woebegone tramp captured its heart. The dime was the country's major medium of trade. One small thin silver coin not only provided the cost of a movie, but a quart of milk, a loaf of bread, a milk shake, a hamburger, a gallon of gas or an adventurous round trip on the streetcar to the center of town and back.

Fresno, California, where I was born, was not a large city. The entire trip from the center of town to the end of the streetcar line took no more than fifteen minutes. One of the few major stops on the streetcar line was the corner of Wishon and Floradora; St. Theresa Catholic church was on the northeast corner and directly opposite, Severance's Dancing School.

Fresno was not rural America, but its location in the center of the San Juaquin valley made agriculture, farmers, and farming the core of its existence. During the heat of the summer months swimming, sun bathing, and drinking lemonade were the major activities. For the rest of the year, people moved inside and resumed their regular routines. Neither the arts nor the sciences were the major focus in this small western town. The leisurely and conservative pace of life was primary.

Severance's Dance Studio was a large, somewhat rectangular, two storied building. It was usually painted gray or, more accurately, it was often painted gray. The one frivolous aspect of its existence was its constant change of color from year to year. The building completely occupied its grounds so that the landscaping around it was minimal, allowing it to stand solidly and securely on the property. The outer aspect did little to convey the magic which existed within its walls. It was one of only two major dance studios in the town of approximately 60,000. The other, Polito's Dancing School, specialized in "crass entertainment type activities" such as tap, acrobatics, and baton twirling, but Severance's remained aloof. It trained young aspirants in the fundamentals of classical dancing with a few wild Apache adagios thrown in for variety and spice. Polito's might be the pleasure palace of dance in Fresno, but those who were truly serious about becoming artists aligned themselves with Severance's and never waivered in their loyalty.

The Severance family lived in the downstairs portion of the building. It consisted of Mr. and Mrs. Severance, who to a young boy seemed aged beyond belief, and three daughters: Phylis, Jane, and Harriet. Harriet, the youngest of the three, taught a good many of the dance classes, while Phylis took care of the finances and any "disruptive juvenile delinquents."

The first floor included the living quarters, a reception room, and both women's and men's dressing rooms. Also, there was an atrium-like room in the front which provided a cool and welcome retreat during the hot summer days. A large stairway led directly out of the reception room and split to the right and left at a landing halfway toward the second floor. The second floor was one huge room with a bandstand located directly above the stairway. It was from there that Mrs. Sager accompanied the dance classes with the best of Tchaikovsky, Grieg, and sometimes, for a little life, an Irish jig. The bandstand was also large enough to hold a small ensemble of piano, sax and drums, which at special times played for the ballroom dance classes that were held on Friday and Saturday nights. These classes tried to teach the intricate steps of the fox trot, waltz, and even the Lambeth Walk to all desirous, teenage, social beings.

Because of the ballroom classes there were no barres along the sides of the large upstairs studio, but rather, long continuous benches were built against the walls. These were necessary as places of retreat for the "wallflowers" of the evening ballroom classes. They also accommodated mothers or little brothers, such as myself, who watched in awe their facile and graceful children or older sisters. At the opposite end of the room from the bandstand hung the only mirrors. The mirrors which because of their revealing nature, haunt every dance class. They are the mirrors which, when stared into objectively, discourage many an aspiring Pavlova because of the ruthless revelation found in reflection.

It probably discouraged my older sister, Phylis Anne, or perhaps she was discouraged by the complete physical effort that was demanded endlessly week after week. Whichever, she, in short order, renounced the life of a ballerina for more conventional youthful activities. When her place was taken by my second sister, Barbara, my mother and father soon realized that the die had been cast. Dance was to be a permanent part of the rest of our family life.

We had little extra money, certainly not enough for hiring baby sitters and so I was taken along to most of Barbara's dance classes. For all of my pent up energy, it was the only time that I could be kept quiet and my natural exuberance contained. I either sat in rapt attention, staring at the strange happenings or, surreptitiously, I would stand on the side and, without success, try to imitate the amazing antics of whatever class was in progress.

There was never any question of my becoming an actual participant instead of an audience. For one thing my parents' finances allowed only one child to take lessons of any kind. Even more important, a boy, and certainly a boy in that conservative city of Fresno, would never consider bringing the contempt of his friends down upon his back by enrolling in a dance class. I had already taken enough flack from my classmates at school for participating in a drama group. Much as I may have desired deep inside myself, I would not have tempted fate enough to test just how much ridicule I could withstand by being the lone male dancer in the Severance school.

But I watched. I watched with fascination. The portable barres were brought out for each class and the disciplined ritual of classical ballet began. What the exact structure of the classes was, I cannot remember, but I do remember the symmetry of movement and its lightness. The students seemed to float across the floor hardly touching it, all totally in balance except for a few miscreant souls who completely lacked an aptitude for this art form.

I remember the sweat that broke out on the brows of these lovely, young girls. I remember being surprised that women who were aesthetically involved behaved towards physical activity much the same as did the male ditch diggers who were working outside the studio. I remember repetition, endless and often boring repetition, in order to make a movement better or to make a pirouette possible.

Most of all I remember a sense of performance. Every movement seemed to have a unique quality. Now my new found interest in acting could find release in accord with my exuberant energies. Because of my fascination with this new discovery, I did not evaluate the worth of what I was seeing. I merely reacted with fervor, little knowing that those first classes at Severance's Dancing School might have a strong influence on my future life.

In time the classes at Severance's proved insufficient for both Barbara's training and my viewing. For a while dance totally left the area of my daily routine while I developed more acceptable masculine activities. My only connection with Severance's now was as a teenage ballroom enthusiast and even at that I fell more into the category as one of Phylis Severance's juvenile delinquents rather than as an accomplished student of the fox trot.

My sister Barbara was still in high school but had moved to San Francisco to find more challenging ballet classes. Fortunately, on my mother's side there were four essentially maiden aunts who also resided in San Francisco. They were all quite willing, if not anxious, to help with finances and to act as chaperons for their young niece. It was as close as those marvelous and generous ladies would ever come to satisfying their maternal instincts.

In San Francisco, Barbara's first teacher was Adolph Bolm, a Russian dancer/choreographer who had played a part in the latter days of the Diaghilev era and had worked closely with Michael Fokine. In 1938 he was replaced by Willam Christensen who, although originally from Salt Lake City, had recently been teaching in Portland, Oregon. The three Christensen brothers, Willam, Lew, and Harold had already made a name for themselves in the world of dance. All three eventually became associated with the San Francisco Ballet, but Willam was the brother who originally established and developed the company.

It wasn't until 1939, when Barbara had left the supervision of our aunts for her own apartment, that I picked up the thread of being a dance observer again. I spent part of my school vacation during the summer living with my sister in San Francisco. As a teenager I was given free rein to go where I wanted. Instead of indulging in the usual teenager's pursuits, I was to be found every day sitting in a class or a rehearsal at the San Francisco school. Barbara attended classes and rehearsals and I followed right along with her. Again I became fascinated, possibly even more so than I had been in Fresno. My future brother-in-law, Deane Crockett, tried to persuade me to don tights and try dance first hand as a participant rather than as an observer, but

I could not. It still remained for me a nonmasculine activity and I could not break through that prejudice much as I might have wished.

During many of the summers, Ballets Russes de Monte Carlo would come to San Francisco to perform at the Opera House. On these occasions they would rent the front studio from the San Francisco Ballet for their classes, extra rehearsals, or auditions. There was always a throng around the open door of their studio trying to watch the full fledged touring professionals at work. To my untrained eye the Ballet Russe dancers seemed of no greater ability than the developing San Francisco Ballet members, only more romantic in concept.

From all those watching, I would overhear constant critical analysis. This one had no elevation. That one's extensions were turned in. Others had poor pirouettes, obscure positions or bad port de bras. I realized that there was much more to dancing than I had discovered in my obviously rose-colored-glasses state. At that time I also began to learn that jealousy was a powerful factor in the dance world. It was only a little forewarning, but a necessary bit of information for later use.

The change in the approach to dancing from Fresno to San Francisco was phenomenal. What had been a recreational approach, an approach whose reason for existence had been nothing more than to give young girls a certain amount of grace, had now been altered to professional training and development of a professional dance company.

Willam Christensen had been followed to San Francisco by many of the dancers who had studied with him in Oregon. They were combined with the San Francisco dancers who were already in training on his arrival. To my young eyes, they were miracle workers in movement. I could not help but observe their tremendous improvement from one summer to the next. Their names and faces to this day remain etched in my memory: Janet Reed, Jacquelyn Martin, Zoya Leporsky, Ronald Chetwood, Zelda Nerina, Mattlyn Gavers, Norman Thompson, Ruthie Rickman, Onna White, and Harold Lang among others. They all created a world of glamour and magic for me.

This professional approach to class was much more demanding than what I had seen at Severance's. There was definitely an increased seriousness of intent. Also an element of desperation had appeared. At this young stage, it was still not greatly in evidence, but each individual seemed to begin the inevitable balancing of desire and reality. As time passed, if reality increased in proportion, desperation intensified.

Perception, itself, was greatly heightened both because of the demands of the teacher and because of the dancer's own demands, clarified by the image in the mirror. The mirror and the teacher each became focal points of the class. The contest for approval of the mirror lay in the evaluation of one's own image in reflection. The contest for approval of the teacher was much more complex as it lay not only in the abstracted image, but also in so many interwoven personal factors. The ego-self and the teacher both were ruthless. To perceive what the teacher wanted and to respond in kind, creating an ideal reflected image could satisfy both, teacher and self. This was the criterion of success and success was indeed the end result for which everyone strove.

By watching the San Francisco Ballet not only had my technical knowledge increased on an academic level, but I began to become consciously aware of the intricacies which lay underneath the surface of dance. In a masochistic way, rather than deterring my interest, it whetted my appetite for further knowledge, and perhaps even eventually some physical involvement.

In the ensuing years, along with my interest in drama, dance lurked somewhere in the back of my consciousness while college, the navy, World War II, and travel took the focus of my attention. In 1946, back at college, in graduate school, I became involved in acting once again; I decided to give theater a serious try at the end of the school year. I finished my school work in June 1947, and with trepidation headed east to New York.

The Neighborhood Playhouse School of Theater provided a secure introduction to the big city. Friends and associates became easy to acquire. The monumental task of finding my way through the theater world of this enormous metropolis was deferred for a time by my attendance at the Playhouse.

Besides this rationale for entering the drama school, one of its more exciting aspects was the requirement of taking almost daily dance classes. The classes were included as an integral part of the curriculum. It stated in all of my preparatory brochures that unless a doctor's excuse was provided acknowledging irreparable physical disability, one was required to attend all dance classes. Obviously, from this warning, there had been problems in the past; this should have forewarned me that there were probably going to be problems in the future.

On the second day of classes our motley crew of students assembled to be viewed by Martha Graham and her assistant Marjorie Mazia. Although in 1947 Martha Graham did not have her reputation fully established, she was well known to all of us both as a powerful theatrical personality and as a figure of fear. The second year students described her as such in great length, as they, had already been lashed by her abusive tongue.

Unfortunately the Neighborhood Playhouse had not yet moved into its newly renovated building on 54th Street. Instead we were having to put up with rather cramped studios in the old building until the reconstruction work could be completed. It didn't help that half of our class was made up of rather large muscular ex "G.I.s" who occupied more than their fair share of the available space. As veterans of World War II, we were provided with education by the government – even in theater. Many G.I.s were taking advantage of the opportunity to test their thespian prowess.

Our first glimpse of Martha and Majorie was enough to put the fear of God into all of us for the rest of the year. They opened the door to the studio and these two small women stepped into the chaos of the room. Books were flying as well as people and the screaming, I am sure, could have been heard as far as Staten Island. Few students noticed the teachers entrance and those who did paid no attention.

Martha let out a blood curdling scream, stated something about never seeing us again, turned on her heel and marched out. Margery, who was much more docile, allowed a smile to show at the corners of her mouth which seemed to indicate that there still might be hope for another day. I was crushed. The failure of my first dance class I took as a personal defeat.

Marjorie was correct. Two days later Martha returned to a subdued student body and classes began. The first sessions with Martha were exciting. We were to discover that she taught two days a week. Margery who was a bright, warm, and most charming woman, demonstrated for her and then taught the class one day on her own.

It was not unusual throughout the year for Martha to repeat many times the reactions that she had to our first class: to open the door, walk into the classroom, take one look at our chaotic state, turn around, and storm out. Some weeks we were so unruly that we missed her classes entirely.

Her reaction toward us may have been intensified by the frustration of her being Miss Hush for the March of Dimes campaign. Miss Hush was the mysterious woman who spoke weekly on the radio giving hints of her identity, hoping to be discovered by someone anywhere in the country who could solve the riddle about herself which she recited secretly over the air waves. It took months for Martha's identification to take place and with each week of failure, her anger seemed to be rapidly intensified. Each week when no one guessed correctly who Martha was, the riddle was further extended.

During this time, in one class which was held at her 66 Fifth Avenue studio just before we moved into the new 54th Street school, she became so enraged that she made us all gather in one corner. Martha then placed a chair in the center of the room. She directed us to walk to the chair, sit in the chair, stand and walk off. It seemed a simple enough task. She finished by stating "and by the time you walk off, I will know everything about your sex life". The parade began. I don't remember Martha's reaction, but I watched the action with great humor. Some of our young debutantes nearly fainted on the way to the "revealing chair" while others performed with the purposeful wantonness of loose women of the night. Even some of our muscular G.I.s had trouble keeping their equilibrium as they marched to the chair and from it. It was obvious that this small, dark haired, vibrant woman could cause havoc at will. There seemed to be a mystic, hypnotic power about her.

At the beginning, Martha, giving way to the G.I.s who had no knowledge of dance and were obviously rebelling against it, dealt with us on more dramatic terms. I remember hanging from the ballet barre and reciting Shakespeare or reciting well known plays while doing deep pliés or some other physically demanding activity. From time to time Martha would return to the more formalized training, especially after we moved into the beautiful, large, third floor studio in the new school. Even then she often gave up the technical approaches to the class as she could not stand to see our total inadequacies when we attempted the more formalized task. She would always fall back on her inspiration of the moment to fulfill the class. Her imagery was constantly inspiring and powerful, and her ideas for movement were ever challenging. It was this method of working that benefited actors at the Playhouse year after year. Marjorie, could deal with us better when teaching the technical classes. Plies, relévés, brushes, and jumps were her forte. Prances were her specialty. It was with Marjorie that I learned my first dance "steps" and felt the first excitement of technical accomplishment.

At the end of my second year at the Playhouse when I decided to become a serious dancer, Marjorie recommended that I not go to Martha's school as I was too short. "Martha", she said," likes tall men so your chances of ever working with her would be slim." It would be better if I associated myself with another teacher/choreographer. I followed the advice. My only knowledge of movement up to that time was as a ballet viewer combined with the smattering of Martha's technique that I had gained at the Playhouse. For me, Martha's technique had proved too strange and removed from my understanding of dance. As a person, she was too overpowering. I recognized her greatness, but it was not for me.

It took almost four years before I was to feel mature and experienced enough to return to the Graham training. In the interim I had studied and danced with many different teachers and choreographers. My opinions and prejudices had been changed greatly by my experiences.

One summer while I was dancing with the Dudley-Maslow-Bales Trio at the American Dance Festival at New London, Connecticut, Martha taught the first week of classes. On a dare I attended them. I found Martha's classes now to be totally compelling. When I returned to New York at the end of the summer session of '52, I headed for the 63rd Street

Graham studio, enrolled in the beginning class and did not leave that studio for sixteen years. After sixteen years, I left still feeling challenged, still feeling that I had never quite accomplished either the technique or the style as it should be danced, or as Martha wanted it to be danced.

Martha's method of training the body for dance is very definitely a technique. One trained within its structure, learning a way of developing and working the musculature of the torso, legs and arms which is easily translatable to other dance forms.

Technique in opposition to style deals closely with universal principles of movement. These principles are used by dancers the world over and, once learned, can be applied to most methodology. A style is the particularized way of moving devised by one person or group of people in order to express his or her indigenous qualities. Still, there can be no clear cut division between the two. There is no such thing as pure technique, for as long as a human being is devising a method or even a technique class, no matter how uncluttered he tries to keep it, his personality necessarily places a certain individual style upon it. Conversely, a style is accomplished only via a specified technique. Style is highly specialized and usually emphasizes only one area of the body; however, a certain technique is still necessary in order to acquire any facility.

Martha, as an individual and as a dancer, had a unique way of moving and so her method of movement became highly stylized. The style became layered on top of the technique, but never lessened it. This became even more evident in the later years as the third dimension of the spiral of the back was added to the more two dimensional style with which she began her work.

In her original search, she purposefully countered the *danse d'école* in order to start fresh, unhampered by preconceived notions. She returned to the more primitive shapes and movement structures. From this basis she began a slow development through the years, constantly enriching and enlarging upon her method until it stands today as a fully integrated way of developing the human body for dance.

Certain detractors of Martha's work have said that hers is not a method which deals constructively with a man's body. Martha being a woman, it was said, had only developed the technique on her own body not taking into account the tighter pelvic area of the male. A counter argument to this rather reverse sexist statement is that, in the early historical development of technique, the dance forms which led to the creation of classical ballet were devised by male teachers for females. This, definitely did not limit the capabilities of the women with whom they worked. The problem is not solved by female teachers teaching only females, and male teachers teaching only males, because they have only an understanding of their own structures. Rather, the necessity, is for a teacher to be able to see beyond his own body and to bring his theories of body movement into a more universalized world. Martha was obviously intelligent enough to be one of those teachers who could transcend the boundaries of her own physical structure. When creating her unique technique, she allowed it to move in a direction which equally developed both the male and the female physique.

Being a woman, much of Martha's imagery was logically feminine; however I am sure that such a phrase as "Breathe from your vagina", was used in order to shock rather than instruct. The source of energy flow in the human body has long been sought by investigative teachers. Isadora Duncan felt the source was the solar plexus. Martha, despite her Jungian training, seemed to relate to the more Freudian hypothesis and place the source in the genitals. This, I think, had more to do with her predisposition, curiosity, and awe of sex and sexually related matters than any fundamental philosophy of movement.

Martha's investigation of movement was intuitive rather than analytical. The analysis of the principles was left to the teachers of the technique. She, herself, had an innate sense of what worked and what did not, what was constructive and what destructive, but the process of analyzing movement bored her. Her emphasis in teaching was on immediacy, the heightened awareness of "now" as the primary factor of performance. Performance was what all technique was about. Except for the bounces at the beginning of the class, everything within her method had been performed in some dance or had the possibility of being performed. The technique usually existed first in the dances and then was brought back into the classroom. Once the movement was made a part of the class, Martha would examine its validity for developing the body, not by scientific analysis but by instinct. If it worked, it was made a part of the technique. If it did not, Martha rejected it without qualm.

Martha developed a deeply probing, human technique. There are things lacking within it, but in dance, because of the vast area which it encompasses, it would be impossible for one form, any form, to be complete in every element. There is a logic about the technique. Its developmental process is clear and clean: floor work, to standing center work, to locomotion. Martha loved the floor work and felt that it was as vital an area for dance expression as any other. The floor work in the more advanced classes at times is taught almost by rote. The teacher can walk into the room, say, "and", and the exercises will begin and continue without stop for the next half hour.

Extensions are demanded but were seldom developed or improved by practice. It was always a mystery to me as to how they were to be acquired. Turns, except for triplet turns, and isolations are nonexistent. A very good aspect of the technique is the lack of codified phases of movement; there are a few but they are minimal. This leaves room for creativity on the part of the teachers and variety for the students. The falls, always at the end, finish the class with a feeling of affirmation.

In teaching, Martha was an extremist. To correct something that was in error, she would emphasize the opposite. The technique was thus always changing, and never lost its sense of freshness and spontaneity as long as she was directly involved with it. Things were always being added or dropped. It was difficult to keep up with the latest changes. Besides Martha, every teacher had his own version, and although the principles remained basically the same, the students were hard pressed to keep up with what Helen wanted, let alone what Bert, Bob, or Ethel wanted in terms of style.

Martha's teaching was polarized in both inspiration and violence. Her imagery was powerful. It was not that every movement had a meaning, but rather that the person who was dancing gave the movement meaning. In clearer terms the dancers gave the movement truth from their own, unique point of view. In the forcefulness of her speech, in her belief in the power of "I have to; therefore, I can", I have seen Martha inspire students to reach heights that had never previously seemed obtainable.

I have also seen her use violence in her frustration while trying to make an unwilling or placid body react correctly to the shape of the movement. I have seen her scratch until blood rose to the surface. I have seen her strike until welts stood out on the skin. I have seen her in class slap a girl across the face, for what reason no one ever knew, least of all the girl. One trembled before the whip of Martha's tongue and the whip of her hand when she was angry.

Martha's hypnotic presence dominated the classes, flooding them with fascination, but etched in fear. She was greatly inspiring as images poured from her mouth in her full, deep-throated, chocolate voice. Proof of her genius lies in the product she created which has lasted long after her personal teaching ended. Her technique has now moved into the mainstream of dance and will remain there both as an entity unto itself and as an influence on all the rest of the art form.

In 1949, I left the Neighborhood Playhouse late in my second year of work in order to study dance intensively. My involvement with the dancing which was taught at the Playhouse had only increased my curiosity about it. Dance seemed to satisfy both the dramatic and physical aspects of theater which I found so attractive. I used the last of my G.I. Bill and shifted to the Theatre Wing, a school that worked as an umbrella under which I could take an array of dance classes.

At twenty-four years of age I wanted only what I considered to be the best training available. Because the dancer's life is so short. I felt I must not waste any time. I spent two weeks watching every dance class in New York, and then decided on three.

   1. José Limón. José Limon, teacher. José had taught a few classes at the Neighborhood Playhouse. His powerful expansive movement seemed to fit well on my body. He appeared interested in my potential in dance, which always is appealing to a student. I knew him personally slightly through my former roommates Peace and Carmen Alvarez.
   2. Ballet Arts. Dorothy Etheridge, teacher. The concept of ballet was still very difficult for me. As a male I still could not break through my original prejudices, but secretly I appreciated its technical values and the demands that it made of endurance and strength. Dorothy Etheridge was a delightful teacher: positive, clear in presentation, and to the point in correction. Ballet Arts School was attractively situated in Carnegie Hall Studios which appealed to my sense of history.
   3. Hanya Holm. Hanya Holm, Oliver Kostok, Alwin Nikolais, teachers. The class that I observed in Holm technique was taught by Alwin Nikolais. I was totally lacking in any knowledge or association with this technique, but by the end of the class I found myself unconsciously standing up on the viewer's bench, clapping wildly in rhythm with Nik's drumming while the dancers turned furiously in locomotion across the floor. I knew with certainty that here was to be the main focus of my training in dance, even though Nik must have had great misgivings about this strange creature becoming a member of his class.

Hanya Holm technique seemed to embody all of the elements which first attracted me to dance: physicality, dynamics, rhythm, drama, focused technique and freedom of movement. Hanya's classes were jammed. During that period she was creating the choreography for Broadway musicals. By the time that I arrived on the scene she had already choreographed *Ballet Ballads* and *Kiss Me Kate*. Now, through the Theater Wing and individually, dancers flocked to her classes, hoping to be seen or discovered so that at Hanya's next audition they would be recognized and thus make it past the first cut. This atmosphere must have been completely different from that which she had created with her original school and company, established shortly after her arrival in the United States. For this German immigrant who had literally fought her way into prominence, the new found popularity and acceptance must have been a great pleasure.

During the period in which I studied with her, Hanya taught each of her classes once a week, except for a special class which she taught three times a week. The latter, which I was not qualified to take because of my technical level, consisted mainly of twelve to fifteen Broadway show dancers of some name or note. They, along with well known ballet dancers who were trying modern dance for a first time, came to the classes to be seen and evaluated. Even the intermediate level which I was taking, every day was exciting for one never knew what dancers of prominence would be in class, Dancers poured in and out, often coming late and leaving early, trying to fit into one day all of their theatrical training.

Hanya had a clever mind. She followed the class format established by Mary Wigman but continued its development much further in her own manner, influenced by her new American environment. The class development from floor, standing, and locomotion, as in the Graham technique, seemed logical. The pedagogical structure of her three year program for the development of a dancer was excellently conceived; first year, centered work; second year, off center work; third year, Laban swings and complex phrase structures. In each year emphasis was placed equally on alignment, coordination, strength, and rhythm. The use of one major theme in a class proved useful in developing material sequentially, but as a principle could easily be overdone, thus failing to incorporate every required element of the daily training of a dancer.

The floor section of class was based on Pilates' exercises without the use of his well devised machines. Hanya kept herself fit by working out at the Pilates' studio several times a week. I accompanied her once to her workout and she approached it almost as a religious ritual. Even without the actual machines, the exercises were valuable in building strength and flexibility. My only objection to them was that, unlike the Graham floor work which had all the elements of performance, the Holm exercises were gymnastically oriented.

Of the main progenitors of modern dance, Hanya was the one to be known for her development of teaching methods and as a teacher per se. With her success in the musical comedy field, however, she began to lose interest in her teaching abilities. After so many years of struggle, it was understandable, but it did prove difficult for her students and the reputation of her school.

The best classes that I ever took from Hanya were at Colorado College in Colorado Springs in the summer session of 1949. Divorced from the pressures of New York and influenced by the open spaces and the clean air of Colorado, Hanya seemed to be much more pedagogically inspired. Her classes had a freshness and zest which were lacking when she taught in New York. I have fond memories of following this woman who, now seeming young for her age, danced energetically across the floor from one side of the room to the other. After our usual warm ups, bodies flew in locomotion. No words were spoken the entire time. She led and we, the students, along with the pianist, followed with intense perception: vibrations, double, single, double, single, turns with endless variations, bounding elevations, and isolations. I have a feeling that at those moments, Hanya was at her happiest. She was instinctively comfortable creating movement in this manner. It was something that all her intelligence and analytical abilities could never give her.

For all of her fame as a teacher, during this period of her career, Hanya's New York classes became repetitious and uninteresting. Certain essential developmental movements were always omitted and one could sense her lack of enthusiasm and involvement. What had once been her primary function in dance now took secondary importance to her choreographic acclaim. The classes of Alwin Nikolais, her main teacher, were much more constructive and informative.

Nik taught not only at Hanya's studio but in the Fall '48, at the Henry Street Settlement House in the lower east side of Manhattan. As Hanya was noted for her teaching, she was often invited to lend her expertise to many different schools. During this time as she did not want to increase her teaching load, she would accept these positions in title only and then send one of her instructors to actually do the teaching. That was how Nik began his classes at Henry Street.

When I returned from the summer in Colorado where Nik taught classes along with Hanya, I felt his classes to be of particular value for my dance training, I took advantage of his teaching at both Hanya's and Henry Street by studying from him in both. Nik taught a very exciting and physically demanding class. His classes at the Henry Street Settlement House were even more inspired than those he taught for Hanya. Wherever he was, he always taught with full concentration and energy. At that point of my career, I could not have found a more inspirational teacher. Nik constantly presented challenging material and always in relation to the level of the students with whom he was working. It was almost impossible to become discouraged in his classes as his presentation was so upbeat and positive. One constantly worked surrounded by a feeling of affirmation.

Nik's other talents played an important part in the context of his classes. His gift as a visual artist led to the creation of highly sculptural shapes in well structured phrases. The linear flow of movement was always pleasing. His training as a musician lent exciting rhythmic variation and syncopation. Nik always accompanied his own classes on the drum or piano. He was excellent at both and this ability usually helped build the class to a smashing climax, with dancers whirling across the floor for a finale.

The ending of classes seems in general to fall into two categories. One theory is that the technical difficulty and energy level of the class builds throughout so that by the termination of the class, the dancers are left exhausted, sweaty, but inspired. The second theory which is more in tune with present day ideas of "warming down" the body, treats the class as a cyclical event, bringing the energies of the students back to their beginning predisposition. Nik's classes were very much of the former variety so, as a rule, students left his class exhilarated, exhausted, and wanting more. Sometimes, but not always, one felt that the end of Nik's classes were stimulated artificially for the sake of exhilaration alone. Movements whose basic physical rhythms were meant for a slow pace were sped up beyond what was physically possible. Excitement in such cases became an end in itself.

The structure of his classes followed exactly that of Hanya's, but his movement was much more immediate and demanding. The stretches, as with Hanya, were placed at the beginning of the class before the body was totally warmed rather than at the end. Sometimes he became a little ruthless in the demands that he placed on an individual's body during the floor work, the premise becoming one of forcing rather than stretching.

I also never really believed in his "pure movement" theories. In his attempt at achieving unadorned movement, he arrived at a very personalized, stylized manner of moving. Gladys Bailin and Murray Louis were the major proponents of his work and philosophy. Stylized or not, they were beautiful dancers. I still use his "canned fruit cocktail" image which he applied to all dancers whose movements had a uniform sameness of quality.

When I started to dance, turning was an impossibility for me. A certain part of every Holm class was devoted to turns. This was fortunate as otherwise I never would have gained any facility. I was so incapable that my flailing arms and body were a danger to every other dancer in class. I would bang off one wall and rebound full force to the other, hurtling on strange tangents while attempting to get across the floor. Finally, in self-conscious desperation, I would stop and walk stealthily the rest of the way to the other side of the room, hoping to appear invisible. "No one ever learned to dance by giving up and walking off. Never stop trying." These prophetic words from Nik applied not only to dance but the rest of my life as well. I have thought of his words often and will always be grateful to him for his training and advice.

Dance Players was situated uptown on 56th Street between 6th and 7th Avenues. It was a building where many dancers and choreographers rented studios in which they could work when they chose rather than undertaking the huge task of developing their own rehearsal studios. The rooms of Dance Players were small, dirty, and crowded, but cheap. In 1949 José Limón chose to work out of these studios. José's life was so full of dancing, choreography, and teaching that he had no time to develop any business instincts that might lie dormant somewhere in his subconscious.

José's forte was not teaching. At that period it was only a means of earning a living. In the capacity of a teacher, he traveled to Boston, Westchester, Connecticut, and any other place that would pay him well enough. All this was combined with his own classes in New York. His schedule was breathtaking; only Jose with his amazing energy and drive could have successfully encompassed this.

He, like Martha, spoke well and could inspire a class with ease, but José's classes were erratic. They followed no line, or form, or build. The movement itself was very bold and broad, strong, drawn with large strokes, masculine. When I first studied with Jose I did not know much about what he taught. It was just as well as I was not yet sufficiently knowledgeable to evaluate his classes. I just knew that I liked the movement and I liked him.

Outside of class, José seemed a caring and focused human being. In class, he was a different person, still gentle, and affable, but unfocused, diffuse, with a wandering mind. Often in the middle of a correction or in giving a phrase of movement, José would totally lose track and had to ask Pauline (Pauline Lawrence, his wife, who was accompanying him at the piano) what he had intended to say. She then, a bit acidly, would help him bring his attention back to the subject.

The plan of the class had no flow; it bounced from one subject to the next. It was really a matter of whatever came to José's mind at the moment. Body bends would almost always begin the class, but from then on it was purely chance whether or not the body would be completely dealt with, during any one class. Pliés, floor work, jumps, locomotor movements, extensions in center, falls, all were presented at random.

One time at the American Dance Festival at Connecticut College, I was again taking some of José's classes while teaching the Graham course. Betty Jones was assisting him. Betty and I were talking while waiting for José to arrive. She said in conversation, "I must speak to José before he starts class and make sure he doesn't begin again with the hopping in attitude on forced arch." When he arrived Betty did speak to him. "Yes, yes my dear, Yes, yes. I won't use it", he answered. In a few minutes he gathered the class around to begin and started by hopping in attitude on forced arch.

Probably he totally forgot what Betty had just said, never giving it another thought. His mind was on his own dancing and choreography for the up coming festival performances and not on teaching.

Betty Jones and a few others have worked valiantly to make a viable technique out of José's style of moving and they have succeeded. Usually the Limón class is taught with a ballet or individually devised warm up. The movements or movement qualities which are so powerful and so beautiful are presented in the later part of the class.

José Limón's two main teachers, in fact his whole background in dance, except for a few ballet classes, were Charles Weidman and Doris Humphrey. His movement style and quality certainly showed their influence, but he had directed his movements into even more expansive, extroverted channels. The only one of his two mentors with whom I studied technique was Charles Weidman. Maybe if I had followed the logical progression from Charles to José rather than of José to Charles, I would have had a better understanding of his method. One always benefits from having a knowledge of the roots of whatever method one is studying.

When my G.I. Bill ran out, I had to cut back on my classes for financial reasons and with my withdrawal from Hanya's at the end of my first year of dance training, I needed to find new directions. Charles Weidman still taught technique class, but now by himself, at the old Humphrey-Weidman, 16th Street studio theater. Knowing that he was choreographing for the New York City opera, I decided that this would be an opportune moment in which to learn his particular style of moving.

Charles was an unusually pleasant man with an exceptional sense of humor, and he presented his classes in an enjoyable and positive manner. At times, however, he could become irrationally angry. This mainly occurred when he was challenged by a student or he found himself in an uncomfortable situation trying to explain an individual movement or phrase of movements. Charles was not good at confrontations and rather than solving the situation, he often became petulant and his stuttering, which was always evident to a degree, increased. At such times people were best advised to stay clear of his emotional turmoil.

Charles' classes always started with the same body bounces. Usually the instruction then progressed with a warm up of legs and feet through pliés and brushes. At times some movements were given without the body being prepared carefully enough for the anticipated activities. Charles did not always follow form. At the beginning of one class that I took, without any preparation, Charles gave the movement series which was based on a parallel first position drop into low plié, thrust into back bend with pelvis pushed forward, followed by the unrolling of the vertebrae back to a vertical stance. It was an exciting and enjoyable exercise and I threw my body into it with full force as it progressed through its variations at a faster and faster pace. The next day I was unable to move and was laid up for a week with my first experience of agonizing back pain.

The warm ups which Charles taught were set into patterns that he could refer to by name. They were numerous and could be varied in arrangement in order to allow for variety. These warm ups were followed by other set movement or "dancing" patterns which consisted of set phrases from previously choreographed dances. The phrases were taught and corrected in relation to shape, time, dynamics, and quality. Once the phrases were learned along with their names, they were repeated and worked on for excellence. These movements were never approached as underlying physical movements of dance which could be transferred from Charles' class to another form of dance. They thus dealt more with the individual Weidman style rather than a universalized technique. Beatrice Seckler, a former Humphrey-Weidman dancer, described the technique as "increasing" as you accomplished another movement, because this, then, in turn, extended one's total movement vocabulary."

Eventually, with repetition, monotony set into the Weidman classes, resulting in lack of interest and concentration. The same movements may only be repeated a nominal amount of times, following which the repetition dulls rather than enhances the learning process.

The Weidman classes were exciting as long as the movements remained fresh. Once I had learned the phrases and had achieved a certain capability, the urge to move ahead to more challenging material predominated: however, I have an enduring physical memory of Charles' love for dance and his easy and humorous approach.

In their classes during the fifties, the modernists prided themselves on the specific analysis of movement and its direct application to each individual student. This could have slowed classes to a snail's pace because of the time taken for explanation, but corrections were often made during the exercises as well as after them, speeding up the process.

The opposite extreme to this teaching approach is to be found in some classical indigenous forms of dance; Balinese dance is a clear example. This style is taught hands on. The feet and the hands of the master teacher carefully guide the limbs of the young students via direct contact, helping to establish an immediate kinesthetic correctness. I have seen this method also used by Noh masters in their teaching.

At the beginning of the Twentieth Century, ballet fell somewhere between these two theories. It was usually taught by the teacher presenting material either orally or visually and then, the student transferring that material into action. In all three methods, the ability to duplicate the movements presented by the instructor was the prime requisite for progress.

I once asked a ballet teacher as to why she did not give more explanations and corrections. She answered that she felt that there were always too many people attempting to dance and with this method of teaching ballet, the untalented eliminated themselves in short order while the talented became stronger because of being forced to rely on their own resources. I'm not sure whether this was sheer laziness on her part or the words of a wise woman.

Recently ballet and modern dance classes have reversed roles. Modern classes have become those of actuation without explanation. Movement is fed to the student at a rapid pace and the students are presented with phrases of movement of considerable length. Ballet now teaches the breakdown and analysis of movement, and gives individual correction. With this change, worthwhile modern dance classes are difficult to find. Instead, modern dancers have discovered, and are now flooding, the newly analytical ballet studios.

I never felt really comfortable in a ballet class. My impressions and prejudices, formed many years previously, remained with me always. I attended ballet performances avidly and was equally impressed by the technical prowess and movement fluidity of the dancers. I fully realized all the benefits derived from a well taught ballet class: increased turn out, heightened and better placed extensions, flowing arms, increased elevation, softened pliés and well honed feet.

Feeling one should experience all things at least once, I even found a female student who generously allowed me to don her toe shoes for a trial run. At that time some men used toe shoes in class regularly, trying to turn their club-like feet into much more expressive instruments. Lifting through the body and legs, the rise onto point seemed simple enough. It was the descent that was frightening. On every attempt, I crashed with an enormous thud which sounded as if either my ankles or the floor had to give way.

I tried every ballet teacher in Manhattan: Dorothy Etheridge, I mentioned earlier; Antony Tudor and Margaret Craske, at the old Met, each a marvelous contrast to the other; Benjamin Harkarvy and Karel Shook, the eternal rivals whether at home or abroad; Aubrey Hitchens, the modern dancers favorite, who looked so bad demonstrating for his classes that every modern dancer felt talented in ballet by comparison; Madame Anderson with her cats and watering can, both of which endangered life and limb. All were equally eccentric and fascinating. My favorites were actually at the School of American Ballet. The Russians were superlative. Mr. Vladimiroff, who never stopped bowing as he entered the classroom; Madame Tumkovsky, with an all seeing eye; Mr. Oboukhoff, the king of all teachers, who could never understand what I was doing in his class; Madame Doubrovska, the only teacher that I ever made cry.

In one grand plié combination at the bar, Madame Doubrovska stood directly behind me and every time that I descended, in what I thought to be a near perfect grand plié, she uttered in a painful, suffering, Russian accented voice, "Puulie". With each plié the sound of her voice became more pained and more Russian accented. When we had completed the first side, I looked at Madame Doubrovska for a little more explanation as to the great pain that I was causing her, but I was rebuked only with a hurt look and tears trickling down her cheeks. No words. No explanations. We turned and started the second side and with my first grand plié, the words cut painfully through the air again, "Puulie". There was never a further word of explanation from Madame Doubrovska.

At the School of American Ballet, the classes were filled with young teenage girls in training for the New York City Ballet Company and a few of us modern dancers who were complete misfits. With the attention of the class being on the budding ballerinas, we modernists were allowed greater ease in participation and openness of observation.

The Russian teachers often seemed fond of belittling their students and on the least occasion would begin a tirade that sometimes consumed most of the class. Tears became a regular ritual along with the barre work, petite batterie, pirouettes, and révérence. No one ever left the room in their tearful state, but rather cried isolated in the corner (the shy type) or while dancing (the more determined type). No matter how intense the tirade became, sometimes almost to the point of violence, one accepted and lived through it. In a strange way, one anticipated it; in a masochistic manner one somewhat enjoyed it.

The Russian teachers had a special aura. There was something indescribably commanding about them and their classes. They were performers. They had already accomplished the deed of dancing and had reveled in the glory, to which the rest of us could only aspire. They all performed their classes which could have distracted from the structure of the class itself, but, instead, inspired the students, both technically and qualitatively. One did not just take their classes; one was required to perform them.

The tirades were accepted because one always felt they came out of the instructors feeling of care and love. There was an honest concern for the student's progress and development, and love for the art of ballet. It was deeply and passionately felt so that when we, students, destroyed and mutilated their much loved world, it almost became a personal affront. Even the younger students felt the emotions and reacted to them instinctively. The Russian teachers overflowed with their feelings toward dance, and the students, with acceptance, reacted in kind. The two combined together to produce some of the most beautiful and productive ballet classes that I have ever experienced.

The structure of the ballet class provided the modern dancers with a clear form and reaffirmation for both their bodies and psyches, which they usually did not receive from a modern dance class. Once a modern dancer achieved a level of freedom and total body coordination in modern dance classes, he used the daily ballet class to bring himself back into his center. Also, for the most advanced modern dancers, ballet classes provided a new challenge. The human being, at least in the Western hemisphere, is essentially an achiever and seldom accepts the status quo for long. Challenge is a hunger that in most must be fed. When one starts the study of ballet past the age of twenty, one is assured of being challenged. As a result, the tide of dancers flowed with a much stronger current from modern dance to ballet, than ballet to modern dance.

There obviously are as many ways of approaching the presentation of a technique class as there are people involved in their teaching. The first modern dance classes were exploratory. They were attempts to find new ways of training the human body which would shape the dancer into a physically expressive entity.

The strong belief which each of these teacher/innovators had in his theories and methods made it easy for him to transmit his ideas to others and thus to gather together a cohesive group of followers with whom each could experiment.

These instructors were the master teachers and they created the master classes of their time.

2
ON DANCE SPACES

The physical surroundings that are required when creating or training in any art form is usually more related to the personal needs of the individual artists than to the art form itself. Nevertheless, generally, writers often want a serene atmosphere; painters want special light; musicians want rooms with pleasing acoustics; actors want an open uncluttered space. In contrast, dancers have explicit requirements which must be fulfilled for successful completion of their tasks. Sufficient space, ventilation, and proper flooring are all absolutes. Correct lighting and temperature are highly desirable.

Despite all of these specifics, most dance studios are created from make-do situations. Even in newly constructed art centers, very little thought is given to the organic needs for a space which meets the requirements for dance training and creativity. The Academy for The Performing Arts in Hong Kong is one definite exception to this. It is a beautifully conceived structure that provides both quality studios and quality theaters for dance. The surroundings in which one works can be extremely affective, coloring most everything which takes place within. Our senses respond immediately to our environment and our emotions respond directly to our senses. To obtain the major benefit for the greatest number of people, the environment needs to be given careful thought and consideration.

One of the favorite studios in my memory was far from ideal in size, but it had a delightful ambiance. I was at the beginning of my dance career having just left the Neighborhood Playhouse. Nina Fonaroff, who assisted Louis Horst with the composition classes at the Playhouse, was desperate for one more male dancer for her new choreography, *Masque*. She asked me if I would be interested. It didn't matter that the rehearsals were held all day Sunday; I was definitely interested. The Sunday meetings were necessary as the only affordable studio available for Nina's rehearsals, was that of a friend who allowed Nina to use her space during the weekend at a very reasonable rate.

The studio had originally been intended as the living room of what would have been a spacious bohemian apartment. As a living room, the area was truly large, but it was of minimal size for a rehearsal studio. Of necessity Nina's dance became intimate in quality and confined in movement.

Small or not, it was a joy to work there. The room was kept immaculately clean, which in New York was a treat, and it had a most magnificent skylight. On a sunny day, the light poured into the room with sparkling intensity, brightening even the darkest corners. A rainy day turned the room into a romantic Parisian atelier of which even Mimi of *La Bohème* fame would have been envious. On those rainy days I loved to lie under that skylight and listen to the rain beat down against the glass panes, all the while inhaling the pleasurable atmosphere.

Nina also seemed affected by her surroundings. Her rehearsals moved productively ahead with little of the trauma and stress which usually accompanies such creative endeavors.

In contrast to that light and clean rehearsal space, there are studios in which one never feels truly comfortable, studios in which one always feels confined and limited. During classes or rehearsals one spends almost as much energy in overcoming the physical liabilities of the space as in actually creatively dancing.

In 1961, I was invited by Lia Schubert to teach at her Balettakadamien school in Stockholm, Sweden. As there were no windows in the studio where I taught class, I often spent weeks on end during the winter months without seeing any daylight. The enclosed feeling gave the classes a sense of isolation and withdrawal.

To make a nondance space into a viable studio is not an easy undertaking. Factors which seem to be of no possible importance during the original creation of the space, suddenly arise and become predominant and determining elements in its later use.

In the beginning of my career I rehearsed in a nondance space near Central Park that previously had been used as a retaining barn for horses. During the winter months all went well, but the smell in the summer made it impossible to work there and all rehearsals ceased.

Lack of money can always create difficulties. Irving Burton rented a space and in order to make it viable for bare foot dancing, he bought some hardwood flooring. Unfortunately Irving purchased used wood that had been torn up from an old house. After we carried the wood up three flights of stairs, he discovered that it was so warped that it was unusable. Pleading friendship, Irving inveigled us to carry it back down the stairs so he could return it and get his money back. It wasn't until months later that Irving was able to purchase new, usable wood and complete his studio.

Building studios from scratch is obviously easier than remaking an already existing space. It is, however, much more time consuming because of the painstaking planning of every element. Although one studies all possible available examples of past constructions, the fallibility of the human being makes mistakes an integral part of every project.

When a multi-purpose space was built within the newly constructed women's gymnasium at Connecticut College in New London every element was thought to be considered before hand to make the facility as near perfect as possible. Although the space was to be used for various different activities, its use as a dance studio during the American Dance Festival was the focal point of its existence.

The studio was situated on a side of the building where the sun beat down the entire afternoon. This allowed a vast amount of natural light to flood the room as the wall was constructed almost entirely of glass. I was never there in the winter to see the reaction of sun, glass, and room during that season, but in summer it was disastrous. Although the natural light was superb, the power of the sun worked constantly against the glass all day, greatly raising the temperature of the room.

Added to the heat was a tremendous glare which for many hours of the day blinded both teachers and students. There is a well known photograph of Martha Graham teaching in this studio wearing dark glasses. The glasses, far from being an affectation on her part, were an absolute necessity.

In relation to what creates a productive atmosphere, the balance between the people who use a dance space and the dance space itself is very delicate. A dreary space can be overcome and can be made productive and exciting whereas a beautiful, well thought out dance studio without the proper input remains empty. My experiences in Japan, Mexico, New York and San Francisco seem to emphasize this point.

In 1985 in Japan, Marni (my wife and former Graham Company dancer) and I were invited by Takani Hirai to teach at Nara Women's University. We gave class in an old worn out gymnasium where the cold was so intense that we dared not let the students stop for a second lest they freeze to the spot. Such cold is debilitating and very destructive to the body. It creates a tightening of the muscles in an attempt to prevent loss of heat; injuries can easily occur.

In the summer of 1973 in Mexico City I taught for Amalia Hernandez' Ballet Folklorico, where the heat was unbearable. I was very excited about teaching there as I had been told that the new Folklorico building was an assimilated, beautiful, Mexican-Indian looking construction. The idea of giving class in such a structure and atmosphere was most attractive.

The outside of the Folklorico building was in truth, designed to resemble an Aztec temple, and was stunning; however, the inside was as depressing as the outside was exciting. The studios were clumped together, dark, and airless. The ceilings of the studios were so low that if any students with good elevation managed to jump too high, or if they tried an adventurous partnered lift, they risked immediate decapitation.

The building which housed the High School of Performing Arts in New York City was old and dilapidated beyond belief. There was nothing about it which hinted it would house training in the arts. When the High School of Performing Arts was first conceived, there was a desperate lack of funding. The New York City school system thought the concept of establishing an arts high school was a nice idea, but nothing more. Because of outside pressures, The Board of Education, finally agreed that if the school could exist in an old building with little money for adaptation, they would allow it to operate for a trial period. The Board, I am sure, guessed that the high school would fail in a short amount of time because of lack of interest and concern.

The dance studios were located a long climb up to the fourth floor of the building. The modern dance classes had the best of it, being assigned to the largest of the studios. This studio was full of light from the windows on either side, but fortunately missed the direct reflection of the sun. The only drawback was that the ballet room and both the women's and men's dressing rooms lay beyond the modern studio; the only access to them was by passing through it. Many a modern dance class was disrupted in order to stop a wild melee of blows and shouts that came tumbling out of the men's dressing room, overflowing into whatever class was in progress.

The ballet studio was the same width as the modern studio, but was much smaller in depth. It required a great deal of creativity on the part of the ballet teachers to make it functional. The main technique classes for each major were held in these large studios, but there were two other supposed studios in which both technique and academic classes were held. These were no larger than a small regular classroom. We all dreaded being assigned to these rooms, even for a subject such as dance history or acting, subjects in which space was not a vital factor.

The rooms were not kept particularly clean and the dressing rooms were terrible. Worst, the building was a fire trap. We knew that the school was condemned. When the doors that led from the modern studio onto the fire escapes were barred shut because the fire escapes were in disrepair, we had difficulty in remaining calm. As the days rolled on and nothing was done about it, our panic increased.

With all of these disadvantages, the High School of Performing Arts was one of the most exciting places in which to teach of any I have ever known. Rachael Yocom, the Administrator of the Dance Division was a major factor. She had a deep love for the school and the strength and the patience that it took to make the division come together constructively. The major instructors: Nina Popova, Bella Malinka, Gertrude Shurr, and Norman Walker, felt that teaching at the school was much more than just a job, and contributed great amounts of free time. The students were training at what they loved to do, what very few teenagers in the entire country were able to do at that time: combine the study of an art form of their choice with a strong academic education. The desire and excitement far outweighed the lack of an adequate facility. Obviously, there were the usual personal difficulties from time to time, but these were minor and did little to disturb the wonderful energy which filled the school. It made for a special bond which continues to this day.

To my knowledge, the most thoroughly and carefully researched building which has ever been constructed specifically for dance is the building designed for the San Francisco Ballet Company and School. As one sees its dressing rooms and lounges for every category of participant, as one judges its different studios designed for different projects, as one sees the administrative offices and counseling rooms, all beautifully functional, one marvels at the person or group of people that were insightful enough to realize the grand concept of this building, and its financial feasibility in the current climate. These people perceptively worked with loving care to see that every aspect of the planned structure was considered and properly constructed. Any necessary compromises were made with obvious intelligence and integrity, and did not destroy the total concept of the building.

Marni and I taught in this building for a very short period of time. We found it completely physically congenial and pleasant. There was easy entrance to the building by a roadway which drew right up to the front door; pleasant and well equipped faculty dressing rooms; functioning elevators to all classroom levels; spacious and well lit studios, excellently sound proofed; good pianos; hallways which were large and uncongested. Everything that students need in order to keep them excited and motivated in their quest for a dance career was abundantly provided.

The more one is given in all the facets of training, the greater is the responsibility of student, teacher, and administrator to make constructive and productive use of it. I know nothing of the attitude of the San Francisco Ballet Company itself but, unfortunately, the spirit of the San Francisco Ballet School was missing. Dissatisfaction seemed rampant. As I moved through the elevators and halls to and from class, I heard constant complaining, far beyond the usual negativism and grousing. In the class, a good portion of the students were unpleasant, surly, and more disrespectful of teachers, pianists, and other students than in any other place that I have ever taught. The negativism of the students defeated the purpose of the building. In my 45 years of teaching, the only class that I have walked out of and refused to teach was the top class at the San Francisco Ballet School. The disciplined, directed, and passionately involved students who fill a space with life and energy are always more important than a beautifully conceived, but basically empty, structure.

I was never a part of Hanya Holm's first studio, but by reputation I knew it to have been filled with people whose interests were centered in creativity and artistic enterprise. When Hanya decided to lessen her concentration on modern concert dance, she left her downtown school and moved uptown to Michael's Studios on 8th Avenue.

As Hanya rented the studios at Michael's by the hour and had only a limited number of classes, the spaces were also used by other rehearsing ensembles. The only space that the Holm school had permanently assigned to it was a small office on the studio level, occupied by Elsa Reiner, Hanya's secretary. Michael and Hanya had a strange marriage of interests. He obviously had great respect for her and her artistry; she lent an aura of tone to his establishment. She, in turn, had respect for him as a successful entrepreneur of a fascinating business enterprise.

Michael was a short, heavy set, bald headed man, with a strong accent of unknown origin. His spirit as well as his body always occupied the premises. Because of the constantly changing clientele, the studios needed a great deal of attention and care. Every nightclub act which played the eastern seaboard worked out of Michael's Studios. Exotic dancers, tap dancers, adagio teams, and fire baton twirlers were predominant, but the animal acts and the tap dancing ice skaters were the most fascinating. Michael's was Show Biz and at that point so was Hanya. They just arrived at it from a different point of view.

The atmosphere at Michael's was one of a fun loving, transient existence. Other than Hanya, the people who rehearsed there changed from day to day. Hanya's ability to teach in such surroundings was proof that she could adapt with ease to every situation. This ability was what allowed these strange bedfellows, Hanya and Michael, to arrive at a most pleasant and constructive working relationship.

A few years after Hanya made her move from downtown to uptown, Martha Graham followed suit. The direction of the move from down to up was the only thing the same about the relocation of these two prominent, dancer/teacher/choreographers. Hanya's move was made in order to help open out her sphere of activities and to bring her into contact with a larger and more materialistic world. Martha's move was to bring her increased dignity as a self-contained concert artist. Hanya aimed toward the further advancement of her Broadway career while Martha wanted a chance to develop and grow within the concert field in a surroundings without outside distractions.

Another great difference was that Hanya had to find her own way uptown and make her own arrangements; Martha was well taken care of. Over the past few years, Martha had developed a close friendship with Bethsabee de Rothschild, the daughter of the French House of Rothschild. Bethsabee had gotten out of France during World War II and emigrated to the United States. Her already established interests in dance, particularly modern dance, drew her to Martha's studio at 66 5th Avenue.

The timing was excellent. Martha was ready and eager for the opportunity to move into her own quarters and by now had built a reputation of such a dimension that she could substantiate this kind of move. Bethsabee wished to establish a foundation in which she could not only get a tax break but could also help to foster the arts and sciences.

After a prolonged search and much consultation, Bethsabee purchased a building at 316 East 63rd Street and established her B. de Rothschild Foundation for the Arts and Sciences. Technically, Martha rented the studios and offices from Bethsabee's foundation. The building had many uses, but the tenant previous to Bethabee was a children's theater school. The project was an exciting undertaking, but to make the structure suitable for the new activities, a great amount of renovation was necessary.

The building was self-contained and had three studios plus a huge garden with a fountain. There were offices and storage spaces. Adjoining the downstairs large studio was a door that led to the kitchen. This was company territory and its facilities of refrigerator and hot plate made the long hours of classes and rehearsals possible. Here Martha cooked her egg drop or garlic soup and lectured us, as any well intentioned mother would, against the evils of leaving our dirty dishes in the sink. Beyond the kitchen was Martha's lounge and dressing room which we all used when she was not there.

The rooms had excellent light without glare and, good accessibility. Although the third floor studio had its problems with heat during the summer, the temperature in the rooms was usually comfortable. Mirrors were provided in all three studios and, although not always of the greatest quality, they were sufficient. In a short time we all got to know which mirrors reflected thin and which mirrors reflected fat, and the students were clumped together in direct relation to where the thin mirrors stood.

Bethsabee not only wanted to provide Martha with a space of her own in which to work, but also a place where informal performances of great artists could be given. Curtains to cover the walls and mirrors were made and tracks for hanging them were constructed. A simple arrangement of lighting was organized from an upper balcony which overlooked the intended small stage. Isamu Noguchi designed an array of marvelous wooden benches and chairs that could be arranged to create different levels of seating for a small audience. This space, along with the 16th St. Weidman studio, were the very first studio theaters.

Because of working in this building, Martha became even more isolated. Unlike Hanya, she was not forced to adapt to new surroundings in an outside world. She had never been known for her ability to work in cooperation with other dancers. Thus, the situation was ideal for her. She did not have to share the space with anyone except for the few performers brought in by Bethsabee, and even that was terminated after a few years. It is rare that an artist is presented with such a gift. While Martha was extremely fortunate, her dedication and devotion to dance plus her extraordinary gift as a dance artist made her merit all that she was given. She never forgot her debt to Bethsabee and was always a most gracious and thankful recipient. It was an excellent example of a building found by good fortune, created with care, and put to good use.

I was brought by the University of California, Berkeley in the fall of 1967 to look into the possibilities for establishing a dance program there. The idea for bringing dance into the university's curriculum came from Travis Bogard, who was the Chair of the Department of Dramatic Art. The idea arose because, after one hundred years, the university finally built a viable theater complex, which allowed for many new programs to be considered. At our initial meeting, one of the first questions that Travis asked was, "Where do you think that a suitable dance studio could be found on this campus?". Because I had graduated from U.C. Berkeley, I had an old but still fairly accurate knowledge of the buildings and so, I had already developed a very good idea of what I wanted, only in my wildest imagination did I ever think that what I was imagining could actually come to pass.

I had learned to my relief that the beautiful old Unitarian Church which I had occasionally attended when in school, had not been destroyed in the construction of the Zellerbach Theater complex. It still remained perched on its corner of Dana and Bancroft Way, looking atmospheric, but, now, a little out of place in relation to the monolithic building beside it. On my way to the meeting with Travis, I made a point of passing by that corner to see the new theaters for the first time. I was delighted when I saw the lovely, old, brown shingle church building still standing. It was obviously still in use. All the doors were wide open, but I could not see what the people were doing inside. Unfortunately the windows were broken and dirty, with vines entwined through the windows and around the inside beams. It was very evident that the building was no longer being used as a church. The thought crossed my mind that this would make an excellent dance space. All of the essential, fundamental elements were in evidence, especially the old fashioned sprung floor, instead of the usual concrete base. Putting the thought aside as too idealistic, I hurried on to my meeting.

Because a special space in which to teach dance was of primary importance, I was not surprised by Travis' question about finding such a space.

Feeling a bit too intimidated to mention my ideal example, I stuttered out something about, "Maybe in Zellerbach?" I was totally amazed at the powers of subliminal suggestion when Travis answered, "What would you think about the old Unitarian Church?" The answer was obvious.

We walked across the campus to inspect the proposed structure. It was being used as the scene and paint shop for the Drama Department, and was filled with machines, sawdust, sets, and paint. It didn't take much imagination, however, to see its potential.

There was still much ground to traverse before I was to be hired by the university, and the church was to be secured for dance use. By the next spring, after many committee meetings and decisions, both my being hired and the assignment of the building to dance, had come to pass.

I did not know how slowly things moved in academic circles and arrived in Berkeley to find nothing done to the studio. I was given temporary quarters in which to teach, quarters that were satisfactory for a short duration only. The delay in remodeling the rooms did allow me to be on the premises while it was being done. I could guide the change over from church/scene shop to modern dance studio, first hand. I had arrived with plans and letters containing specifications for size and general essentials for a dance studio. It took all the papers and more, plus many hours of argumentative meetings before I was able to convince the authorities of my strange needs: an oak bar at an exact height; interlocked maple floors, sanded but left unfinished; mirrors with no distortions imported from eastern manufacturers; paint in simple pale colors of cream and beige; dark wood; a small area in place of the pulpit for a raised stage which was to be used for the viewing of classes by guests. All these demands were finally, fully met. Only three rooms were originally remodeled: the large studio, a student entryway, and my own office which had been the minister's study. By the beginning of the second quarter the studio was completed and usable: a magnificent dance space had been created.

The studio was large but not so enormous that a class became lost in its confines. It had entry to the room from two sides and the cathedral ceiling gave a soaring sense of endless overhead space. The walls were of light beige at their lower level and a light cream the rest of the way up. The beams were a dark wood, brown color, and created a sturdy, massive atmosphere. The mirrors covered one long wall and were of excellent quality. Natural light poured into the room through four double sized windows, gracefully curved at the top, made totally of amber glass. On the west wall was an enormous, round window, also of amber glass. The whole room was the most beautiful dance studio that I had ever seen.

We eventually took over the entire building creating, one more, small studio, a second office/dressing room for the women teachers and two bathrooms. It was not sufficient as a total dance complex as too many necessary elements were lacking, but the large studio was absolutely compelling.

After a long day of continuous teaching from nine in the morning until six in the late afternoon, if I did not have to rehearse until seven thirty that evening, I would usher out the lingering afternoon students, lock all the doors, and sit on the edge of the stage facing the huge circular amber window, completely quiet and alone. Even the energies that were propelled through the room during the day seemed to slowly ebb away. On certain days in late October just past six, the sun would begin its journey downward at exactly the correct placement in relation to the circular window, striking the amber glass. It painted the window with a blood red color which slowly seeped down the entire space. The red spread from pane to pane until the window was ablaze with a color so intense that it filled the entire room. Then slowly as the sun finished its descent, the color faded away leaving the room in deep shadow, extraordinarily silent and peaceful.

One year, as I sat watching this transformation of light take place, I thought back to my rehearsals with Nina Fonaroff and the inspirational skylight. It reaffirmed that a room which has some special element about it, whether it be an enormous, round, amber colored window facing west or a beautiful skylight peppered by endless raindrops, creates an atmosphere that is highly conducive to creativity. Feeling suddenly refreshed and renewed, I moved through the shadows and out the door ready to return, after a brief dinner, to face the evening's rehearsal.

Severance's Dance Studio, Fresno, California. Photographer: Phyllis Anne Tidyman.

Barbara Crockett (Wood) in *Don Quixote*. Photo credit: Crockett Estate.

Joanne Jones Woodbury, David Wood, Debbie Choate, and Mel Fillen at Hanya Holm's Summer School, Colorado. Photo credit: Wood collection.

Ellen van der Hoeven, Betty Jones, Juan Valenzuela, Beatrix Flores, and David Wood back-stage at the Juilliard Theater for *El Grito* in the choreography by José Limón. Photo credit: Wood collection.

Anne Westwick and Christopher Dolder rehearsing in the dance studio at the University of California, Berkeley. Photographer: Jon Marlowe. Photo credit: Wood collection.

3

ON LIVING SPACES

Just as dance studios can affect the creativity that occurs within them, so the living situation of the dancer can have an equal affect on his spirit and attitude which in turn creates a direct influence on his work. At the beginning of a dancer's career, the most important part of the day, in terms of both time and energy, is occupied by dance classes and/or various types of physical training. Outside jobs which the dancers undertake for financial support make up an important, second, time consuming category. The remaining short third slot which one spends at home "off hours" can provide a "quality period" which may greatly enhance the working hours of the dancer. This is true whether the living conditions in which the "quality time" is spent are in permanent daily lodgings or if they lie in the transient, eternal hotel rooms which all touring performers must eventually occupy. In arriving at a viable solution to the living situation, the dancer must consider certain elements.

Obviously finances are a prime factor. Their availability usually determines the ambiance, size, and location of the living quarters. The choice of having roommates or not may arise because of finances, but, in some cases, it may be a choice made to satisfy certain social needs. Commuting is another element. Travel time is a nuisance, but the possibility of space and greenery may far outweigh the disadvantage.

As I had not made any arrangements for living in New York before my arrival there in August 1947, I came into the city without any place to settle even for an overnight stay. I had no friends or even vague acquaintances. The reception room of Grand Central Station yawned frighteningly in front of me as I descended from the train that had brought me all the way from San Francisco via Chicago. I walked into that exciting, vast space with great trepidation; I had no idea what might lie in store for me in this enormous city. A dark, west side, theatrical hotel room sufficed as a place to sleep for two nights, but I began to feel impending financial disaster. I searched each day for lodgings. Finally the third day proved fruitful. The acquaintance of a friend of a friend had a cousin who sent me to a basement apartment in the lower, west village on Houston Street. One of the tenants in an already overcrowded one room studio was supposedly going on tour.

The apartment was occupied by three very friendly men who seemed not at all worried about crowding. For a period of two weeks we all lived together in an harmonious but crowded state. Then one of the room-mates did actually leave for tour, giving the rest of us a little breathing room, especially welcome during the sweltering August weather.

In my naiveté moving into the apartment, I did not question or even wonder about the sexuality of my new roommates. Later, however, their relationship became a puzzling mystery to me, and to this day I have never learned or solved its riddle.

The experience did teach me that homosexuals, the same as hetero-sexuals, usually do not approach or sexually bother anyone who does not want to be bothered. Thus homosexual and heterosexual can live together with integrity, respecting each of their individual preferences. After two months though, the basement apartment became more and more overcrowded. When Peace and Carmen Alvarez offered me my own room in an apartment that they had newly found, I moved in immediately.

Peace and Carmen were half sisters newly arrived in New York from San Francisco. Carmen was a first year student in my class at the Neighborhood Playhouse. I doubt if, even at that time, she had high aspirations of becoming a great actress: a newly discovered sex goddess, yes, but a great actress, no. Peace was in New York to attend graduate school and work for her visiting nurse's license. She also was trying to keep track of Carmen, not only because Carmen was the younger sister, but also the wilder one by nature. The two sisters actually got along amazingly well. Peace was not only older but the innate leader. It was she who had found the apartment, a large space with three bedrooms, a large living room, an eat-in kitchen, and a single bathroom. It was located on 22nd Street just off of 3rd Avenue. The Third Avenue elevated was still in operation and its noisy rumble could be heard and its vibra-tions felt throughout our apartment, both day and night.

No one thinks twice today when unmarried men and women share the same accommodations, but in 1947, it was far from commonplace. The three of us went into the arrangement without any worries about gossip or social disapproval. I even excitedly told my parents of my good for-tune in being asked to team up with the two sisters. My parents never blinked an eye, making no comment or complaint. I was to discover in later years that, although they said little or nothing about it to me, they had a great deal to say about it to each other.

My first year in New York passed delightfully. Peace, who handled all finances, was most generous. She charged me a meager rent of thirty dollars a month, and the large sum of fifteen dollars per week as my contribution toward food. Peace, of course, did the cooking and although it was not French cuisine, it was both healthy and delicious. It was truly a period of male chauvinism. I remember just slightly helping with the dishes or at least washing those that I had dirtied myself. With encouragement from Peace, I also managed to clean my own room. It was Peace who directed all living arrangements, who listened to our problems, who advised us when we asked for it, and who made all things work. She was a rare person, with a vast reservoir for giving.

Through their mother in San Francisco, the two sisters were closely connected with two dance personalities, José Limón and Louis Horst. We had many Saturday or Sunday night dinners with José and his wife, Pauline, or Louis and his friend, Nina Fonaroff. They generously included me at these meals; it was my first personal contact with well known dance personalities. I sat shyly quiet at the table, drinking in the professional conversation and dreaming of the future.

The apartment also had an element of mystery, included with the sublet at no extra cost. The front bedroom, located on the hallway by the front door, was occupied, or more accurately, stuffed with all of the personal belongings of the original inhabitants of the apartment, as well as the inhabitants themselves, an elderly, Italian mother and her thirtyish, single daughter. By prearranged agreement these two were to vacate the premises and to reside in Florida during the entire year of our sublet. I think that they were actually gone for about three weeks. Even when the mother was not there the daughter made her presence strangely felt.

We were all extremely curious about the daughter's occupation. She was a tall, slim, large featured, dark woman who although a bit horsy, was attractive. Many a time in the middle of the night while groping in the dark for the bathroom, I would run into strange men on their way out of the front bedroom or the front door. I had never seen any of the men before and was never to see them again. All of us had similar experiences and arrived at similar conclusions. Our only confusion was what happened when the mother also occupied the room along with the daughter. Whether Mama was present or not, the same continuous stream of men were in evidence. Long before the word kinky became popular, we imagined some odd happenings going on in "Little Sorrento". When the Italian operation finally became too intrusive, it was Peace who took over again and spoke decisively to our landlords. All activities ceased.

Unfortunately, Peace finished her studies and Carmen didn't return to the Neighborhood Playhouse. After a summer in stock at Duxbury, Massachusetts, I returned to New York, homeless again, but now much more knowledgeable.

There followed in rapid succession a few temporary addresses as I migrated from uptown to downtown and back uptown again. I finally settled down for approximately two years in an old brownstone building off of Lexington Avenue in the east twenties. It was rented out basically as a theatrical rooming house and was referred to by the dubious title of the Morgue. According to rumor it had been put into emergency use as a temporary address for cadavers, and later had been returned to its original state as a living quarters. The rooming house was run by Al Moritz who also was producer of the stock company at Duxbury. The rooms were rented mainly to his close, personal, theatrical friends. Marie Hall Laube, a lovely lady who had attended the Neighborhood Playhouse with me, lived there and spoke on my behalf. My pitiful condition was dealt with by assigning me a walk-in closet on the third floor rear. My closet room had a window, a door, and an old fashioned stretched steel bed with a thin ticking for a mattress, not the most comfortable bedding, but something to sleep on. Other than that, the minuscule space was totally bare. As I usually was at the brownstone only to sleep, my closet sufficed. I had no need for luxury in my surroundings; the monastic life was much more appealing to me at the time.

When I did spend spare moments there, the Morgue provided me with companionship and friends, sometimes very difficult to find in New York. All types of interesting people inhabited the premises, but rarely on a permanent basis. At times there was tension among us and even a few fights, but basically there was a great deal of camaraderie. As everyone living in the house was a struggling artist, there was much sympathy dealt out each for one another. I was at the bottom of the heap of the Morgue's residents both in experience and finances. My closet rent was five dollars per month and there were many months when I could not even pay that. Being at the bottom, though, was not so bad, as it often elicited a great understanding of my difficulties.

Meals at the Morgue were done on an individual basis. There was a huge communal kitchen and pantry in the basement. Each of us had our own shelf in the pantry for food. Mine was always bare. I usually ate late at night after the other tenants had gone to bed and everything was quiet. I never actually stole anyone else's food but a lettuce leaf here and a potato there proved to be the sustenance of life for me.

At that poverty stricken period in my life, the Morgue was a "haven in the storm", "an oasis in the desert". I probably could not have survived in New York without its umbrella protection. Besides all of its practical assets, its artistic atmosphere provided my struggle for survival with a golden aura of unreality. I knew that I could not last in those circumstances forever, but in my youthful fervor, I pictured myself as Ibsen's Lovborg or Shaw's Marchbanks. I was sure that the struggle for artistry would develop a greater depth of understanding within me which would give me better sustenance that any food could ever possibly provide.

After two years at the Morgue my next move was to a studio apartment on Perry Street near Hudson in Greenwich Village. Helen Livingston Nickerson, one more invaluable friend from both San Francisco and the Neighborhood Playhouse, lived on one of the upper floors of the Perry Street apartment house. When a small studio apartment became available in the building, she phoned me immediately feeling that it was time that I began to improve on my surroundings. The apartment encompassed a very small living area, only about three times the size of my closet at The Morgue, but ten times the rent. Fifty two fifty was the exact cost. Having my own small Pullman kitchen and tiny bathroom was the incentive for moving. Although by now I was earning a few dollars every week, the rent was still too costly. A roommate was my only choice. Al Srnka was a big, likable fellow that I had met in Colorado Springs the previous summer, at Hanya Holm's session at Colorado College.

It was a miracle that either of us got any sleep at all in the apartment as our living quarters were on the ground floor directly by the front door. We had personal knowledge of all the comings and goings of every inhabitant of the apartment house. Because of the unbearable humid heat of the New York summer, I would leave the front door open. While I never did succeed in my attempt at "air conditioning", I did become acquainted with everyone who lived in the building.

The apartment was too small for even one person; two people were totally disastrous. The fact that we were still friends after one full year had passed is testimony to Al and my basic good natures. At night, when the trundle bed was pulled out, there was only the smallest space left to edge around the room with our backs pushed tightly to the wall.

The single window looked out on a light well and our only view looked directly into the living room of an apartment in the neighboring building where a young couple lived with their small son. In time I got to know the little boy well. His parents treated him poorly. "You want to die?", the mother would scream. "I'll kill you."

This would be followed by anguished cries from the child and slaps from the mother. The little boy seemed constantly to sit by the window waiting for me to return home. Sometimes, when I only had a few moments to clean up and change clothes, I would open the front door slowly and then crawl along the floor on my stomach trying to stay out of his sight, as I couldn't stand the thought of disappointing him by not answering his calls.

"Hello, man."

He never asked my name. I was always just, man; however, I often asked him his name in the attempt to make light conversation. I got a different response every time. Matthew, Donald, Arthur, and, one day, even

Archibald came spouting out of, his imagination. He always wanted to know everything about me; what I was planning to do or had done that day; to what I was going to be when I grew up. Our conversations sometimes went on for hours. After the pressures and anxieties of New York, I found it refreshing to reach back to simplistic conversational levels and to be able to communicate with another human being, even such a little one, just for the pure pleasure of the act itself.

My greatest regret when I moved from Perry Street was leaving Matthew, Donald, Arthur, Archibald to the lonely cruelty of his parents. I often wonder if his actual life ever caught up with his vicarious living.

My apartment in Greenwich Village was followed by many other apartments which took me once again from downtown to uptown, east to west and back. The nomadic instincts of New Yorkers are famous; the average change of a Manhattanite's residence is every three years. Roommates came and went, whenever dissatisfaction caused them to pull up stakes and return to their roots. Most roommates were personages of convenience rather than close friends, so their departure seldom caused any emotional turmoil or feeling of loss.

Shortly after I joined the Graham Company in 1953, two company members, Mary Hinkson and Matt Turney, informed me of a vacant floor-through loft in a building next to theirs. There were actually three buildings in a row on the south side of 23rd Street between 6th and 7th Avenues that had been built as a unit. The buildings had contained, at one time, large, lovely apartments, but industry had taken over and scuttled their insides to make way for office furniture storage. With living space in the 1950's beginning to become a premium, artists and other creative people were trying to reclaim these types of buildings for large, living/working areas.

Mary and Matt's apartment had been totally remade and it was delightful. At three flights up we had connecting fire escapes, but that was all that was similar between their space and mine. The empty loft which was to be mine was huge and completely open from front to back with added space at both ends giving it the look of an inverted "C". The only break in its clear horizon was a six foot high pile of debris that had been left by an artist who had lived and worked there previously. I was told by the real estate management that if I would undertake the task of removing the debris, the place was mine for $75 per month.

My monthly rental was slowly rising, but so were my resources. Still, I couldn't handle the full sum by myself so a roommate again became a necessity. Al Schulman was from Philadelphia and through circuitous routes became involved with dance. He was given a scholarship to Bennington College so that the young dancers of that expensive all girls school would have at least one male partner with whom they could perform. Having finished his schooling, Al moved to New York to test his chances in the big city. He took classes at the Graham school and picked up whatever work, dance or otherwise, that he could. Al would be acknowledged today as a true womanizer. In truth, he just had a marvelous appetite for the feminine gender. We split the rent but the loft was totally mine. I was the person responsible for reconstructing it and furnishing it.

Our immediate task in getting oriented in our new place, was to get rid of the trash that commanded the central area of the main room. The first attempt was a complete failure. Late one night, shortly after moving in, Al and I carried all of the junk down the three flights of stairs and stuffed it into the doorway of one of the many commercial businesses that occupied the ground floor. Unfortunately, among the garbage, Al left an envelope with his name and address on it. At 6:00 the next morning, there were angry bangs at our front door accompanied by exclamations. "Get your crap out of my entryway, now!"

Caught, we, with great chagrin, piled the junk on the stairway as we didn't want to carry it all the way back up the three flights, only to have to carry it back down again. This brought forth the anger of all the other tenants as they stumbled and fell over our garbage on their way out to work.

In desperation, I called Louise Guthman, the only person that I knew who owned a car. After we had filled it to overflowing and we had stacked two full size doors onto its roof, the three of us began to cruise lower Manhattan looking for empty public trash baskets. When we spotted one, Louise would slow down the car and Al and I would get ready. As Louise stopped the car, either Al or I loaded out the debris while the other stuffed it into the city cans. In fear that we might get caught, no more than fifteen seconds were allowed per stop. Then we jumped back into the car and took off in search of more empty trash cans. Three hours and we were rid of all of the car's contents. All that remained were the doors that we had placed on top of the car. We thought that it was a miracle when we passed a truck filled to the brim with doors such as ours. We weren't sure whether our two additional doors would be appreciated by the truck's owners, but we didn't wait to find out. The three of us, exhilarated by success bought a six pack of beer and returned to a new, beautifully empty loft which was now waiting to be remodeled.

The remodeling took time, great physical effort, money, and a hernia before I managed to accomplish it, but all of the effort was worthwhile. I have rarely felt such satisfaction as I watched the rooms take shape under my creative sweat.

In time the three buildings became a dance enclave. Arthur Mitchell and Karl Shook moved in above me after a Greek family moved out.

Louis Johnson moved into the floor below, I never used my loft as a dance studio, but Louis did, and it was great fun to stop on my way home and watch his rehearsals. Karl, because he was the master teacher with whom we all studied classical ballet, became the focal point of the three buildings. We would gather most every evening in his apartment to listen to his stories of past adventures with the Ballets Russes de Monte Carlo and to savor his often given and more often unasked for advice. It was a marvelous time of life, vibrant with energy. Nothing seemed impossible. Just the act of living was exciting and fun. I was teaching, studying and performing, and I was enjoying all of it. Going out on tour with Martha Graham was a tremendous excitement. Coming back home to my loft was a pleasure. It was a haven for me, in contrast to all of the rest of the chaos and furor of my daily life.

Even Martha paid a short visit to my loft one evening. I think it was one of her most selfless moments toward me. It occurred when she learned of my belated case of mumps. I was in my early thirties, and it was considered a little dangerous for a grown man to have such a disease, especially if he intended to produce children. My doctor had ordered me to stay in the loft, lie down, and be as quiet as possible. I didn't mind as it gave me a chance to relax and enjoy doing nothing for a change, and by then my loft was a pleasurable place in which to be.

The day after I was diagnosed, Martha Graham called on the phone. "David, I have just heard about your illness. How awful. How are you? How are your genitals?"

Dear Martha, she certainly could come right to the point. I assured her, after a quick reassuring look below, that all was in good order. Martha asked if I needed anything or if there was something that she could do for me. After a moments thought, I remembered the many esoteric books that I had seen in Martha's studio sitting room, which I had always wanted to read. Since I was now forced to do nothing, it would be a good time to try to gain some philosophical knowledge. Martha said that she would see what she could do to get them to me.

That evening I heard Martha's husky voice calling me from out in the stairwell. Surprised, I moved slowly to the door and opened it. On my doorstep sat a heavy box full of books. Martha had gotten Bethsabee de Rothschild to drive her down to 23rd Street. Martha had climbed the three flights of stairs to my floor carrying the heavy load. When I opened the door, she had her back against the opposite wall and cried out, "Don't come near. I have never had the mumps. Take the books and please go away from the door."

I obeyed, wondering what her devious mind had in store for me. When I had drawn far enough back, Martha advanced to the door, smiled and said, "I just wanted to see how you lived."

She looked around thoroughly, spoke approvingly of what she saw, and then quickly disappeared down the stairs even before I could express my thanks.

When I opened the box of books, I found lying on top of them a strange looking fetish along with a short note from Martha. "David, here is a fetish symbol from Abadan, Iran. I hope it helps you through this awful crisis." It seemed that Martha wanted to make sure that all of my sperm were kept alive and well and ready for active duty.

After two years when I returned from the first Asian tour with Martha, Al met me with the news that he had reached the point of no return. He was leaving New York. He had gotten himself a job selling veterinary medicine out of Chicago. The desire to lead an ordinary life with a secure income had completely overtaken him.

When Al got depressed, he really hit rock bottom. He would stay in bed for days at a time, not shave for weeks, and wear only his shoddiest clothes. During the time that I was gone, Al had hit one of his low points and took to his bed. Finally, hunger pangs got the better of him. It was a cold evening in early February with the snow falling hard and the wind lashing out at every corner. Horn & Hardart was just across 7th Avenue and it provided the cheapest food around. Al stood on the corner waiting for the light to change, becoming more depressed as he fought the ice and the cold that was intensified by gales of wind that beat against his skin through the openings in his thin clothes. At that moment one of New York's indigents came up, put his arm around Al, and said, "Hey, buddy, it's going to be a rough one tonight, isn't it?"

Shocked at such an approach by a completely unkempt stranger, Al shoved the man off angrily and headed as fast as he could for the Horn & Hardart Automat and its warm solace. As he stood in the automat getting change in order to purchase his food, he looked across the counter at his reflection in the mirror opposite. It was then that he realized that his "buddy" on the corner had every right to consider him to be a kindred spirit. In horror, he decided to alter his life immediately. Veterinary medicine and Chicago were not Utopia for him but were a step in the right direction.

Al went home to Philadelphia for a couple of weeks to get reoriented. Late one evening he drove back to New York in his parent's car to pick up his belongings. We sat up until dawn rehashing old events and philosophizing about the future. As the sun rose, I helped him carry his bags and boxes down to the street. We said good-by and he drove off to a new life. I never saw him again.

There were many other roommates who rapidly moved in and out of my loft. A couple of years later I found myself loading my own car and heading out, if not into the sunrise, into the new frontier of marriage.

Marni and I, after a brief and intense courtship, were married in December, 1958. The planned move from New York to Mexico turned out to be a six months working honeymoon.

The apartment that we rented in Mexico City was located, oddly enough, on Calle de Nueva York, near the bullfight ring. We were gringos living like Mexicans in a seemingly Americanized city. It was a lovely situation that appealed to my sense of romance. Our one flight up apartment gave us a perfect view of the wandering street circuses that performed every week directly below our windows, as well as the late night Mariachis who came to serenade. It took Marni many months before she realized that these musicians had not been brought there at my behest for her pleasure, but rather by the enticement of the much more romantic other gringo upstairs for his lady love.

From the time that Marni and I returned to New York until the present, our living situation has reflected both our growing numbers of children, Marina, Raegan, and Ellis, and our growing financial security. A two bedroom apartment on West 87th Street sufficed through two children; then suburbia became a matter of choice. We slipped across the line of upper New York City to a beautiful, large, stone and wood house in Yonkers. At present in Berkeley, we have settled above the campus in a spacious home overlooking San Francisco Bay with the gleaming lights of the cities surrounding us. It gives us pleasure every day that we live in it, much as my 23rd Street loft did in New York.

The main difference is that we have no cockroaches to keep us company. Instead, ants and gophers vie for our attention. It is a long way from my $5.00 per month closet and yet I would never give up the experiences and deprivations that occurred while I lived at the Morgue. I would not want to go through the process again, but I learned values which would have been difficult to obtain in any other place or in any other manner. They are values which still play an important part in the ethics of my life.

The temporary lodgings of hotel rooms on tour, or the residences which are provided for ones living during summer teaching stints all merge into one singular image. Tour begins to blend with tour and a hotel room to blend with another hotel room. The large room with bath provides the necessities of life but little more.

Upon arrival at a hotel, there are always complaints: the ambiance of the various rooms that have been assigned; the size of the room; the view; not near enough to the elevators; too near to the elevators; too high a floor; too low a floor; too noisy or too quiet. Dissatisfaction runs rampant and the dance company management is always at fault. A myriad of questions arise upon each new arrival. Should I unpack right away or should I wait? Should I go out immediately and look for a better place

or should I take my afternoon nap? Did any one find a cheaper room?
How expensive is the director's hotel? Do they have any more rooms
there? Should I have a place away from everybody? Will I be too lonely?
Is anyone else changing? Is everyone else changing?

Of the larger hotels in which I have stayed there are a few which
standout. The Raffles in Singapore feeding off of the reputation gained
from past British generations, lent to those who came to stay there
an aura of mystery and elegance. The Grand Hotel in Stockholm, Sweden,
reeks of solid elegance. The front rooms look out over The Royal Palace,
Gamla Stan, and The Royal Opera House, which stand strongly outlined
above the glittering waters of Lake Malaren and Stroemmen. Nature
and man blend in a spectacular skyscape unmatched any where else in
the world.

The Taj Mahal in Bombay, is now equaled by the Taj in Delhi, but in
1957 it was, alone the most outstanding hotel in all of India despite its
dark, dreary rooms and corridors. The old section has now been renovated and brightened with great care so that none of its marvelous old
British, far east flavor is lost. The Britannia-Europa in Venice, Italy was
probably the most romantic of any large hotel in which I have stayed.
Marni and I rented a good size room overlooking the Piazza San Marco
and the Grand Canal. It had a lovely balcony from which we could
watch the gondolas and vaporettos pass and where we had breakfast
served every morning in the bright sunlight.

The most beautiful of all the major hotels was the old Frank Lloyd
Wright Imperial Hotel in Tokyo, Japan. The hotel was actually built in
two different sections; the original that was designed by Wright, and
a more newly constructed high rise building that was fitted up against
the older part. The original building was a low, elegant structure no more
than three stories high, which created a massive sweep of movement, and gave it a feeling of closeness and stability. It was fronted by
a gracious driveway and fountain that seemed literally to carry one up to
the front doorway. The different levels of its interior gave it a marvelous
sense of space and, Wright, had brilliantly blended the qualities of east
and west into a unifying total. Even amidst the bustle of activity, there
was a definite feeling of serenity, enhanced by the long linear lines of the
structure, as well as the deep colors: of brown, red, yellow, and blue, that
pervaded.

The disadvantage of being prime real estate in an overly crowded
metropolis forced the destruction of the old hotel. It was replaced by
a new, high-rise building of glass and chromium, whose only connection
with the original Imperial is the name and location. The facade of the
original is restored somewhere outside of Tokyo, and the only part of the
old hotel that remains active is the Old Imperial Bar within the new

hotel. As small as the bar is, it still remains a wonderful reminder of times past.

A much better example of bringing a hotel up to date is that of the Oriental Hotel in Bangkok, Thailand. It exists now in three different sections built at three different periods of time. The original Oriental, placed beside the Chao Phraya River, was a small, ideally situated residence which attracted writers from all over the world. The British had a strong influence on the structure and its activities. Even now, tea time is a major ceremony carried out religiously everyday. By the time Martha stayed there in 1956 on our first Asian tour, a large additional section had been built with updated furnishings. The rest of us in the company were residing in a fly infested small hotel around the corner from the Oriental where Bangkok belly was running rampant among us. We could only look with envy at the marvel of the Oriental and hope that we might be invited even for a short visit.

All good hotels are not of giant proportions. Perhaps the most delightful commercial hotel in which I stayed was a little inn or kro in Rødvig, a small village about thirty miles south of Copenhagen, Denmark. Marni and I had been performing in England and Portugal and were driving to Stockholm with our three children for a six week's teaching stint. I had arbitrarily chosen a spot halfway between Paris and Stockholm as a likely point for a week's vacation. Out of a travel book, I picked what seemed to be an accommodating place to stay. We crossed from Germany into Denmark and in a wild storm drove north beside the pounding ocean until we arrived at the quaint village of Rødvig. We drove through the town, rounded the corner, and there, across the road from the angry waters, lay our small kro with its sign banging wildly in the wind. We were given two beautiful and newly redecorated connecting rooms with bath overlooking the water. Some of the best meals that I have ever tasted were served in its restaurant.

On most of the early tours with Martha Graham before I was married, I was fortunate to have Bob Cohan as a roommate. On the Asian Tour we had little leeway for moving around and choosing our own lodgings. In Asia it was necessary to be careful to stay at what were considered to be entirely safe accommodations, but on the first European Tour the choice was ours. Bob seldom liked the assigned hotels, and he had endless energy for finding the best value in every new town. Our flat in London which he found after much searching was huge and dark but had a fireplace. An excellent breakfast was served every morning at our convenience. Because it was centrally located near to Piccadilly Circus, and the now demolished old Saville Theatre where we were performing, the residence finally attracted about half of the rest of the company. In The Hague, Holland, we moved from our assigned elegant hotel to a small family style accommodation around the corner which cost half of the price and had twice the charm. In Paris we moved across the Champs Elysées to a small, truly French hotel which although a block further away from the theater, was completely enchanting. The rooms were inexpensive and many conveniences were provided, The management was also most helpful in giving needed advice about Paris and its environs. Bob Cohan was a hotel finder extraordinaire.

One of the best of his discoveries came about by chance. Over the years it benefited all of us tremendously especially Bob himself. When we arrived in London on the first European Tour, our boat train was met by a young woman, Peggy Harper, with whom Bob and I had a slight friendship. We had met Peggy in the summer of '52 at the American Dance Festival in New London, Connecticut. Bob was teaching for Martha that summer and I was dancing with the Dudley-Maslow-Bales Trio. Peggy became greatly enamored of Bob. This was nothing unusual; Bob often attracted people to him. He had the allure of a matinee idol. Peggy was bright and enterprising and when Bob expressed displeasure with our assigned hotel in London, she suggested an excellent solution. She had a friend who owned a hotel called The Gore in Queensgate. It was located a little way out of the center of town, but the theater was easily accessible by either bus or tube. She called her friend, Robin Howard, to see if the proper arrangements could be made. With the hotel bookings confirmed, Bob and I, along with our music director, Eugene Lester, headed out for the Gore and a meeting with our benefactor.

Robin was a very large, energetic, typically British, man. He had lost his legs in World War II, but managed himself extremely capably with replacements and canes. In fact as we got to know him better, we all completely forgot about his disability. Robin gave us an unbelievable bargain rate for the rooms at his hotel and provided us with fast transportation by personally driving us to and from the theater.

Bob, however, was still unhappy with the situation. He said that he felt too indebted to Robin, and insisted on moving. My sedentary nature made me wish to stay where we were, but I followed along when Bob found a flat in the center of town. Eugene held his ground and remained at the Gore thoroughly enjoying himself.

Robin became a devotee of Martha's and later he gave the company a feast in the Elizabethan Room of his hotel with Martha and Dame Marie Rambert reigning at the head of the table. There never existed two more competitive women and their friendly barbed banter throughout the meal enhanced their appetites as well as ours. Little was Robin to know how much dance, especially the dance of Martha Graham, was to have an effect on his life from that time. Nor did we know how much this man was to have an effect on all of our careers. All of that I will explain further in a later chapter.

The hotel in which Martha stayed while we were performing in Vienna during the first European Tour has become only a vague memory for me, but the room in that hotel in which Craig Barton and Leroy Leatherman, Martha's two managers, stayed remains clearly delineated. It is not that the room itself was exceptional in any manner, but rather that the event that occurred there was so striking. Our tour was ending in Vienna. The last stop preceding was in Bern, Switzerland. Just before our departure for Vienna the company arranged to have a meeting with Gert Macy, our company business manager. We wanted to conclude the financial arrangements of the tour. Gert was a large, rawboned woman, marvelously candid, of strong character, and fair and honest to a fault. Craig and Lee, at their own invitation, also attended the meeting. The financial discussions were without rancor. We asked for certain terminating benefits which were turned down but with clear explanation by Gert concerning why. There was some bantering and bargaining but all ended entirely friendly, with as much satisfaction on the part of both labor and management as could be expected. The point of friction had arisen because the contracts that we had as dancers were not sufficiently specific in detail. The tour was completely financed by Bethsabee de Rothschild, Martha's benefactor. Martha, rightfully, felt greatly indebted to Bethsabee for all that she had done and would stand for no new imposition on the Baroness.

Nothing further would have happened as a result of the company meeting except that Craig and Lee stopped by Martha's room later that evening and related what had occurred from their highly biased point of view. As a result, we all arrived at the railway station the next morning to be met by a stoic Miss Graham with rigid back, high chin, and dark glasses. Our "Good Morning, Martha." was given an icy stare, and a whip of the head, which was quickly followed by the body twisting so that the greeter, who ever it was, was given a full and immediate view of the Graham backside. Once we boarded the train, Martha paced the aisles the entire trip like a tiger lashing its tail, speaking to no one and increasing her regal furor as each righteous hour passed.

We had three free days in Vienna before the first performance and we all spent it running throughout the city tasting its many flavors. Because Martha was at a different, more elegant and more costly hotel, we ran into her very seldom. When we did, we were completely ignored, passed by without even a murmur or a glance of acknowledgment. The day before we moved into the theater for the performances, the orders came: 3:00 P.M. sharp, Craig and Lee's room, a company meeting with Martha. By 2:50 P.M. most of us had gathered in what proved to be a rather small room for the approximately twenty people in attendance.

The memory of that tiny inconsequential chamber remains vivid: an entryway and hallway off of which opened an unspectacular bathroom; a sleeping area filled with two twin beds, crowded in by an armoire on one side and a desk on the other. The desk was on the far side of the room as one entered, at the foot of the beds, by the windows which overlooked a central courtyard. The company assembled, occupying all the chairs of the room and both sides of both beds. We were finally all gathered but one, Yuriko. About 3:30 P.M. there was a phone call from Charlie Kikuchi, Yuriko's husband. Yuriko and their daughter Susan were stuck on top of the ferris wheel in the Prater, the large amusement park in Vienna. She would come to the hotel as soon as she could get down. There were now also many communications with Martha who was waiting in her room, one flight up. She would not budge from her quarters until we were all present. Valiantly, we began conversations among ourselves, but our conversations lagged and became forced with jovialities. The steam from our warm breaths and bodies began to fog the windows.

An hour late Yuriko arrived, full of excitement from her recent adventure. Martha was notified that all were finally present and we now sat awaiting her arrival with hushed expectancy. In short order Martha Graham, dressed for a full social occasion, entered the room and proceeded to give possibly the best performance of her theatrical life. She moved lithly to the focal point of the room, the desk by the windows, and its by now only remaining empty chair. Without noticing anyone of us she took her seat there with regal elegance. She then gazed over us and quietly began to speak. She started slowly and softly and, with calculated theatricality, built momentum.

"It has come to my attention that there has been a meeting of this company without my knowledge and at that meeting you insulted Gert Macy!" Then, in full voice and anger, she shouted, "and I will not stand for it."

With the words, "stand for it", Martha stood; it was not just the rising of an ordinary mortal. Martha's hand smashed against the desk in perfect coordination with the projection of her body upward, her steel spine rigidly at attention and her neck arched like a swan ready for battle. The fight was on and for forty five minutes there was no let up. It raged and stormed. The furor narrowed to two participants, Martha and Stuart Hodes. Stuart had been union representative for the company and so in Martha's eyes was always the enemy. Once Pearl Lang tried to break in by saying something sensible, but she was ignored. Everything in the past relationship of Martha and Stuart was dredged up from the mire and spewed out. The accusations reverberated off the walls and we who were merely observers watched as if we were at a tennis match. We were all considerably in awe and wonder at the professionalism of their volatility.

Finally, at the end of forty-five minutes, Stuart struck a blow. "Martha, have you asked Gert if she feels that we insulted her?" There was a short pause before Martha, forced with the inevitable, confronted Gert and said, "Well, Gert, did they?"

Gert was now on the spot. She knew that it was Craig and Lee who had told Martha the story of the meeting and Gert was close friends with the two men. As always with Gert, her honesty triumphed over all else. "Well, Martha," she drawled, "it was a business meeting. A few things were said, but I don't think that I was insulted."

A sigh of relief went through the room, and then a silence fell, a deafening silence lasting at least three minutes, three interminable minutes. Martha sat down quietly, thinking. No one moved. After the lengthy pause Martha said with total sweetness and complete change of thought, "Has anyone been to the theater yet?"

There were a few light words and pleasantries exchanged about the coming performances and about the end of the tour. Then each of us, one by one, bid good-bye to Martha with a hug and escaped through the door into the fresh air. As I exited, I heard Martha chastising Stuart with her full coquetry. "Stuart, you naughty boy."

It was my first experience with the vagaries of Martha's many moods. To learn that Martha was an emotional chameleon was to help me in working with her in the years to come.

The President Hotel in Jerusalem, Israel, had a combined bar and swimming pool, Most of us could be found beside the pool during the day, but because of the evening chill, not too many of us were to be found swimming after a performance. One evening when we had returned from the theater, the younger members of the company were enticed into the pool by a friendly inebriate.

Whether by dare or suggestion he convinced the dancers to strip to their underwear and dive in. It was in this state of undress that Martha discovered part of her company swimming happily about and having great but cold fun splashing each other. With her puritan background rising to the forefront, Martha ordered the dancers, male and female, out of the pool. The drunken friend, trying to save the situation and having no idea who she was, admonished Martha for ending the fun and tried with his already proven persuasive powers to get her to loosen up by joining him for yet another drink. Martha answered haughtily, "I never drink and no one in my company drinks." She was obviously wrong on both counts.

The dancers were rounded up shivering in their wet underwear. Martha lined them up in a file and berated them for ten minutes as she paced back and forth in front of the line like any common army sergeant. It was hard to make sense out of what she was saying, but she ended her tirade clearly with, "Don't you know that there is no mixed bathing in Jerusalem?"

Martha, on this subject, was just a little behind the times even for Jerusalem. The point, however, was that she was always greatly exacting about the behavior of her company and the impression that we made not only as performers on the stage, but as social ambassadors as well. Whenever any of us veered from the path, we paid the price with many lashes from her acid tongue.

Our hotel in Dhaka during the 1956 Asian tour was certainly not memorable because of its architecture, service, food, or conveniences. If it had not existed in a badly impoverished third world country, the hotel would have been passed over by most Western travelers for a much more luxurious Motel 6.

The day after we arrived in Dhaka, then East Pakistan, now Bangladesh, we were given a welcoming dinner by our presenters, The Rotary Club. The hotel in which we were staying had one large reception room and it was decorated beautifully for the banquet in our honor. Because The Rotary Club was a male only society, the members who attended the dinner brought with them as companions either a wife or a daughter. Out of deference to Martha, they asked their relations to dress in saris rather than their usual black burkas. The burka is a Moslem attire for women which covers their entire head and body except for slits at the eyes; at times even these slits are covered with a net.

When we entered the reception room, the Pakistanis, male and female, were already gathered. They were clumped together in tight groups, the men with the men and the women with the women. We were introduced briefly and without further ceremony were motioned to the table to begin the dinner. Possibly this occasion was not the first time in which these Pakistani women had appeared without being completely covered; however, it seemed as if it must be, by their obvious discomfort.

The women at the dinner were evenly spaced among us. I was seated directly between a wife of one of the Rotary Club members on my left and a daughter of another on my right. The daughter was the most at ease of the two, but even she did not stray from looking straight ahead at the table. She answered all of my questions with a brief yes or no or a nod of acknowledgment. The wife said nothing the entire meal, but sometimes would smile shyly in answer to a comment that I made to her. Without having the covering refuge of their burkas, It seems that the Pakistani women felt exactly as if they were totally naked, openly revealed to all of the world. We could hardly wait for the dinner to end.

One evening in Dhaka after a performance, we were taken to a party by the young U.S.I.S. officer in charge of us. Rather than an official reception, this party was off the cuff. It was attended by a mixture of a few East Pakistanis and many westerners from the various embassies. The party goers were mainly young people of our own generation, which allowed us a freedom of activity and self-expression that was hard to come by for most of the tour. Almost all of the social functions of the company consisted of official parties and receptions given either by diplomatic officers from our own country or officials of the host country.

Taking advantage of our easy state that evening, most of us overly imbibed in the abundantly provided alcohol. By 2:00 A.M. those who were left decided that it was time to return to the hotel before we embarrassed ourselves more than we already had. The only dissenting member of the group was Cristyne Lawson, one of the youngest and newest women in the company. Up until that time, Cristyne had seemed a very nice, slightly shy young woman. This evening she had come into full bloom and now was absolutely refusing to leave the party. Each of us separately pleaded with her. Failing individually, we pleaded together as a body, but to no avail. Finally the U.S.I.S. officer took over. He and Cristyne disappeared into a private corner and after an intense conversation, arrived at a bargain. Cristyne agreed to leave the party if she could be the driver of the officer's car for the trip back to the hotel. Desperate to solve the situation, he had agreed.

Fortunately the traffic in Dhaka at this early morning hour, consisted of little more than two trishaws and one pedestrian. The U.S.I.S. officer sat as close to Cristyne as possible so he could grab the wheel on a seconds notice in case an emergency arose. He was practically sitting in Cristyne's lap the entire trip. Cristyne, aware that all was not well with her faculties of perception drove at no more that four miles an hour. We inched towards our hotel, closing in on it yard by yard. We slowed down to two miles an hour as we turned each corner. After what seemed an endless amount of time, we pulled up safely in front of the hotel.

Everyone poured out of the car giving thanks to the gods that governed all safe journeys. It being late, most of the company disappeared immediately into the hotel after a brief "thank you" to our host. Cristyne wiggled her way out from behind the wheel of the car and in a heavily slurred voice thanked everyone for letting her drive home, giving special thanks to the U.S.I.S. officer for his generosity. With all etiquette accomplished, Cristyne slowly sank to the ground like a deflating balloon and passed into total unconsciousness. By that time, I was the only other person left. I will always remember that our hotel was exactly three floors high, as I carried Cristyne up the three flights and put her to bed. Every step put Cristyne into my debt for the rest of her life.

The Dhaka hotel also became memorable because of the holiday we all spent there together. Christmas in Dhaka may sound like a joyous Bing Crosby movie, but in actuality it was a dreary gathering of alien people. Craig, Lee, Bethsabee, and Martha gave us a "festive" party with presents, food, drinks, and even a mock Christmas tree. We all gathered once again in the hotel's all purpose reception room, dressed in our best party attire and carrying presents searched out in the barren stores of this small town. Everyone was there but Martha. Instead of attending, she sent her presents down to us, choosing to remain in her room. The tour had been a strain on her. She was one of the few members of the company who had never missed a performance. This Christmas holiday respite gave her a chance to recover her much needed energies. Her decision was both necessary and intelligent, but it left the Christmas party bereft of its major personality.

The occasion spun itself out quickly with everyone on their best behavior, but after the presents had been distributed, we all disappeared quietly to our individual rooms. Bob Cohan, my roommate, had gone off somewhere on his own and I was left completely by myself, burdened by my rambling thoughts. I went to bed but after a brief attempt at sleep, I got up, dressed again and went downstairs. At the front entryway a few trishaw drivers were waiting through the night for any possible business.

I picked out the most likely driver, a young man who looked strong enough and warmly enough dressed. It was difficult to make myself understood but by combining my gestures with his few words of English, we finally reached an understanding. I wanted to ride through Dhaka for an hour in the crisp and cold air, hoping that it might clear my troubled mind. Having no idea why this strange westerner wanted a scenic tour in the middle of the night, the driver started off. His purpose was to earn some much needed money while my purpose was to earn a much needed relief.

The city had one main artery from which branched many little winding lanes. These were filled with a few essential shops, many hovels about ready to collapse, and tents pitched in empty spaces with gatherings of people who had no coverings for themselves what so ever. These people were wrapped around wood fires, trying to fight off the elements and maintain some warmth as they slept the night away. My driver and I roamed the small city for most of the hour and then, having run out of places to go, we stopped in front of a hovel which looked especially dilapidated. The driver indicated that he lived there with his family. As I had made so many comments regarding the poverty and the poor conditions in which his people existed, he thought that I might be interested in seeing his home. We approached the hovel and he pulled aside the curtain which covered the entryway. There in a small space of about fifty square feet, eight people of varying ages were sleeping. A mat was thrown on the ground for protection from the dampness that crept up from the earth underneath. The walls looked as if with one strong gust of wind they would cave in. There was no warmth in the room except for that which seeped slowly out from the bodies of the sleeping people. Never has abject poverty seemed to me so immediate and so helpless. I watched hypnotized for a few minutes and then indicated that I wanted to return to the hotel.

When we arrived at the hotel, out of a feeling of guilt or desperation, I gave the driver all of the money that I had in my pockets and all my cigarettes as well. The latter, amazingly, seemed to give him the greater pleasure. I went into the hotel and finally got back to bed again, making another attempt at sleep. I had accomplished my mission. Christmas in Dhaka was wiped from my mind.

The Yarkon Hotel was just around the corner from the beach in Tel Aviv. Actually the Yarkon Hotel was just around the corner from everything. The Graham Company stayed there en masse, in happy or unhappy union depending on the individual. Martha stayed in the far more elegant Dan Hotel situated a few blocks further up the beach. At the present, the Yarkon Hotel has fallen on hard times and now houses only homeless, nonpaying itinerants. Even its surroundings have been down graded and it sits easily in full accord with its poor and tawdry neighbors. When the Graham Company was housed there the Yarkon was not greatly different from what it is today, but somehow, I remember it as a place of great freedom and fun.

The Yarkon was the hotel where Marni and I first decided to get married, so of course for us it carries special significance. Its halls were where Marni learned her first Graham dances. Having gone on tour only at the last minute to replace a dancer with a broken foot, she was forced to become a "quick study". While the rest of the company were tanning their bodies at the beach, Marni and Lois Schlossberg moved through the dark hallways (the hotel always liked to save on electricity) like agonized specters writhing, jumping, and falling as Lois taught Marni the intricate movements of *Clytemnestra* and *Night Journey*. The Yarkon was the hotel where, I discovered my roommate Paul Taylor, stepping out of the shower wearing his blue seer sucker suit, claiming that it was much the simplest way to get it clean. He then stripped it dripping from his body, hung it up and stepped back into the shower to give his body the same cleansing treatment that he had just given his best and only suit.

The balconies of the upper rooms of the Yarkon were interconnecting allowing for a great interplay among the inhabitants Marni woke up one morning to find a strange Israeli soldier in the bed next to her sound asleep. Because of the rather relaxed, simple atmosphere of the Yarkon, the members of the Graham Company generally enjoyed each others friendship more than at any other time that I can remember.

Our teaching residencies from summer to summer provided Marni and me with a wide range of living quarters, from an attic in Connecticut where for six weeks I could never stand vertically upright, to our old, brewery-converted apartment in Stockholm with its long hallway, thick walls, wide windows, and gorgeous kokelugn made of Swedish tile. Perhaps the most fulfilling stay anywhere was in Kyoto, Japan. We were living in Tokyo for six months in 1985 so that I might investigate that country's form of theater called Noh. I was especially interested in its slowly hypnotic dance forms. During the time that we were there, we traveled to Kyoto to teach a modern dance workshop for Takani Hirai at the nearby Nara Women's University. Hirai-San had stayed with us in Berkeley for a week while she was in the United States studying modern dance at U.C.L.A. Now that we were in her home territory, she felt that she in turn should offer us a truly Japanese experience. She found us lodging in Myoshinji, one of the oldest and largest Zen Buddhist temples in Japan. The temple was not a single building, but rather a huge compound located near the edge of Kyoto. Its separate buildings existed side by side in their own landscaping and autonomous atmosphere.

We arrived at the temple late at night; the holy buildings seemed completely enveloped in mysterious contemplation. Priests, dressed in simple robes, appeared easily out of the shadows caused by a bright new moon and just as easily disappeared back into them. The lane by which we wound our way into the compound narrowed considerably, becoming so small that the car was finally forced to halt. A priest met us and, with a low bow, indicated that we were to follow him. We passed rapidly through little gardens and over small bridges before arriving at a large and relatively well lit building. Standing at the door waiting to greet us was our Mama-San, a smallish, thin woman whose main attraction were eyes which were flecked with her warming smile.

Leaving our shoes at the door, we entered the immaculate building and climbed the immaculate stairs to our immaculate quarters. Our section of the temple was used mainly to house novitiate priests, but because it was in between sessions, we were the only tenants on the upper floor. Marni and I had the whole vast space all to ourselves surrounded by the simplistic beauty of tatami mats and shoji screens. We slept on the floor cradled in our warmly protecting futons. Our Mama-San took complete charge of us. She drew our bath every night when we returned, tired from either our teaching sessions at Nara or a day of wandering for hours through the beauty of Kyoto. After our bath we were fed fruit, tea and cakes to help replenish our spirits and to revive our energies. When we arose in the morning exotic breakfasts were prepared in which Mama-San provided a delicious mixture of the best of eastern and western foods.

Mama-San, however, gave us a curfew. Either we were to return to the temple by 8:00 P.M. or we were to call her. Not that the doors were ever locked, but if we had not made contact by the predetermined hour, Mama-San would then begin to worry about our welfare. Not wanting to cause concern, every evening at 7:55 P.M., Marni and I were to be found racing through the temple grounds like two young teenagers trying to avoid punishment for coming home late. I could have made a phone call instead in order to explain where we were and what we were doing, but although my Japanese was improving, it definitely was not good enough for me to meet the challenge of communicating over the telephone.

Our loveliest moments at the temple occurred in the early hours upon waking. The shoji screens allowed the coolness of the morning air into our room, making us sink down further into the futons, our bodies grabbing at the precious warmth for a little longer time. As we moved easily between waking and sleep, the constant low, subdued chanting of the priests while at their morning prayers combined easily with the clacking of their wooden blocks to create a hypnotizing sound. At first it passed over us and then surrounded our very beings. It was autumn and the harshness of the year's ending was softened by the dimming sunlight. Newly fallen leaves crushed under foot and the freshly washed skies glistened clean. For the five days that we resided at Myoshinji, more than ever before the world seemed to us like a beautiful place in which to live.

4

ON EMPLOYMENT

To the professional modern dancer of the 1930's and 40's, a job was thought of as being nothing more than necessary, extracurricular employment. Its singular benefit was that it provided the finances needed for the dancer to continue practicing his chosen profession. The act of working at that job had no connection whatsoever with the dancer's aesthetic interests. It was totally disconnected from his artistic life. Despite the sweat and the sore muscles that often accompanied the process of practicing dance, no one who was serious ever considered dancing as employment.

One worked and then one danced. The two worlds existed side by side in the daily life of the individual, but with the commercial endeavor being completely subservient to the artistic. Dance was thought of as a dedication, worshipped and served daily. Its impracticality caused parents to attempt a variety of devious means to deter their progeny from seriously considering dance as a career; they seldom succeeded.

In the 30's and 40's the devotion to modern dance by the young dance acolytes and the sacrifices that they made closely resembles the attraction of many youths toward the religious cults of the 70's. The major difference between involvement in the two ideologies lies in the fact that the early dancers were not brainwashed by outside forces but rather the condition was self inflicted. Who needed drugs when dance as a powerful stimulant was readily available to produce an easy high?

Having to labor at a job interfered with the aesthetic life of the dancer; however, it was the one time that he came into contact with the outside world. At times this interference was a very rude awakening but at other times it was a much needed relief from the intensity of the dance world. Coming in touch with reality could always open up new depths of perception for the dancer.

Over the years, as a dancer's career progressed, teaching and choreography brought about more financial security. It was an inevitable progression for those who wished to spend all of their life in their chosen field. Upon reaching the age of retirement from performing, seldom did people who had obtained even a moderate level of accomplishment, change their profession. They might leave the centralization of New York for more regional areas, but their involvement in dance never lessened. Having increased their work in choreography and teaching as the years passed and their maturity grew, these dancers were well prepared to move from the performing field into any other, more lucrative dance specialization. Even if the dancers had no great interest in teaching or choreography, the money earned by performing was so poor that the dancer was forced into these additional fields for financial survival. And, teaching and choreography were infinitely more closely related to their immediate profession than any outside jobs.

Beginning with the 1960's most dance companies became incorporated. The tours sponsored by the National Endowment for the Arts provided performing artists with the possibility of full time employment. Because of these two factors, the dedication of the dancers toward their work underwent a large change. Auditions for the major companies now became commonplace. This was true even among the companies that had previously used dancers trained only in their own schools. Because of the high degree of competition for employment, the attitude of the performers underwent a substantial change also.

Dance now became a job. The job became unionized and even developed a certain amount of bargaining power in relation to management. Dancers, although still far from achieving any degree of wealth, could at least, now, seem somewhat respectable. Job employment existed through the greater part of the year. Dance was no longer a hunger which must be fed by the individual performer. The dancer could now earn enough to keep sufficient food in his stomach, a secure roof over his head and presentable clothes on his back. Luxuries were still missing, but there was little time for the performer to indulge in such things anyway. Dance as a profession slowly began to enter the world of the accepted.

Because of the constantly increasing level of competition for the new professional dance jobs, the emphasis placed on technique increased at a rapid pace. Technique was an area that allowed for easy comparison of one dancer with another. As a result dancers began to gain a physical prowess which heretofore had never been accomplished. Times had changed. Now that dance was thought of as employment, it became a salable commodity. In a great many cases, it developed in a short period of time from a labor of love to a labor for profit. True, one dancer could possess both intentions at the same time, but the days of the acolytes and devotees which existed from 1930 to the 60's had almost entirely been eliminated. There has been much criticism that the dancers of the newly formulated companies lack the fire of the old days. It is said that once the absolute level of dedication diminished, the quality of the dancing became brilliant, but uncreative, singularly technical, and mechanized. The judgment of this, for good or bad, I feel, lies with the taste of the individual viewer. All things must grow, change, and develop; dance is no exception.

Upon arriving in New York, almost all dancers, unless they are fortunate enough to have parents who are endlessly generous, must find some
kind of supplemental financing in order to exist. Food, rent, and transportation as well as the ever necessary dance classes have always cost,
even at post World War II levels of the 1940's, a vast amount of money. In
the 90's, the cost of these same necessities has become exorbitant.

Today it is difficult to find jobs which pay enough money to cover all
of the expenses of a dancer. In the past, the possible earning power was
more closely aligned to the budget of an economizing dancer.

The cost differential in the past could be covered by a much greater
array of jobs than it can be at the present. Nowadays the cost of living is
so great that the minimal amount of wages earned in part time employment does not nearly meet the basic requirements for daily existence.

There are a few dancers who for various reasons are never placed in
the position of seeking employment. They move straight from schools
into connecting companies, progressing directly from the protection of
their parent's finances to immediate employment in their chosen profession. Because I was given a stipend to cover my living expenses under
the G.I. Bill when I first came to New York, I also was able to forestall
having to find a regular job in order to support myself. The purpose of
the G.I. Bill was to provide veterans of World War II a chance to reha-
bilitate themselves following wartime activities by trying to find new
directions and careers without having to fight great financial pressures.
No one ever became wealthy from the income of the G.I. Bill, but it
helped to provide a simple sustenance. My G.I. Bill provided me with a
year's graduate study at the University of California, Berkeley, two years
at the Neighborhood Playhouse in New York, and one session under the
Theater Wing, also located in New York.

In addition to the G.I. Bill there was the 52–20 Club. All veterans who
were unemployed could receive for fifty-two weeks a weekly payment of
twenty dollars. Between the first and second years of the Neighborhood
Playhouse during the summer of '49, a group of us from the theater
school apprenticed as actors at the Duxbury Summer Theater in
Massachusetts. As apprentices we were given room and board, but no
more. Being unable to be further employed because of our rehearsals and
being veterans of World War II, all of us made use of the 52–20 Club.
Early every Monday morning before rehearsals began, we all hitch-hiked
our way from Duxbury to the nearby town of Plymouth, where the government office was located, to sign for our weekly unemployment
checks. If the authorities had ever found jobs for us we would have had
to accept them or lose our benefits, but that never happened. In those
days, twenty dollars could cover a multitude of expenses, but we were so
occupied with rehearsing and performing at the summer theater that

there was not much time in which we could spend even this small amount. As a result most of us ended the summer with quite a few extra dollars left.

Back in New York the carefully counted extra money was rapidly spent and we all soon found ourselves living again on the edge of poverty. All of our daytime was spent at the Playhouse studying acting or other related courses. Out of necessity, we became experts at all sorts of free evening and weekend entertainment. Near the end of my second year at the Playhouse, my desire to concentrate on dance training finally got the better of me. I began cutting acting classes in order to find various part time jobs to earn enough money to pay for the extra dance classes.

It wasn't too long before I discovered the futility of this plan; I was getting neither acting or dance training. I withdrew from all of the classes at the Neighborhood Playhouse except for Louis Horst's dance composition class. Until I began my session with the Theater Wing, the financial support from my G.I. Bill ceased and I was forced to work for the first time and to fully provide for all of my living expenses.

Poor paying jobs at poor hours were easy to find, especially jobs with dull and uninteresting companies. I readily got a job with a well known insurance company. Working for that type of company was considered to be at the bottom of the list for opportune employment. Rock bottom was a file clerk on the swing shift exactly the job I undertook in order to stave off imminent hunger.

My interview for the position was given by a severely dressed authoritarian woman who smoked French Galois cigarettes constantly. My interrogation by this woman consisted of a few impersonal questions evidently meant to reveal something about my honesty and integrity. These questions were followed by a challenge to recite the alphabet forwards and then, a special challenge to recite it backwards. Having completed the tests with flying colors, I was put to work immediately.

Because of present day computers which compact endless amounts of information into minuscule areas, it is hard to imagine the many rooms filled with row after row of files which in turn were filled with row after row of white cards. After every normal day's work at the insurance company, we, file clerks, were left with stacks of those small rectangular cards which were to be dispersed among the already filed information.

Each day, within an hour of beginning our work, ennui overtook took us. Monotony compounded monotony. It took little time to find out how to pass the long evenings while doing the minimal amount of constructive work. The supervisors only made their rounds every hour or so and were quite lax even in that task. As they neared every group, the word of their imminent arrival was passed on ahead as if we were a part of some secret and mysterious underground pipeline. As the inspectors passed, cards flew rapidly if inaccurately into some file or other, any file cabinet would do.

My co-workers were much in the same position that I was, trying for a short period of time to earn a small amount of money while our "real" life lay somewhere over the horizon. Our common point of view made for an easy camaraderie. In between the supervisors rounds our personal relationships blossomed. We were quite evenly divided between male and female; the pairings among us were accomplished very easily, naturally, and without stress. The little alcove by the back row of files in which the water cooler had once stood proved to be a marvelous nesting place. None of us took each other seriously, but those brief relationships made the hours of unbelievable tedium pass rapidly and pleasantly. The monotonous activity of putting cards alphabetically in place took on an increased excitement and stimulation because of those short liaisons.

There were now too many days in which large stacks of file cards remained untouched. Supervision increased and all of our romantic activities ceased. With the pleasantries removed, being a file clerk became a purposeless task, boring beyond endurance. I quit the job without notice, not that it made any difference to anyone, but as I walked out of the door for the last time, I felt an increased determination to accomplish something in theater so as to avoid being doomed to such a future.

Being a file clerk had not solved my financial problems, and I could not let many days go by without finding another job. Through other students at the Neighborhood Playhouse I had heard that there was easy money available for little work by doing life modeling at the Art Student's League of New York. All one was required to do was to sit or stand quietly for lengthy periods at a time so that an art class, using a living model, could learn to draw the human body. I had never done anything like it before, but the whole concept of modeling seemed simple and easy. My only reservation was that the focus of attention had to be on the body's muscular development. Thus, a bare unclothed physique was required. The one covering that was allowed to be worn by a male model was an athletic supporter. I had a fairly well developed body, gained from all my physical activities. Although I was still overflowing with energy, I could also be quietly contemplative if necessary. This I assumed would aid me in getting through the long static hours.

The audition for life modeling was more related to the purpose than was my interview for being a file clerk. It was obvious that I could not be hired until my body had been completely inspected. It was easy to strip to my briefs before my detached interviewer. All I had to do was to imagine that I was on a sandy beach, basking in the warm sun, and preparing for a swim. The beach of my imagination was obviously muscle beach, for I was asked to flex and stretch more muscles than I had ever known existed. I was not immediately hired. After being accepted as a possibility, I was put on a long list of potential models.

After about two weeks, the call came from the Art Student's League. I was told to arrive the next day with an athletic supporter and a covering robe. Also, I should arrive cleanly bathed. I was insulted. I hoped that the statement was a general one, given to all new models, rather than as the result of my recent audition.

I arrived a half hour before the scheduled 10:00 A.M. sitting in order to have time to carefully analyze the situation. As the time drew near for the official unveiling of my body, the palms of my hands began to perspire. To be caught unaware in one's athletic supporter in most situations would not, even in the early 50's, make one suffer much embarrassment but there was something about the disrobing with all those eyes probing my body at one time, inspecting and evaluating my pectorals and abdominals and who knew what else, that caused me to feel discomfort.

Then there was the other matter of the basic male uprising. I remembered with self-consciousness as a youth in junior high school how, after I had been sitting for an hour in an English or history class, I began to feel my manliness grow just as the bell rang signaling a change of classes. Hands went desperately into both pockets, making big fists so as to disguise the disturbances that had arisen. Now, if while modeling, this self-consciousness should happen to arouse the same instincts, there would be no possible place to stick my fists for cover. I need not have worried. The only thing that arose on my body were goose bumps from the chill in the air.

My mauve colored robe felt good as it covered my nakedness and for a time I doubted if, in reality, I would ever be able to shed it. The room was filled with twenty or more eager artists ready to get to work. Relaxed, setting up their pens and ink, conversing among themselves, the students hardly knew that I had entered the room. For my part, I was sure that all eyes were riveted on my every move. Each step toward the posing dais became more difficult and tripping while mounting the small raised platform didn't help my feeling of security. A deep breath and the robe dropped. Silence. There were no gasps of wonder or exclamations of approval much to my disappointment, but there were also no catcalls.

Once that moment was past, the rest was simple. Biceps were tensed. The body was curved. "Don't move for ten minutes." Rest. Bring my muscles into action for another ten minutes. Quick studies were easier than prolonged full drawings during which monotony set into both mind and muscle. Crawling insects were destructive to stillness as well as occasional strangely placed itches.

To earn more money I took on private sittings. Posing for individuals proved to be more profitable as well as more pleasant. I had three clients, two elderly men and a mid-life woman. All were undemanding, letting me rest whenever I wanted. The woman, I think, liked the breaks better than the work sessions, and with each pause, she stuffed me with delicious food from exotic places. The pay was fair so I continued to model and this work helped me to exist through the spring days of my Theater Wing session. A casual sexual approach by one of the elderly men in addition to my departure in the summer for Colorado combined to end my modeling career. When I returned to New York at summer's end, dancing by choice, began to take over my entire life.

All of my G.I. Bill had run out by now, and so I was forced to find work immediately. My friend from the Morgue, Marie Hall Laube, was acquainted with a doctor who practiced at Columbia Presbyterian Hospital on the upper west side. A few words from him got me a job as one of the service boys with Harkness Pavilion, the exclusive section of Presbyterian Hospital. I opted for the swing shift once more as working the hours from 4:00 P.M. until midnight left me the greater part of the day for dance classes and rehearsals. I enjoyed the idea of working in a hospital. In my younger days, I had always wanted to be a doctor. Helping to cure others seemed like such a marvelous profession. Now that I was employed at a hospital, I toyed with the idea that fate was directing my foot steps and that I was destined to become a physician.

My major task at the hospital, however, was much less grandiose. My job was to take all the pregnant women up to the labor room to give birth. I would meet the ladies at the door with a wheelchair. I assured the attending husbands that all was well and after securing a large size tip, I disappeared up the elevator with the imminent mother in tow, while she moaned and groaned, counting the minutes between contractions.

The hospital was almost always filled with celebrities, some dying, some birthing, some merely being repaired. Another of my tasks was to pick up the records of the incoming patients and transfer them to the Harkness section. Although all records were supposed to be kept secret, I always took a peek into the folders learning who was having a face lift or other type of cosmetic or vital surgery. Reporters were continuously hanging out around the waiting rooms to get the latest tidbits of gossip. Bribes were always offered in return for information about the celebrities who had been recently admitted or to help in gaining entrance to a higher floor. The hospital job paid poorly, but was intriguing and never dull. Everyday offered some new adventure.

One day shortly after I had come on duty, I was sent by the woman at the admitting desk to try to entice a female patient back into the hospital. The woman had been placed in the Harkness neurological room, a room designated for patients who were of questionable stability. These people were supposed to be watched carefully as their behavior was often erratic. This woman had managed to escape the nurses' all-seeing eyes and was now holed up in a cafe across the street. She was calling into the admitting office quite often informing everyone of both her whereabouts and her increasingly upset state of mind; however, she refused to return to her room in the hospital.

I spotted her right away in the cafe. She was easily recognizable by the hospital attire that she still wore underneath her slightly open long coat. We struck up a conversation and I soon discovered that there was nothing basically wrong with her. She knew immediately where I was from and why I was there. It took me almost the length of my entire shift to convince her that she would be better off at the hospital than in the cafe. Once she was convinced, we made the trek back to her room. The woman at the desk in the Harkness downstairs admitting office winked at me as we passed her on our way to the elevators, but said nothing. The head nurse on the floor where the neurological room was located also did nothing as I arrived with the patient, only nodded in recognition. When we came to the door to her room, the woman refused to go into it until I entered first. Once I was inside, she darted into the room behind me, quickly locked the door, and with a cry like a banshee, stripped off all of her clothes. This was not exactly what I had in mind, but I was trapped and she knew it.

I stealthily moved away from her to the opposite side of the room across from the door, trying to remain as nonchalant as possible. She edged away from the door and began to walk slowly towards me. Our eyes remained riveted on each other and our breath began to come in short pants because of the tension of the situation. At the right moment I rushed past her, unlocked and opened the door, and ran out. I sped all of the way to the elevator which fortunately was still waiting for me. As I passed the nurse on duty, I cursed her roundly for leaving me alone in the room with the woman. When I arrived at the bottom floor, I raced past the lady on duty at the desk shouting that I was leaving immediately for the night. I did not stop running until I reached the subway and into safe territory far away from the hospital.

The next day when I returned to work, I was told that during the night the patient had escaped from the room once again and this time she was gone for good. I breathed a sigh of relief.

Just one week after that traumatic event, there was yet another and much more demanding happening. A taxi pulled up at the Harkness entryway. As usual I opened the door of the cab with my wheelchair ready to take the expectant mother upstairs. One look inside and I discovered that not only was the poor woman alone in the vehicle, but that the situation was already in a disastrous red alert state. The head of the baby was completely out and the rest of it was rapidly progressing towards birth.

The taxi driver screamed, "Get her out of my cab. She's already having it."

I, in turn, screamed, "Get a doctor immediately." Chaos reigned. It took no more than five minutes for the doctor to arrive but by that time, a little girl had entirely entered the world.

I guess it was then that I realized that I would never become a fit doctor. It was a nice altruistic concept, but it was more than I could handle. Shortly thereafter I began teaching for Hanya Holm and my days with the highly touted medical profession came to an abrupt end.

There were other jobs, most of them short lived and purely utilitarian. A soda jerk in a Whelan's Drug Store on the corner of 8th Avenue and 42nd Street provided some humorous moments balanced with tiring hours of standing endlessly on my feet. Once I started teaching at Hanya's, I had a weekly income on which I could rely. While it still did not allow me to pay my rent, classes at the Holm studio would now be free.

To give me a little more leverage against poverty, I answered an ad for a Western Union messenger boy on Wall Street. The Western Union office was located right next to the New York Stock Exchange and was filled with bustling activity during the day. As I could only work the job on weekends, the one shift available to me was from midnight until 8:00 A.M. At first I refused to consider taking the job, but then decided to give it a try. The position turned out to be the best and most beneficial of all my extracurricular employment.

There is something very special about lower Manhattan and its financial district. During working hours, the streets are jammed with people, cars, and delivery trucks, all carrying out tasks with inflated importance. Then a delicate quiet comes as dusk settles over the concrete valleys. The streets are quickly deserted and left in silence. The district's complete change of character gives it a magical aura as if a master conductor is leading a human symphony through intricate rhythmic changes to a fast and loud crescendo followed by a quiet lengthy final coda.

Each weekend when I arrived at work at midnight the area was entombed in darkness except for the few shimmering lights of the night clerks in the various buildings. Most businesses maintained these men on duty in case of emergencies and their incandescent illuminations glowed like welcoming beacons in each edifice, as I delivered the "vastly important" messages. The money was good as most of the night clerks contributed to my income with large tips. After many hectic weeks of racing from class to class, teaching and rehearsing, these weekends of wandering through New York's man made canyons, in the dark, quietly alone, were a refreshing respite; they were a reminder that life and humans existed beyond the world of dance. During those long hours until the world became once again filled with light, my mind and imagination were given time to explore in complete freedom. Sleepy as I might be, I always returned to my bed with a feeling of being refreshed, renewed, and much better able to handle the coming week.

Because several choreographers with whom I was dancing at the time required Saturday and Sunday rehearsals, I somewhat regretfully had to cease my wanderings as a messenger boy in the financial district. Also, by now I had started to teach additional classes under Hanya's aegis at the Mill's School for Girls in Manhattan and Adelphi College in Long Island. Teaching these classes provided me with additional money so that I had no need for extra outside jobs.

I was now even earning enough money to pay off the debt I had previously incurred for back rent at the Morgue. When that debt was paid off, I was able to look for better, if not more spacious lodgings. Life for me, in general, began to take on a new, shiny, professional look. Even at the beginning of the summer, immediately after I stopped teaching at Hanya's, I continued to garner a sufficient income by teaching at The New Dance Group. Although my weekly earnings were reduced a slight bit because of the fewer classes, I still had a steady amount of money.

With no outside jobs, I could concentrate completely on my dancing. At the New Dance Group, I was allowed to take any class that I wanted without paying. Also, after a few weeks of paying for classes with Charles Weidman, I was presented with a scholarship for as many classes as I wanted to take. The only classes for which I had to pay were the ever challenging daily ballet classes which I never missed. Also I was able to audition for everything that I heard about or read about on the dance studio's bulletin boards.

Through Elsa Reiner, the secretary at Hanya's, I learned of many television auditions that needed men qualified both in acting and dancing. These were usually the popular network dramatic shows, Studio One or the Philip Morris Playhouse. A great many of these jobs seemed to be created specifically for my training. Most of the time, the other males who were auditioning could out dance me by far, but had little talent or training in vocal matters. As most of the dancing was relatively simple, the shows could more easily deal with inadequacies in that area rather than with inadequacies in acting. During that period, television shows were performed live and were full of excitement and real immediacy. That excitement is almost impossible to recreate in the present day taped television shows, even with a live audience present.

Sometimes I was just an extra, part of the background of a scene taking place in a dance studio or a theater rehearsal hall. At other times I was given a few inconsequential lines to speak. Whether the dialogue was inconsequential or not, I was paid a great deal more money every time I opened my mouth. The more lines that I spoke, the more money I received. Thus, the assignment of lines was awaited anxiously for financial reasons as well as artistic ones. I finally appeared on so many Studio One shows, that I was almost considered a regular. The producers would bypass Hanya's and call me directly if they needed an actor/dancer for a small part.

My favorite television role was in a live production of Alice in Wonderland, presented on one of the major networks. In it, I had the role of one of the three highly costumed playing cards that painted the rose bushes red. Besides speaking a few lines the three of us had a short but lovely little dance to do, choreographed by Dorothy Jarnac. As profitable and as much fun as these productions were, they began to pall as my desire to concentrate on concert dance grew increasingly intense.

In my entire career as a concert dancer, I was required to audition only a very few times in order to join a modern company. In the 50's and 60's dancers still entered the concert field by first establishing a devotion to a choreographer and then, by being extended an invitation to join his company. My first audition for a modern dance company was for the Dudley-Maslow-Bales Trio in 1951. The company was connected with the New Dance Group Studios. As I was already teaching there, it was really what one would call an "in house" audition. Jack Moore and I were actually the only two dancers who were being seen. Jack had arrived in New York from Iowa at approximately the same time that I had arrived from California. Through our common interests, we became good friends and eventually, as a joke, set up a competition concerning who could work with the greatest number of noted choreographers. I think, we finished our dancing careers fairly even except for the Dudley-Maslow-Bales Trio.

A few years later I had a similar "in house" audition; this time it was for Sophie Maslow alone. Again there were just two of us and on, this occasion, I was in competition with Alvin Ailey. Sophie chose to use both of us in her concert. Alvin got the solo in the jazz piece *Manhattan Transfer* while I was given the marvelous part of the fiddler in Sophie's *The Village I Knew*.

The auditions that were really exciting and which I thoroughly enjoyed were those held for the various Broadway shows during the 1950's. I probably had a completely different approach to auditioning than the other hopefuls. I had no expectations for ever getting chosen. In fact, with my direct focus on becoming a concert modern dancer, I really didn't even want to be one of the chosen few. I was auditioning for the experience and the sheer pleasure of it. I felt sorry for the Broadway gypsies whose very existence depended upon getting hired. If these dancers were lucky, they would eventually get into a hit show which might last from two to four years. This allowed them to make big financial savings. When the show closed, these financial savings would then tide the dancers over until they could make it into another spectacular, long running hit.

The pattern would keep repeating itself until the process of aging began to overtake the dancers. The dancing chorus of the Broadway shows was a young people's world. All the chorus boys and girls were required to be seemingly if not actually, vital and fresh looking. The means that the dancers devised to head off the aging process were sad, full of a terrible sense of desperation.

As I had gotten my equity card during the summer at the Duxbury Playhouse, I was permitted to audition at the Chorus Equity tryouts. This was much better than having to deal with the masses of people crowded together for the open auditions. Not that the equity auditions had a lack of dancers trying out. At most of the union auditions in excess of one hundred male dancers attended; at the open auditions there were often two hundred to two hundred fifty men.

Usually in the 50's everyone who auditioned got a chance to be seen dancing for at least the first time around. A phrase of movement would be presented by the choreographer or his assistant. Then, usually in groups of ten, each dancer would get a chance to perform. Following this, most dancers were greeted by the phrase, "Thank you very much." which actually meant that you were eliminated and would you please leave the premises as soon as possible. It was only in later years that most of the auditioning dancers were eliminated on type without ever getting a single chance to display their terpsichorean abilities.

At each audition, equity and nonequity, in a few hours applicants were cut down from the masses to twenty or thirty men and twenty or thirty women. These lucky dancers were brought together for the final selection on a later day. At that final audition, a few movement phrases were given to the remaining dancers, and one more cut was made. That ended the dancing section of the audition. The final choice was left not only to the choreographer but also to the director and the producers of the musical. All of the people that remained were entirely usable as dancers by the choreographer; selections were now made with regard to type, size, and the overall look of the entire group together. Most musicals required the dancing chorus to be able to contribute substantially to the choral singing in the show. Thus, the dancers often were asked to offer up a rendition of one of the latest popular ballads.

I looked forward to each audition with anticipation and excitement; I knew that it was the only time that I would ever get to dance with or rather for, some of the great choreographers of the dance world. There was no other means to see those outstanding creators at work, first hand. In a short period I danced for George Balanchine, Michael Kidd, Agnes DeMille, Onna White, Anna Sokolow, Helen Tamiris, Jerome Robbins, Ron Field, Jack Cole, and Hanya Holm. Each one of these choreographers was entirely different, having his own particular style. Some never left the audience area of the theater, letting their voices create the movement as they called out orders from that vast shadowy expanse of seats. Others never left the stage, but hovered over those of us who were auditioning with devastating control. Some of them were outrageously arrogant and some were warm and friendly. All were ruthlessly decisive, especially when it came to those dreaded words, "Thank you very much."

Hanya Holm had the most interesting way to make cuts. Each person auditioning did a seemingly simple dance walk across the stage, after which they were either eliminated or allowed to stay for further viewing. From that walk, Hanya felt that she could easily determine alignment, general carriage, rhythmic awareness, coordination, and presence. It was a great deal to be revealed by such a supposed simple movement.

It wasn't too often that I got past the first phase of dancing at an audition, but once in a while I would make it all the way through the preliminary tryouts into the final one. That, in itself, helped to feed my ego. Three times I even made it all the way through the final audition to the last selective process.

In 1952 the Theatre de Lys (now the Lucille Lortel Theater) in Greenwich village was presenting for its gala opening a production of *Frankie and Johnny*. It was a musical version of the story, written by John Huston. The rumor was that Huston had actually written it when he was about twelve years old, and that it was written for puppets. Vonn Hamilton was to be the choreographer. Jazz, tap, and ballet were the required movement forms. None of the latter named styles were a specialty of mine, but Lavina Nielsen, a friend from the José Limón Company was also a good friend of the choreographer. She was kind enough to put in a positive word for me. Even with this inside influence, I would not have been hired if Mr. Hamilton could have really heard my taps, but even to his knowledgeable ear, my soft ballet shoes camouflaged the ineptness of the sound created by my feet striking the floor. I was hired. The satisfaction that I might have had from being selected was diluted by the fact that I knew that I was in the final group only because of Lavina's kind words.

Wendy Toye, an English choreographer, was brought over to create the dances for the production of *Peter Pan* in a version which starred the movie actress, Jean Arthur. At the audition she selected me as one of the dancers for the show. Unfortunately, the director of the production who had to give the final approval was not in attendance at the audition. We were supposed to sit in the theater and wait for him to arrive. I was teaching for Hanya Hoim at the time and the hour for my class drew near. Being an unbelievably responsible or, actually, a completely naive person, it never entered my mind to call Hanya's studio and say that I could not make class that day. Instead I ran up 8th Avenue to Michael's Studio where Hanya's classes were held in order to teach my scheduled class. I hoped that I would be able to get back to the theater before the director arrived. I knew that I was definitely taking my chances on getting into the musical, but I thought I had no other choice. By the time that I returned from teaching, the director had come and gone. I was left to be the first replacement somewhere in the nebulous future. This was another diluted feeling of satisfaction.

The minute the final audition began for *Plain and Fancy* in 1954, I felt that I was going to be selected. Helen Tamiris was the choreographer. As each phrase of movement was taught and each group of dancers was selected, I was always the first or second person chosen and placed in the "inside" group. I had made the final audition easily; with eagerness I danced my way through this second audition right to the final selection. We had to sing for the producers but singing was no problem I could carry a tune well enough. The men who were left at the end of the audition had to wait for the women's audition to finish, so that we could be placed in line with them and be shifted around in various orders and arrangements. Finally nine males and nine females were picked. This time my satisfaction was complete.

Being selected to be in a Broadway musical was an accomplishment, but the actual experience of being in that musical certainly did not live up to expectations. The real feeling of exultation came at the point of being selected, at being one of nine men who had been chosen out of the three hundred to three hundred fifty males who had tried out. One can call that feeling ego, one can call it an affirmation of finally belonging to the professional dance world, or one can call it both. No matter. At that moment it gave me a marvelous surge of satisfaction.

It also gave me a solid salary that along with my other teaching and performing, enabled me to pay all of my many old debts, I was finally able to buy new and, by now, badly needed clothes, and to move a further step up the ladder in bettering my whole status of living. I was making progress financially and I felt that I would never again have to turn back.

5

ON HEALTH

Dancers rely on their bodies not only to earn a living, but also as the instrument for communicating their creative ideas. The necessary focus that is placed on the body's physical fine tuning at times causes an almost pathological attention centered on its inner conditioning and outward appearance. The ever-present classroom mirror, which continually casts back the dancer's own image, is a diabolical contributing factor. The reflection of each newly gained pound, each newly added facial wrinkle, each newly developed muscle, is carefully analyzed with devastating accuracy.

Jerome Robbins' ballet, *Afternoon of a Faun*, is a beautiful choreographic example of this type of self-involvement. Robbins takes the theme of sexuality and narcissism which Nijinsky derived from a poem by Mallarmé and develops it one step further. Robbins gives us two dancers, one male and one female, brought together in a studio involvement before an imaginary mirror. They are both so caught up in their own reflected images that the two can only fleetingly relate to one another. Then, with a sense of prolonged relief, they each return to their own masturbatory self involvement.

This focus on one's own physical well-being starts with the routine of daily classes and wends its way through all types of physical necessities built into the dancer's daily modus operandi. Activities such as sleeping and eating become rituals, rituals that, once established, cannot easily be dropped or altered.

The dancer's responsibility for maintaining a performance level of conditioning extends beyond himself into a whole sociological interaction of choreographers, other dancers, musicians, stage technicians, and the audience itself. The interlocking link with other participants and their physical interdependence in a choreographer's work is often so complex that it is impossible to hold any constructive rehearsal if one of the dancers or any of the other integrated figures becomes incapacitated.

Dancers are the instruments with whom a choreographer invests his creativity. No matter how vivid his imagination, it is nearly impossible for him to create a moving sequence of images without having the actual bodies present. An intelligent choreographer creates within the abilities of his dancers, finding what lies within their capacities and what does not.

The capabilities of the dancers for certain movements can only be tested by their presence in the studio. Injury and illness totally disallow this process.

The dancer is required to maintain his physical peak of strength not only through proper nutrition and sleep, but also by working carefully and intelligently while in the process of training, rehearsing, and performing. The dividing line between injury prevention and overindulgence in self-protection is hard to recognize. The only person who can clearly read one's own body's capacity for strength and endurance, is the individual dancer. He has been provided with a beautiful system of nerve endings and sensors which give clear warning about when the body's limitations have been reached.

The individual dancer as a professional enters this world of increased responsibility, he discovers his own way of working within it. As the years pass and the dancer continues to mature, the ritual of physical care and performance preparation increases, sometimes so much that these preparatory measures seem to take precedence over the actual act of dancing. But most often through years of work the mature dancer finds the care which he needs for his own body, and works within its boundaries.

In the Graham company in the 60's, Martha Graham, because of aging, needed as much energy, artificial or otherwise, as she could possibly obtain. Her doctor, Amos Cobert, came to the theater an hour or so before every performance to give Martha a vitamin B12 shot. What was good for Martha soon became good for the rest of the company and, in short order, a new ritual was developed. Most of the company's buttocks were bared as Dr. Cobert made his rounds from dressing room to dressing room, jabbing his sharp needle filled with vitamin B12 into every nude backside that was presented to him.

From the time that one enters the theater the rituals increase. Signing in, walking the stage, checking costumes, checking props, laying out make up, setting in place good luck figurines and pictures, changing into warm up clothes, and even going to the bathroom all are done in as many different ways and arrangements as there are individual dancers, but each dancer establishes his own routine and seldom varies from it.

Dancers are not always thorough in preparation. Because of indulgence and laziness, at times short cuts are used to replace those laborious but necessary rituals. Pills and liniment become a ritual in themselves. While their positive effect is immediate, over a long period of time, the negative aspects can be disastrous.

On one tour, I shared a dressing room with a dancer who, wanting to save time and energy, liberally applied Ben Gay to his legs and body, thus stimulating his blood vessels and hopefully, warming his muscles, ligaments and tendons. It seemed to work well for him for a short time;

he was fortunate in that he had a flexible body. I think that fact, rather than the Ben Gay, was the prime reason that he was able to maintain his performance excellence. The same dancer relied on a series of amphetamine pills which he took ritualistically before every performance, starting two hours preceding curtain time and spacing them at even intervals until the curtain rose. This brought him to a peak of energy just as the performance began. His own personal life was rather demanding and definitely draining. Because of his nightly dissipation, the only way that he could meet the energy requirements of his performing was through the artificial stimulation of Ben Gay and amphetamines. After a few months his tendons began to show strain and his nervous system became badly damaged. After a year or so more, all dancing ceased. He had cheated his own body to a fatal degree.

When I was dancing on tour with the Dudley-Maslow-Bales Trio, I remember being completely amazed at Ronnie Aul's ritual of eating before each performance. I never knew exactly what the concoction was that he put together, but I became fascinated watching him brew it, measuring out each element meticulously before it was added into the total. It seemed to have a marvelous effect as he was an outstandingly beautiful dancer.

Of all of the dancers that I have run across, Daniel Nagrin is probably the person that maintained the most highly developed rituals of preparation. Ointments, bandage wrapping, padding, socks, shoes, food: all were a part of the physical care that he went through religiously before every rehearsal or performance. Such care, as well as his generally good eating habits, prolonged Danny's performing career far beyond the age when most dancers have stopped. The last time that I saw him on stage was at the Zellerbach Playhouse in Berkeley, California. By that time he was well along in years, but still maintaining the physical capacity of a much younger man, he performed with a passion and strength.

While on tour the simple question of just what time is best to eat becomes a major contributing factor to dissension within a company. Some dancers need the energy gained from absorbing food before a performance and if they are forced to dance on an empty stomach, their dancing suffers greatly. Others refuse to eat anything until after the performance and then are often left bereft in small towns where all of the restaurants seem to close at an early hour. The before and after people make up two entirely different groups with two entirely different personalities, each group totally dependent on its own metabolic structures. They constantly clash on any bus tour, no matter how well structured it is.

There is also a third group of dancers who eat constantly, nibbling like rabbits on anything available. Their loneliness on tour and inactivity while traveling from place to place is soothed by the constant shuttling of food from hand to mouth. This has an immediate effect on the size of their bodies. It is sometimes referred to as "the ballooning of the American dancer."

I know of a young female performer who was engaged to be married following a rather long extended tour. She took with her on the trip a special dress which she was to wear on the day of her return home. Her intention was to meet her future husband in full and elegant regalia. The one thing that she did not take into account was the amount of weight that she happened to gain during the tour.

The arrival dress was kept carefully folded in a corner of her suitcase, never seeing the light of day in such exotic performance venues as London, Paris, Copenhagen, and Vienna. The dress was always kept in abeyance, awaiting that marvelous future moment when the couple would at last meet again. When the momentous day arrived, the dress was carefully taken out and an attempt was made to step into it. It was only when the zipper refused to close by more than an inch with her bulges of flesh pressed hard against the material of the dress that the woman realized the tragedy which had occurred little by little over the months. Not all the tears she shed could overcome her indulgent consumption of food.

At the other end of the spectrum lie the eating disorders of anorexia and bulimia. Although providing an immediate solution to the problem of excess weight, both disorders are completely destructive to an individual's strength, muscle tone, and body development. Each human body has its own uniqueness; its ability to lose or gain weight most often occurs because of the individual's metabolic rate.

Although often overemphasized, the lean, thin body has been accepted for quite a few years as aesthetically necessary for the incipient dancer. In times past, the voluptuous Italian ballerinas were looked upon with great favor, but with the passage of years, the long-legged slender Balanchine dancer has changed the entire look of both male and female performers all over the world.

Like any athlete, the dancer can function at his best when there is no excess weight encompassing his body. As with the athlete, "excess" is defined more by body structure than by an attempt to achieve the slender lines of a fashion model. Bone size and muscular development are the true determining factors. By working within these boundaries, not only does the line of the movement become more visually effective, but, more important, the pressures placed on the joints, tendons, and ligaments are greatly lightened.

The dancer puts great strain on his body because of the continual physical overuse during classes, rehearsals, and performances. If either excess weight or excess thinness is added to this activity, the situation for the dancer can become dangerous. If there is any confusion on the part of the dancer, he should see a doctor so as to define a workable weight.

I have found that almost all nontraumatic injuries occur with dancers whose weight is out of proportion with their structure in either direction. This is true especially with regard to the ankle joints and knees which receive most of the force. Thus it is logical to predict that the need for properly proportioned dancers evolved so that the dancer could function in the most affective and efficient manner and with the greatest safety. In time this developed into the aesthetic rule of thinness with which we are all so familiar and which often becomes an onus for so many young and budding performers.

If the dancer has little self control and any tendency toward neurotic or psychotic behavior, both anorexia and bulimia can very wrongly seem the easy answers to the unsolvable problems of weight. Fortunately these two disorders today are approached as illnesses and can be treated affectively over a period of time if the individual is so willing.

There are many methods of working with the body which are not directly oriented toward dance alone, but are also used by the general populace. They are studied by the dancer not so much to increase his technical prowess, but rather to keep his body in the best, centered, working order possible. Striving for a perfectly aligned performing body is an infinite process; nevertheless, the dancer never ceases the constant search for perfection. Some of these methods are deeply probing and demanding. Some present themselves as the miracle short cut to training, with desire replacing reality. None can replace dance as an actuality. The technique required for dance performance can only be achieved in regular classes specifically directed toward technical growth.

This is not to say that the various ancillary methods cannot enhance the dancer's training. What works for one individual cannot be denied its value for that individual. The physical and the psychological are so interwoven in dance performance that it is hard to separate the two. More often the effect of any approach is one of totality for the individual encompassing both the mind and the body.

When viewed in performance, dance is seen as a vital physical activity, whereas dancers spend endless hours of dull inactivity in rehearsal. Lengthy periods are spent sitting by the side of the room as choreographers try to transfer into physical actuality their intricate concepts and imaginative plans. Particularly in past times, choreographers were placed under tremendous pressure since the dancers were giving their time freely, without recompense. The chance to dance was the only reward for these performers and all unused time was a waste. During this period dancers spent restless, dissatisfied lives moving from choreographer to choreographer and company to company, seeking not only the opportunity for better parts but also the sense of being occupied and useful. Only if the dancers were totally devoted acolytes to a major dance personage, was time a gift easily given.

Today the situation has changed. Dance for the most part is a paid occupation. Salaries are even paid during the rehearsal period. They are undoubtedly at levels well below those that are contracted by dancers during a performance period, but nevertheless, some of the pressure is removed from the employer/choreographer. Once the dancer is paid for rehearsal, the dancer's time belongs to the choreographer to use as he sees best.

Thus dancers are often left to their own devices during extended rehearsal periods. During these times, the dancer's body can cool down to such a degree that it becomes dangerous to plunge into movement immediately. Even so the dancers often, on command, attempt to satisfy the choreographer's expectations, thus perhaps endangering their own physical safety. They choose self-inflicted injury in order to please.

The only way to prevent this is to keep one's body in a proper state of preparedness during the period of inactivity or to take the time to fully warm up the body and legs again. Certainly for the benefit of both the dancers and choreographer, the former method is greatly preferable over the latter, although it requires much greater use of continued applied energy.

The greatest example that I have ever seen of the constant attempt at keeping the body in a ready state during a rehearsal period was that of José Limón. José must have had one of the tightest bodies that ever existed among professional dancers. As one watched him prepare for performance, one could not help but wonder how he ever managed to create his powerful, free flowing, magnificence of movement.

To watch José in a studio rehearsal was a marvelous lesson. I first was given this opportunity while rehearsing for a performance at the American Dance Festival at Connecticut College in 1952 of Doris Humphrey's *Variations and Conclusion from New Dance*. This dance of Doris' consisted of several solos, a duet, and a trio within a group of dancers. Doris always divided the rehearsal time among the different sections leaving those not working to our own devices for long periods of time. We were left to practice our own parts or to sit on the side and gossip and rest until our individual turns came.

Most of us used the opportunity to sit and gossip. Not José. If he was not rehearsing or assisting Doris, José was always in the corner of the room practicing his solo. If he wearied of that after a time, he would move to the ballet barre and work on adapting technical demands to his tight body. He labored endlessly and meticulously, learning how to cre-ate an illusion of flowing movement within the limitations of his own physicality. By doing this he not only benefited himself but he always remained in a state of preparedness for Doris to make use of him whenever she wished.

The above-noted physical difficulties are integral to the process of making dances and therefore have a logical reason for their existence. On the other hand there are physical difficulties which are self-induced and are probably even more detrimental. Cigarettes, alcohol, and drugs both mentally and physically destroy the constructive activities that the dancer undertakes to bring his body to a prime operative level and his mind to a bright clarity of vision.

Smoking is the most frequent of these habits. Endurance is a much desired quality of the dance performer since dances often make great aerobic demands. One needs only to stand in the wings during a performance, watching the dancers enter and exit the stage, to realize how important the intake of oxygen is to the dancer. Unlike singers, dancers, because of the special carriage of their bodies, must use shallow breathing techniques instead of the deep abdominal intake of breath. This, combined with the aerobic demands of a choreographer's work, leaves even the dancer in the best of shape gasping for breath. The demand is so great that, in high altitudes, oxygen tanks are often provided to make it possible for the dancer to perform. The lungs of a smoking dancer are so congested that they must struggle for the needed oxygen, often leaving the performer writhing in deep pain.

If smoking is so detrimental to dancers, why is it that so many dancers are addicted to it? I have never seen such featured dancers as Martha Graham, Hanya Holm, José Limón, and Helen Tamiris smoke, but the same cannot be said about Doris Humphrey and Charles Weidman. Louis Horst constantly had a cigarette dangling from his lower lip with its ash slowly falling from it, but then, endurance was not a necessary qualification for his piano playing and caustic criticism. There are innumerable personal reasons contributing to why each dancer smokes, but the many hours of waiting in rehearsal rooms, dressing rooms and hotel rooms are extremely strong enticements. Once the habit is established, it is very difficult to break. Both the nicotine, itself, and the physical act of handling the cigarettes becomes addictive.

I smoked for approximately twenty years, finally consuming more than two packs of cigarettes a day. I was teaching in Stockholm, Sweden, with Marni and our newly born child, Marina, when I decided to quit. My salary in kroner was not vast but the cost of Swedish cigarettes was exorbitant, incentive enough to cease. I lit one cigarette in Stockholm before I returned to New York as a test case. I was afraid that when I returned to my old habitat, I would once again pick up old ways. This time the cigarette seemed flimsy, too light in weight to be held comfortably.

I felt sick to my stomach and dizzy, much the same as I had felt when I originally began smoking. That was enough. I never again desired another cigarette. It is the only time that I have ever used sheer will power to overcome anything; this time, fortunately, it worked.

Over the years I have often seen what a devastating toll overindulgence in alcohol has upon the dancer. Drinking liquor in excess is physically detrimental, as it strips the individual both of mental acuteness and physical coordination. In the near term, immediate harm occurs when a performer is intoxicated while attempting to dance, leaving himself unable to control his mind and body during a performance or rehearsal. Greater harm develops over time as excess drinking begins to attack the organic structure of the individual, causing possible irreparable damage to his entire muscular and nervous systems.

As with smoking, the causes of habitual excessive drinking are many and individual but are often exacerbated by the loneliness and inactivity during any lengthy tour. With nothing else to occupy one's time following a performance, after hours bars act as magnets and become the focal point for the gathering of a good portion of a company's dancers.

I didn't even have the excuse of being on tour the one time that I tried to dance while under the influence of alcohol. The parents of my friend from Perry Street, Helen Livingston Nickerson had come to New York for her birthday. They threw her a plush cocktail party at an elegant apartment somewhere on the upper east side. I was dancing with the New York City Opera Company at the City Center Theater. Helen's party was given on a Saturday which forced me to squeeze it in between a matinee of *The Love of Three Oranges* and an evening performance of *Aida*. On that Saturday, dinner was out and martinis and peanuts were in.

I was enjoying myself and my martinis so much at the party that I lost all track of time until Geneva Reed, a young dancer friend, suggested delicately that I put down the drink that I had in my hand and get myself into a cab headed toward the City Center Theater. I was about to miss the evening performance. She being an exceptionally sensitive woman, quickly recognized my state of intoxication and understood that I would not even be capable of getting downstairs to the street by myself. Geneva took me by the hand, led me downstairs, hailed a cab, dumped me into it and gave the driver explicit directions.

While sitting in the cab, riding through the streets of Manhattan I began to worry about my physical state. I felt that I could fake most of the evening's performance as the dancing in *Aida* wasn't exactly difficult. For the greater part of it, the men just carried around Marina Svetlova, the lead ballerina, in a split, while making unofficial and uncouth remarks much to her entertainment. Grant Murodoff, the choreographer would be there, but he had featured himself in the triumphal ballet scene and so would be busy doing his own thing. At his age he had enough troubles just dancing. In my drunken state, my worries focused on a balance on one knee near the end of the ballet. I was sure that there was no way that I could handle that movement; I kept picturing myself, over and over again, crashing to the stage floor never to rise.

The taxi pulled up to the stage door on 56th Street. Somehow I paid the fare and got up the steps to the backstage entrance. As I passed, the stage door guard made a few snide remarks about both my lateness and my condition. Fortunately there was an elevator that could take me to the male dancer's top floor dressing room. When they saw my condition, in no time the other dancers stripped me of my clothes and pushed me into a cold shower. When that proved to be of no avail, they quickly dried me, dressed me in my costume, created a hasty make up and practically carried me back downstairs and into the wings. There they left me to my own devices, wishing me luck as the dance began.

My concentration kept shifting in and out as the dance endlessly progressed. I constantly kept telling myself to follow the group wherever they went; lift Marina whenever they lifted her; turn whenever they turned; and jump whenever they jumped. There were so many people and so much activity on the stage that I was sure that no one would notice my strange actions. But the specter of that one knee balance haunted me increasingly as the ballet progressed. Eventually I was in such a state of panic over that one movement that I gave serious thought to making a mad dash for the wings.

Finally the terrible moment arrived. There was no way out. I closed my eyes and plunged head long for the floor. Completely by luck, there I was, balanced perfectly on one knee. The sweet smell of success surged through my body. I had overcome the hideous specter. I had won, but now I couldn't move. I was locked in place. The dance continued around me, but for the rest of the ballet I stayed on one knee basking in success. I would probably still be there today if at the ballet's end someone hadn't run past and told me bluntly to put my leg down and to get the hell off the stage.

Both Charles Weidman and Martha Graham had great reputations for their constant consumption of alcohol. Both of them reached a point at which their drinking began to take a tremendous toll on their creativity as well as their dancing. Both of them, using great will power, completely stopped when it became a choice between drinking and their physical and mental deterioration. Both never regressed in this habit once that they had completely stopped. Charles and Martha were extremely lonely people. Charles, as well, had a feeling of insecurity woven into his personality which Martha did not seem to possess, at least not in any obvious manner. Both, according to second-hand information, started drinking at very early points in their careers. Doris once said that

Charles' drinking sprees were one of the major difficulties that she had when working with him and a major cause of their separation. Louis Horst, upon hearing of our complaints concerning Martha's heavy drinking, stated that he had never known her at any time when she did not drink in excess. He relegated it to her inborn Irish nature.

In the one performance that I danced with the Weidman Company, Charles was certainly not interested in drinking. Quite the opposite. He was dreadfully sober in a desperate attempt to get through the performance as best that he could. By that time, in 1951, his age made the simple physicality of the performance almost impossible for him. Martha, however, at times became so disoriented on stage by her drinking that, on occasion, we feared that the performance would have to be stopped and the curtain brought down in order to forestall complete disaster. I remember with shattering clarity one performance of *Clytemnestra* in Munich, Germany. The whole evening became a horrifying experience.

I had gone to Martha's dressing room long before that evening's performance had begun. I was attempting to get Martha to tell me which dancers she wanted to use in a lecture demonstration that we were scheduled to perform for the U.S.I.S. the next morning. As rehearsal director, this was one of my responsibilities.

That evening in Munich I knocked on Martha's door and waited. There was no immediate answer. The theater in which we were performing was terribly old, drab, and dilapidated. It has since been refurbished, but at that time everywhere back stage the paint was peeling from the walls and the plaster was beginning to crumble away from the lathes behind it. As I knocked on the door, I noticed that some paint even flecked off the panels with each rap of my knuckles. Finally I heard a faint, "Come in." The sentence finished with an upturned inflection indicating a question rather than permission. I opened the door gingerly. Straight ahead of me was a small dark passageway that led into one side of the main room. As I entered the main chamber, I was startled by Martha, sitting at a dressing table directly to my right. Because the entrance way ended so abruptly, I passed a few steps beyond Martha before I was aware of her; I ended standing slightly behind her.

Like the rest of the theater, her dressing room was tawdry and worn. Only the required necessities were apparent. A bare electric light bulb hung from a dangling wire in the center of the room. It supplied such little but harsh light that it took a few seconds for my eyes to become accustomed to it. Against the near wall was an old battered dressing table at which Martha sat. The mirror of the dressing table was cracked and freckled brown with age. It was in such poor condition that it was difficult to see one's own image in it. Half of the light bulbs that surrounded the dressing table mirror were burned out.

Martha was wrapped in the Japanese yukata that she usually wore while preparing for a performance. All of her street makeup, which had over the years become quite heavy, was wiped from her face with cold cream leaving a glistening thinness to her skin. She had taken her hair down and it was hanging loosely about her face. In actuality, her hair was surprisingly thin and wispy and seemingly unkempt. Martha was leaning with her arms on the dressing table staring directly at herself in the ancient mirror. A glass of some kind of white alcohol, gin or vodka, was standing on the dressing table, half finished, along with the bottle from which it had been poured.

Martha didn't move. She didn't even seem to breathe. There was no awareness that I was in the room at all. Everything was seemingly static, locked into place and time.

I was so hypnotized that I also did not move, afraid to disturb the delicate equilibrium of the room. I stood there staring at this woman, this torn genius, who kept gazing at herself drunkenly in the broken mirror. What did she see? There, certainly, in the forefront of the mirror was reflected the Martha of the present day in all of her aging reality. Behind that image, hidden further back in the mirror, she probably also could discern in reflection the hundreds of other Marthas one after the other, Marthas that had passed before in a younger and more physical period of her dancing life. All had sat there at the dressing table at sometime, if not in Munich then in London, in New York, in Paris, or in Tokyo. And now, at that moment, the layers of images were all sitting there together, none of them knowing if this would be their last time, if this would be the final act when the Martha of the present moment would step onto a stage never to return. The frightening prospect of never finishing some performance because of age and turmoil must have constantly haunted her.

We were frozen there: Martha staring at her time swept flow of images; I staring at Martha in front of me. Still I didn't dare move. We remained transfixed in that manner for at least three minutes, and then Martha slowly became aware that I was standing behind her. With blurred speech, she asked what I wanted. I told her briefly and she said that she would call me at the hotel before I went to bed. I was released and fled out of the room in relief.

Martha had a difficult time dancing that night. The prologue of *Clytemnestra* contained three duets that were performed between Martha as Clytemnestra and the figure of Hades danced by Gene McDonald. Gene steered Martha around the stage as best as possible, but it was to little avail. At times Martha would lose her balance and literally fall off stage only to hit a metal railing in the wings and bounce back. Craig Barton, Martha's manager, and Bethsabee de Rothschild were in the audience. They raced backstage thinking that this must be the end of Martha's career.

Somehow the prologue finished and the curtain fell. Martha was gathered into the bosom of Ursula Reed, her costumer and dresser, and taken to her dressing room. The intermission was longer than usual and when Martha returned she was amazingly sober. She performed the rest of *Clytemnestra* if not brilliantly at least satisfactorily. When Ursula was asked what she did to accomplish this feat she said, with her own secret slyness and revealing, beautiful smile. "Tea and coffee. Lots of tea and coffee." and then after a short pause, "and a little faith."

The use of drugs in the fifties and even into the early sixties was much less prevalent than it is today. Dancers might have experimented in private with the use of a drug from time to time, but the habitual intake of any drug was an exception rather than a rule. The smoking of marijuana was given so little consideration by the authorities at the time that it was easy to carry the substance across borders from one country to another and even into the United States without worry. During the early fifties, I never knew of any dancer who performed on stage under the influence of drugs, but we often speculated among ourselves what the results of such actions would be. We conjectured what would happen to one's physical control, balance, and endurance. Even more important was what would happen to a dancer's state of reality both in relation to himself and to the other dancers with whom he was working.

Unlike most other areas, there is a difficulty in experimentation with drugs. If a person is physically or emotionally in the least susceptible to the habitual use of any drug, the door is left wide open to proceed from experimentation directly to addictive abuse. The chances are slight that experimentation will turn into major addiction. But they are great enough, hopefully, to become a major deterrent.

Usually in order to test one's reaction to any drug, it is necessary to indulge in its consumption more than one time. At a party following a performance of the Graham Company in London, I remember Sir Frederick Ashton stating that at one time or another he had tried every drug that he knew existed and had access. He averred that his rule was to try each of the drugs only once as he wanted to leave no avenue open to addiction. Thus for him, experimentation was a total waste. Almost all of the drugs that he tried made him sick on the first attempt. The only reaction that he could remember was nausea.

On both the European and Asian tours, some of us carried marijuana across the borders of many countries without any concern or worry, "experimenting" with its use from time to time. This was true even when we were involved with tours sponsored by the United States State Department. We operated without having any awareness of what the consequences would be were we to get caught. Years later, when I twice took our university group, The Bay Area Repertory Dance Company, to

Europe, I sat the members of the company solemnly down and gave them dire warnings about incurring my wrath if I ever caught any of them carrying drugs or consuming them during the tour. It wasn't until much later, in retrospect, that I realized how hypocritical I had been. Hypocritical or not, I still think that my warnings were correct in intent and beneficial in outcome.

My first attempt at smoking marijuana was a complete failure. A short time after we arrived in London on the first European tour, four of us gathered in my large and cozy flat just off of Piccadilly Circus. We decided to test the potency of the marijuana that one of us had brought along on the trip. Our actions would be commonplace by today's standards, but in 1954 we were entering strange and untried territory. I have a feeling that my three companions from the company had tried marijuana before as indicated by their familiarity with the procedures of smoking it. Also, the effect that the marijuana had on each of them was immediate and complete. I, on the other hand, in my novice state, had no idea what sensation to look for. As my friends moved into those strange worlds, I began to feel that I was being left far behind. The harder that I tried for some reaction, the more any sensation eluded me. I finally stopped trying, disgusted at both my ineptitude and lack of sensitivity.

My next attempt at reaching a high didn't occur until a few years later. We were in Dhaka on the first Asian tour. Dhaka was a city that didn't quite know where it belonged in the world of Asia. It was divorced from its origins and was lacking in progress. There was nothing at all happening in the city in arts, sports, politics, or any other area. We were booked into it for four or five performances. Most of the company became sick at that point of the tour, or, if they weren't sick, they were complaining drastically. Everything that happened in Dhaka took on major proportions.

Out of sheer boredom one hopeless afternoon, two of us lay back on our beds and began to smoke some recently purchased marijuana. This time I felt myself slip across the edge of consciousness easily and immediately began my wanderings into silliness and idiocy. Just as we were reaching what we thought to be a marvelous high, the phone rang. Leroy Leatherman, Martha's personal manager, was on the other end of the line asking if we wanted to join him and Martha in their newly rented luxurious car for Christmas shopping. The offer obviously provided us with additional entertainment for that afternoon. We considered asking Martha and Lee if they wanted to participate with us in our smoking pleasures, but then thought the better of it.

The two of us sat in the back seat of their chauffeur driven car laughing constantly and making inane remarks. Martha and Lee were obviously irritated and confused by our strange behavior, but had no idea from what it stemmed. On the first chance possible, they left us, in a jewelry shop in the middle of town. They drove off in great relief, making us find our own way back to the hotel. Even at that time, I felt that we were beginning down a rather dangerous path and should carry out our operation with a little more care and discretion.

Upon our arrival in Burma, on the same Asian tour, we were told that it was possible to purchase drugs easily and cheaply. One of the first evenings that we were there, before our first performances had started, two of us hired a trishaw and headed into Rangoon to buy hashish and whatever else we could find. The rumors that we had heard proved to be true. The trishaw driver took us directly to a dealer in the center of the city and we bought extremely inexpensively quite a stash of hashish and some supposed opium.

Upon our arrival back at the hostel where the entire company was being housed, the news of our successful purchases was passed by word of mouth from one company member to another. Most of the younger members of the company along with a few of the older soloists gathered around us like bees around a hive of honey to share our bounty.

Rising out of the bedroom of two of the women dancers was a mysterious dark stairway that led to a circular, unlit area up one flight. This space surrounded the base of a cupola that sat on top of the hotel. We discovered that another stairway arose out of the pitch black section and up one more flight was an area similar to the first but smaller. It also was pitch black and it surrounded the top of the cupola. This second section was completely encased in windows that allowed for a magnificent view of all of Rangoon. It was a beautiful and exotic atmosphere, lit only by a bright new moon. Here we felt that we were safe enough to begin our drug experimentation.

It was a bizarre evening in which, high above a beautiful and strange city more than half of the Graham Company became stoned on hashish. As we did not have to perform that night, I have to admit that it was a most enjoyable way to spend an otherwise ordinary and boring evening. No harm came from it, but I doubt if the potential danger of the discovery of taking drugs while on a state department tour, was worth it. The pleasures gained from the event did not really justify the act.

We tried the opium later, but could seldom make it work. Either our technique for smoking the drug was wrong or the pipes we used for toasting it were faulty. Somewhere further along on the tour, I gave up trying to use the opium and tossed it down the toilet along with any other aspirations toward drug addiction. I found that the highs on drugs were not nearly as satisfying as the natural highs received from certain happenings in "normal life". No drugs that I have ever taken have made me feel such exhilaration as those gained from sex, the birth of a child, being selected from among hundreds at an audition, the rousing applause of an audience after a difficult performance, a beautiful sunrise, an indescribable sunset, or a bright new moon on a clear night. There are so many fantastic natural events in life that lift one to unbelievable heights. Living is not meant to be carried out in a constant state of ecstasy. As human beings, we fluctuate like the swells of an ocean and our highs are emphasized by the troughs that surround them. We are meant to move in a natural, constant rhythm from one point to another. This rhythm of life, then, repeats itself endlessly throughout our existence. False and purposeful disruption of it can only be destructive.

Not all of the conditions that prevent an individual from performing are self-induced. Accidents to the dancer do occur at unexpected times. Viruses can infect a dancer or even a whole company, passing through it like the plague. On tour the dancer is particularly susceptible. As the tour progresses the dancer becomes increasingly worn and tired and the resistance to injury and sickness seems to diminish as the exposure to outside influences multiplies.

There are sometimes ways to overcome these sicknesses and injuries so that one can follow the well worn axiom of "The show must go on!", but these methods must be used with great discretion. Novocain or other numbing agents, which are used as temporary pain killers, are dangerous panaceas. Pain is a purposeful way in which our bodies warn us that the injured area is in need of rest. When the pain is reduced or removed by artificial means those warning signs cease and the injured area can become increasingly damaged.

Early in my career as a dancer, I developed a chronically injured ankle which limited my movement tremendously. It lasted for months and in desperation, I allowed a doctor to shoot Novocain into the ankle in order to test how it would react to increased mobility. After the Novocain shot, I felt no pain allowing for increased action, but when the Novocain wore off, I became totally incapacitated and had to stop dancing for a couple of weeks.

Back injuries are even more dangerous to try to correct in such a manner. The spine and its surrounding muscles are so interwoven into an individual's carriage and the body's complete muscular and nervous systems, that these temporary corrections should always be disallowed.

Traumatic injuries which happen during a performance are usually chance accidents which are impossible to anticipate. In Copenhagen, Denmark, while watching the Royal Danish Ballet perform George Balanchine's *Symphony In C*, I saw a ballerina tear her achilles tendon in the middle of the performance. The ballet continued without pause as the dancer, in obvious great pain, slowly crawled off stage through the legs of the rest of the company's dancers, much to the horror of the audience.

Although injuries are always a disappointment for the dancer to whom they occur, they can sometimes offer an opportunity for someone else to dance a role for which they might otherwise never have the chance. During the week that the Graham Company performed in Djakarta, Indonesia in 1956 we were treated royally by everyone. The company was entertained by the Indonesians with parties, indigenous dance performances, and as many trips into the interior of the country as our performance schedule would allow. On one trip into the hinterlands we were taken to a swimming pool which had a magnificent view of the rice paddies beautifully sculpted out of the Javanese rolling hills. After an hour's refreshing swim, just before we were to leave, Stuart Hodes, one of the company's major male dancers, attempting a playful stunt on the edge of the pool, slipped on the wet surface and broke his big toe. The injury put Stuart out of commission for two or three weeks, but it gave unexpected opportunities for many of the other male dancers in the company. For me, it was the first time that I was able to dance the male yellow figure in Martha's *Diversion of Angels*. After one rehearsal with Helen McGehee, my new partner, I went on to perform that role for the rest of the Indonesian tour and in Burma.

On another tour with the Graham Company, I was given an opportunity to dance the Seer in *Night Journey* for the first time because of the illness of Bob Cohan, a leading male dancer with the company. We were performing in Belgrade, Yugoslavia, when Bob suddenly came down with a sickness that closely resembled ptomaine poisoning. The illness left him weak and unable to leave the bathroom for more than five minutes at a time. We were all, except Bob, at the theater for a scheduled rehearsal of Judith when we received the word that he was too ill to perform that night.

Martha, Craig Barton and I, as rehearsal director, headed back to the hotel immediately to settle what was to be done. *Secular Games* was to open the program. Bob was not cast in the work so that solved one problem. *Acrobats of God*, the closing dance, could be done by just eliminating a couple of dancers here or there. *Night Journey* was a different problem as Bob was performing Tiresias, the seer. It was probably Martha's favorite dance and Jocasta was her favorite role. She steadfastly refused to relinquish this performance of it.

Craig asked, "but Martha, who will do the Seer?"

Martha looked straight at me and said clearly, "David will."

With that she disappeared up to her room to rest in preparation for the performance.

I began my feverish preparations for learning the role. I first visited Bob in his room where he did his best to teach me the part in between frequent trips to the bathroom. With that knowledge gained, I headed for the theater to rehearse with our musical director, Eugene Lester. Gene played the piano reduction of the Schumann score for me and was most helpful, giving me much valuable advice. Ursula, the costumer, brought me the huge cape that the Seer wore, so that I could learn to move with it. She had to shorten the costume drastically to accommodate my small stature. Other than the costume and the Seer's staff, I was not able to work with the other important elements for the dance such as the set, other props, other dancers, or the orchestra.

I hardly had time to do my make-up before the evening's performance began. I went through *Secular Games* as if I were in a trance. My mind was completely elsewhere. At intermission I had little time to devise a make-up for the Seer before it was time for *Night Journey* to begin. On stage before we started, everyone wished me luck.

Everything went well during the performance except near the end of the piece. As I moved around to the back of the Noguchi bed in order to mount it, I suddenly realized I had no idea how to lift myself onto it as was choreographed. There was no time to meditate or conjecture. I just took one good look, put my foot on the piece, and prayed. One thrust from a strong thigh and I was there, a little shakily, but I was there. Moving down the bed was simple, but then came the next problem.

I was supposed to push my foot against the ropes that were holding Bert and Martha together and, with a thrust, knock them to the floor. At the same time, I was to step past them, descending from the bed. Never having practiced, I could envision myself totally entangled in the ropes that represented the umbilical cord, ending the entire dance struggling for freedom. Having tempted fate once already and won, I felt that I couldn't count on that kind of luck twice. I gave the ropes a strong thrust with my foot and then directed my step off to the side, entirely clear of the ropes, Martha and Bert. The direction of destiny was altered a bit, but at least it was not completely destroyed. It was a coward's way out; however, it saved my nervous system.

I made my final entrance at the end of the dance with great relief, but also with a wonderful sense of accomplishment. These are rare but very special moments to be treasured in one's career.

Another chance accident not only altered the dance opportunities for two women, but changed the course of my own life drastically. In September 1958, the Graham Company was scheduled for an Israeli tour under the sponsorship of Bethsabee de Rothschild. Martha had flown to Tel Aviv a week ahead of the company and as a result, most of our daily rehearsals had stopped.

Marni and I had just begun dating a few weeks previously. She had graduated from Sarah Lawrence College that June. During the summer I invited her to demonstrate for the last three weeks of my teaching stint at the American Dance Festival in Connecticut. Lois Schlossberg, my regular demonstrator, had to return to New York for rehearsals. On the last night of the festival, I had invited Marni to a special dinner to celebrate our working together. It was during the appetizer that the idea of marrying her entered my mind. By the time that we settled into the main course, I had definitely decided that it was a good idea. As we ate dessert, I almost jumped across the table with enthusiastic ardor. With the coffee, however, I controlled myself, as I felt that a marriage proposal was a little premature. At that point I wasn't sure that I would ever get another opportunity as things were being made difficult for the development of our relationship by the impending tour to Israel, and a move from New York to Mexico that I was planning after the tour.

On learning that we had one free day before the company's departure, Marni and I decided to take a quick journey to Green Mansions, a resort located in the Catskill Mountains of New York. I had promised to visit three of my students from the High School of Performing Arts who were dancing there: Rosalyn Cohen, Louis Occhicone, and Jaime Rogers. Also my old friend Louise Guthman was the production director and lighting designer for all of the weekly shows.

After five hours of driving, we arrived at the resort to find that I had been paged over the loud speaker system every fifteen minutes for the last couple of hours. On investigation, I discovered that Martha's personal manager, Leroy Leatherman, had tracked Marni and me to the Catskills through my roommate. He wanted me to call immediately.

I was in a panic. I was sure that our plane to Israel was leaving early and I would be caught stranded in the Catskill Mountains hours away. Instead, the news was that a young dancer in the company, Carol Payne, had broken her foot in class on the previous evening, and could not make the trip. It was one of those terrible accidents of fate.

Lee had heard Martha speak most favorably of Marni earlier in the summer. He decided that she would make the best replacement for Carol if Martha felt that a replacement was necessary. He had wired Martha to ask if he should bring Marni, and was awaiting the answer. Not wanting to turn around immediately and drive all the way back, I told Lee that I would keep calling him every hour on the hour to learn if Martha had answered his wired request. I kept trying each hour as arranged until midnight but there was still no word from Martha. Lee informed us that we had to return immediately anyway. If Martha were to say that he should bring Marni, she would have to be in New York to get herself ready for the trip. We finally agreed to return at once and by approximately five in the morning, we arrived back in Manhattan. I delivered Marni to her apartment and returned to my loft to await the results. In an hour Lee called. Martha had said yes. Marni was to join the tour.

Marni had a busy day ahead of her. She met Lee at eight in the morning at the passport office in Rockefeller Center where he swore to the officials that he had known her for years. Actually, it was the first time that he had ever seen her. Marni visited Dr. Cobert to receive the regulation shots for traveling, signed her contract, had one rehearsal at the studio, and bought her white gloves for the trip.

No woman ever went on tour with Martha in those days without white gloves. No matter what the company looked like while in flight on the plane, whenever we arrived at a new destination, Martha's company had to be impeccably groomed.

By seven that evening Marni was at the airport, fully prepared and ready to fly to Israel as a new member of the Graham Company. Most of the older members of the troop had never seen her before that moment and had no idea who she was. For Marni, it was an unbelievable dream come true. For me, it was an easy answer to all of my romantic problems.

Upon her arrival in Israel, Marni had to learn *Clytemnestra* and *Night Journey*, so her life remained extremely busy for a few days. On opening night, by the shores of the Mediterranean in Tel Aviv, I asked her to marry me. My timing was right. By now, too tired to resist, she said yes.

Being a physical activity, the vagaries of a dance career often prove unpredictable. In one day the immediate futures of many people can become permanently altered by a chance accident. Paths are interchanged leaving some bereft, and others in a world of unbelievable wonder.

Physical and mental health are powerful factors in the development of a dancer. As the dancer matures technically, his increased knowledge of how to deal with his body must keep close pace. As one's career progresses the demands on body and mind reach tremendous proportions. At times the dancer must learn how to work around his injuries, making unnoticeable accommodation for them. At other times, the dancer must be realistic about totally incapacitating injuries and act accordingly. Although doctors and practitioners can and should advise the dancer about his injuries, only the individual can accurately evaluate the state of his body and its readiness for dancing.

Martha Graham and Louis Horst in the early 1930s. Photo credit: New York Public Library Dance Collection.

Helen Tamiris and Daniel Nagrin. Photographer: Hugo of Hollywood. Photo credit: New York Public Library Dance Collection.

Doris Humphrey and Charles Weidman in performance. Photo credit: New York Public Library Dance Collection.

Hanya Holm. Photo credit: New York Public Library Dance Collection.

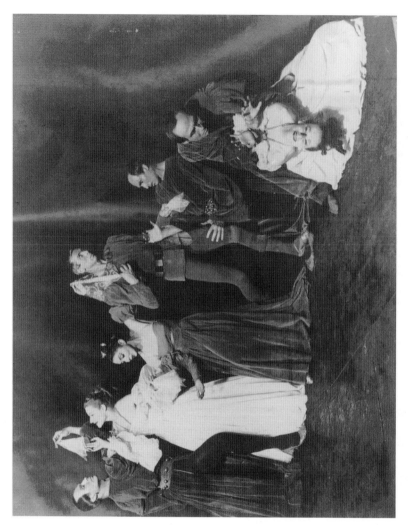

José Limón, Betty Jones, Pauline Koner, and Lucas Hoving in *The Moor's Pavane*, choreographed by José Limón and costumed by Pauline Lawrence. Photo credit: New York Public Library Dance Collection.

David Wood in the Neighborhood Playhouse production of *The Arbitration*, directed by Sanford Meisner, choreographed by Nina Fonaroff, and costumed by Martha Graham. Photo credit: Neighborhood Playhouse Archives.

Marni, Marina, David, Raegan, and Ellis Wood in Berkeley, California. Photographer: Betty Guy. Photo credit: Wood Collection.

6

ON REHEARSALS

One of the major reasons that I was drawn into the field of dance was my complete enjoyment of rehearsing. I have always found the process by which dance movements are created and then placed into a structured concept, to be thoroughly intriguing.

I was fascinated watching the creative procedure of a choreographer unfold. It provided the chance to observe the continuous growth of a choreographic work from the inside out. In later years, as a choreographer, I continued to experience the same fascination for rehearsing. My interest with choreography lay not in the communication of any great philosophic concepts or even abstract movement ideas. Rather, my fascination was aroused by the circuitous route which the slender thread of an idea would take in its development. This delicate thread seemed eventually to create a life of its own.

In the Eastern part of the world patience is a great virtue. There, involvement with the process of learning holds sway over any desperate need to race toward the final performance. In Eastern theater, learning and growth are lifelong activities out of which fruition via performance is a natural occurrence that develops in its own time.

Attitudes toward rehearsing vary greatly. Often, the young dancer, because of a freshness of approach, will find the rehearsal a more invigorating exercise than will the older, more experienced dancer. Still, the basic reason for liking or disliking rehearsals results from the individual's involvement either with the process of creating, on the one hand, or the desire to reach immediately for the end result of performance, on the other hand.

Rehearsals fall into many different categories. With each of these various types of practice sessions, it is necessary for the dancer to alter his working approach to reach the desired result with the least effort. In choreographic rehearsals, where the actual creative process takes place, rehearsals are often the most frustrating, both for the choreographer and the dancers. When the choreographer's well of creativity temporarily runs dry or when his preconceived ideas refuse to be transferred into a satisfactory physicality, desperation rises. The dancers are then, required to wait for lengthy periods of time while the choreographer works out his specific ideas.

Replacement rehearsals have their own unique difficulties. When only one or two dancers are new in a piece in which the rest of the company is well versed, the learning situation can become extremely difficult.

The first rehearsal that I had for learning a role in Martha Graham's *Diversion of Angels* illustrates the problem. Late one afternoon Martha sent the three men who were already in *Angels* Bertram Ross, Stuart Hodes, and Robert Cohan, with me into the small studio of the 63rd Street building. The three of them were to teach me all of the sections which the four men danced together as a unit. We spent approximately two hours in the studio while the three argued at great length over every movement. Each of them had his own private version of the dance, and each insisted on its absolute correctness. Teaching was forgotten while playful argumentation raged on and on.

After two hours, Martha called us all back into the large studio and asked to see what we had done. It was an embarrassing moment for me. I followed behind the other three men, glued to their every movement, trying to convince Martha that I had indeed learned something. When we were finished dancing the sections, Martha, seemingly unperturbed, suggested kindly that it would take a bit more rehearsing before I was ready to perform the part. Fortunately for me, Martha could at times be a master of understatement.

Rehearsals for revivals of dances that have not been performed for many years have their own special difficulties. If possible, with revival rehearsals, old company members are brought back to clarify movements, relationships, and qualities. These veteran dancers often can give insight into the original conceptions of the choreography which even the choreographer, has long since forgotten.

Brush-up rehearsals usually contain the fewest difficulties. In these, the dancers are already trained in the work. Brush-up rehearsals may be called because the performers have not danced the work for a long time, or some element of the dance has gone askew and needs to be corrected.

Spacing rehearsals are basically used to adjust to each new theater or area in which the company performs. The decision concerning from what wings to enter and into which to exit is of great importance. Adaptation also must be made to the size of the stage. The movements of the dance are expanded or confined in relation to its proportions. When we performed *Diversion of Angels* at the Greek Theater in Los Angeles, drastic changes were demanded because of the huge size of the performing space. Pearl Lang, as the woman in red, was forced to extend her ecstatic runs, streaking across the stage, to a one hundred yard dash of Olympic proportions. For Pearl, her endurance became a more vital factor than her extravagant technique.

Dress rehearsals are only held when a work is completely new. It is usually a chance to hear the true sound of the orchestra for the first time, if a choreographer is lucky enough to afford an orchestra; it is a chance to see the costumes in relation to movement and lighting, if one is lucky enough to have a costume designer who has finished his work on time.

In the *Snow Queen* with choreography by Sophie Maslow, based on the fairy tale by Hans Christian Andersen, the dancers were literally sewn into their costumes as the curtain rose on the first performance. In order to depict the feel of the ice and the cold, a silver lamee material was used. The weave of the material required it to be lined in order for it to hold its shape, but in this instance there was no time for such exactness. During the opening night performance, as the dancers moved, the costumes slowly disintegrated, lending a marvelous effect of melting ice to the wintry scene taking place on stage. By the conclusion of the performance the costumes hung in melted shreds from the dancer's bodies.

Backstage, after the performance, people marveled at the wonderful effect that the costumes gave. Sophie graciously thanked them for their kind comments, but stated that she doubted that she could afford such an effect at every performance. With a proper dress rehearsal for the *Snow Queen*, Sophie could have saved herself much trouble and financial strain.

There are times when the amount of rehearsing required by choreographers is a type of compulsive behavior. In the mind of such a choreographer lies the logic that the more that one rehearses the better will be the performance. This thinking denies the reality of the wear and tear which over-rehearsing places upon the dancer's body and psyche.

When I was on tour with the Dudley-Maslow-Bales Trio, I was not prepared for the constant intensity of that group's rehearsals. After each evening's performance, we would board a bus and travel through the dark of night to our next day's location. Arriving at our destination in the early hours of the morning, we got into bed as fast as possible only to be awakened after a few short hours of sleep. We were then transported to the awaiting theater. There we spent the entire day, spacing each dance, phrase by phrase, and lighting each of the works until a supposed absolute perfection was achieved.

Dinner was brought to us in the form of coffee and sandwiches while we prepared ourselves for the coming performance. When that performance was finished, the entire process repeated itself once again. Luckily those tours were of short duration; after a week of such a schedule we were all completely exhausted. The unions of today have helped to alleviate this kind of endurance contest of travel and rehearsal, but even today with some smaller companies this condition still exists.

Some dancers enforce compulsive rehearsing upon themselves. Pearl Lang, during the time that she was performing in the company of

Martha Graham, never stopped working on her solo roles even while the performances were in progress. In a work such as Martha's *Canticle For Innocent Comedians*, Pearl, as the Figure of Death, did not enter onto the stage until very late in the choreography. During the entire first part of the piece, while others were performing, Pearl was dancing in the wings, going over and over her part.

When other members of the dance had quick entrances and exists, they would have to duck rapidly around Pearl in order to prevent deadly head on collisions. Pearl's actions seem to serve two purposes: by constantly dancing, she kept her body in a warmed condition, physically ready to perform; she also kept herself mentally tuned so that she could gather increased momentum as time for her entrance drew near. Certainly the power of her performance in the work displayed the benefit of such concentration.

The different mediums of dance require approaches to rehearsing which are unique. Each of these forms (television, stage, opera, film, and concert dance) seems to vary in what they desire to communicate to an audience.

Because of being given only brief practice periods, dance specials on television, are required to make use of dancers known in the television vernacular as "quick studies". This term implies that the dancers are capable of learning the necessary movements on sight and can immediately, reproduce them with accuracy. Most of the choreographed routines are based on flashy, eye catching movement. Fundamentally they do not aim to develop any depth of performance. For these shows, performance techniques have to be readily accessible and rapidly reproduced.

On present day television, there are few remaining shows which utilize a chorus of dancers weekly. During television's inception and for many years thereafter, musical revues were always at the top of the list of audience favorites. *The Paul Whiteman Show, Your Hit Parade,* and *The Gary Moore Show* were just some of the noted weekly revues which made constant use of male and female chorus performers. Each week the dancers had to learn three or four newly choreographed works, cramming them into mind and body in a few days. These shows were usually performed live in the studio and, on some occasions, with a studio audience in attendance. The nervous energy of a regular theatrical performance became a factor which added to the physical drain on the dancers.

The major difficulty of rehearsing this type of a show lay not in the weekly learning process, but rather in the physical drain on the dancer's bodies because of the constant and intense demands that occurred week after week.

Along with the overuse of one's physical structure was the additional element of dancing on cement for long periods of time. This hard surface places a great strain on the dancer's backs, legs, and feet. While most of the actual rehearsing was done on resilient wooden floors, the television studios where the final performance day was spent almost always had a rock hard surface. That one full day of working on the cement flooring, inevitably took its toll.

Although, for the first few years of my career, I performed in a good many television productions, they were usually isolated occurrences. I was not placed under the pressure of constantly learning different routines each week. The only occasion in which I did become involved in this kind of grind was in 1950 on a show called *Country Style*. It was seen on the old DuMont Television Network located in the basement of the now defunct Wanamaker's Department store in Cooper Union Square.

I had heard about the audition for the show through Elsa Reiner, Hanya Holm's secretary. On this occasion I managed to be hired without having to rely on my acting training. The show employed a chorus of four men and four women who were brought together from a variety of dance training and diverse experience.

The theme of the show was exactly what its title indicated, country music, even though the show took place long before country music had achieved its national popularity. As dancers, we performed lots of hoe downs and do-si-dos accompanied by loud whooping and hollering. Every so often Burl Ives was one of the major performers on the show. Many lovely soaring dances were shaped to accompany his singing of lyrical ballads. I preferred these flowing routines to the more raucous, extroverted barn dance numbers.

The show was performed live every Saturday night during the summer months. The following Sunday was our free day and each of us used it to recover from rehearsing and performing all day on the hard concrete surface. On Mondays we met to begin to work on the two or three new dances that were to be featured on the following Saturday's show. Rehearsals were always held in a studio uptown on regular wooden floors. I don't believe that it would have been possible for our bodies to sustain a week of practicing on a concrete floor.

Performing on *Country Style* was rewarding for me not just because it was one of my first professional paying jobs, but also because having to learn the dances at such a fast pace, I acquired immediately a tremendous amount of self-confidence. If I had gone only the regular modern dance route, it probably would have taken me years to acquire an equal degree of assurance.

Country Style lasted for only one summer; by the time of its demise, I was ready to stop. Being a "quick study" was not really the direction in which I desired to develop. My choice was to work in areas where I would be able to probe more deeply into the performing experience, rather than trying to forget the dance routines that I was performing as fast as they were learned.

I feel a little sad that today the demand to be a "quick study" has crept over from television dancing to other fields of performing. The search for the dancer who can immediately reproduce movements seems today to be of prime importance rather than the discovery of the dancer who is qualitatively capable of constant development within a performance role.

There is also little required of the chorus members of Broadway musicals in terms of growth in performance. Like television routines, Broadway shows make use of the obvious in an effort to reach a paying audience. The pace by which dance routines must be learned for Broadway shows, however, does vary greatly from that of television dancing. The majority of musicals rehearse from a month to six weeks. During that period the dances are choreographed, the songs are learned and staged, and the show, in general, is put together by the director. Following the rehearsal period, the show begins performances with out of town tryouts or Broadway preview showings. Both are trial runs in which the audiences reactions can be evaluated under performance conditions. Songs and dances are sometimes cut from the show during this period and new production numbers may be added. Chorus Equity, the show dancers union, has strict rules concerning the number of hours that can be spent rehearsing once the actual performances are underway.

After the pre-Broadway showings have been completed and the musical has officially opened, very few rehearsals are held. Brush-up rehearsals are called if the dancers begin to grow stale with the passage of time and replacement rehearsals are called when dancers leave the show and new chorus members must be added. Basically there is very little that breaks the routine of a show's performance. Most chorus dancers inevitably become bored. The constant repetition of the same dances without change makes one performance begin to seem exactly like the next. But no matter how much boredom is felt, once the orchestra begins playing the overture, the adrenaline starts to flow and renewed energy and excitement build to performance pitch.

The first musical in which I was cast was located a long distance from Broadway in every aspect. It was the production of *Frankie and Johnny* that was performed at the Theatre de Lys (now the Lucille Lortel Theater) on Christopher Street in Greenwich village. The theater was actually being constructed while we were rehearsing. In order to save money, the producer made us rehearse in the half built barn-like structure among all of the splinters and sawdust created by the construction. Because the building laborer's union was much more powerful than that of the dancers, the carpenters were given the preferable working hours in order to get the theater built on time. At six P.M. after the workmen had finished for the day, the cast of the show arrived on the scene.

We practiced in the space from six o'clock until two in the morning, working on all of the different routines of the show. The management, although rather unprofessional and not exceedingly generous, did take pity on all of us because of the late schedule, and brought in mattresses. This allowed us to take catnaps during the early morning hours whenever we were not required to be on our feet rehearsing. It became a close race to the finish line between building the theater and putting the show together. With a little extra effort on everyone's part both the construction and the musical direction were completed just in time for opening night.

We opened one night and closed the next. The reviews were the total disaster that we had anticipated. The only people from the show who finally got paid were the dancers. For some unexplained reason, the producer loved the dancers. To our benefit, he loved us enough to give us our two weeks closing pay, a rarity for dancers in the nonunion theater world.

My other experience with a musical production was on Broadway in the show *Plain and Fancy*. The musical was a low budget operation and so it was forced to rehearse in the warehouse that was owned by one of the producers of the show, Yvette Schumer. Packing cases of various sizes were available to be used to mark the dimensions of a stage or as indicators of future scenic effects.

Being new at the whole procedure of rehearsing for Broadway shows and overcome by the glamour of it, I was anxious to be used in as much of the show as was possible. Every time a crowd scene or a simple crossover was to be staged, I made sure that I was clearly in the director's line of vision so that I would have a fair chance to be selected.

In the first few weeks of rehearsal I had become good friends with Robert Lindgren. Bobby had arrived on the Broadway scene after years of performing with Ballets Russes de Monte Carlo. By the time of *Plain and Fancy*, he had definitely claimed the title of one of the more experienced of the Broadway gypsies. He took one look at me and correctly evaluated my lack of experience. He then took me aside for a bit of friendly advice about rehearsing for Broadway musicals.

Involvement in the dance element of the production was one thing. Every dancer wanted to be in as much of the choreography as was possible. In every other facet of the production, the advice was to stay removed from the director's view. If the dancer didn't follow this procedure, once the show opened, he would find himself continually occupied by running on and off stage just to be a body in the back of some nondescript arrangement of performers. The clever Broadway show dancer, so Bobby said, avoided that situation and, as a result, would be able to sit quietly in his dressing room between dance numbers, sipping his evening coffee.

It was excellent advice and I quickly put it to good use. Every time that either of us saw Morton De Costa, the director of the show, casting his eye over the dancers, looking for extra participants, we would sneak behind one of the packing crates, until the danger of being selected had passed. In the entire show there were only a few full size group numbers for which Bobby and I were conscripted.

Certainly the most chaotic of all rehearsal periods are those for opera productions. Within this one art form there are combined a multitude of diverse artistic elements. Between the orchestra conductor, the orchestra musicians, soloist singers, chorus members, stage directors, lighting, set, and costume designers, choreographers, and dancers, there is more artistic temperament released into the atmosphere than in any other performing medium. There exists a refined hierarchy in the chain of command. It starts with the General Director of the opera company at the top and spirals rapidly downward to the chorus dancers and the supers (walk-ons) who occupy the bottom rungs.

Part of the difficulty in producing operas lies in the vastness of the operation. There are always a great many people involved in every aspect of an opera. Each human element feels his own creative importance in the total production and fights for his rightful place within it against infringement by any of the other artists. Basically it is the stage director's job to bring into accord these diverse elements, guiding the artists so they are each seen as best possible.

Added to the difficulties of producing opera are the stringent financial restrictions placed on almost all companies. The cost of a full dress rehearsal of any opera production is astronomical. The most costly of these practice sessions are reserved only for new productions. Only for these productions are all the elements brought together before the first performance occurs. Opera revivals, those operas which use the same production elements as in previous years, but have not been performed on contiguous seasons, are sometimes given a partial dress rehearsal. Enough major elements are removed from these rehearsals to drastically lower the cost.

Repertory productions are the operas which suffer the most because of lack of integrated rehearsal of any kind. They operate under the misconceived assumption that everyone concerned has a thorough knowledge of all of the idiosyncrasies of that specific production. In truth, many of the soloists may be totally new to the opera. Within the singing and dancing choruses there may have been large changes of personnel. The orchestra conductor may not have had any experience with the specific production at all. All of the disparate elements do usually have sufficient rehearsals before the opera's first performance, but each exists in its own world. On the night of the season's first performance, all of the related elements of a production gather together on stage and pray for a successful outcome, but in most cases, chaos is the direct result.

Because of insufficient integrated rehearsals, I have seen an orchestra conductor in a rage during a performance throw his baton at a singer on the stage. In return the soloist singer picked it up and threw it back in the conductor's face, hitting him directly on the forehead. I have seen a female chorus member refuse to leave the scene as she had been previously directed to do. Finally an assistant stage director disguised in a fright wig, entered and took her off surreptitiously. I have seen a tenor storm onto the scene completely overcome with anger for some unknown reason and tell a costumed and frightened assistant director in full voice exactly what he thought of him. I have seen a solo dancer caught on stage at the end of a performance because the cape of his costume had become entangled in the stairs of the set. He was left struggling to free himself as the final curtain descended. I have seen a bloody fight between a chorister and a super take place during a performance, directly in front of the audience. I have been in a chorus of dancers who entered the scene hoping to perform their well-rehearsed choreography only to find that there was not even an inch of empty space on which we could dance.

One can easily see the humor of each situation in retrospect, but at the moment of occurrence, such events are usually viewed as complete tragedies. None of these misfortunes would have occurred had there been proper preparations for the performances.

During my tenure as a dancer with the New York City Opera Company, Grant Murodoff and Charles Weidman were employed as the company's resident choreographers. The operas that Murodoff choreographed: *Don Giovanni*, *Manon*, and *Aida* were all classified as new productions. Charles choreographed the larger amount of the operas and thus had the problem of dealing with a majority of the repertory productions. One of his assigned operas was Bizet's *Carmen*. In it, Charles explained, was a trio consisting of two women and one man who performed during the tavern scene.

I was fortunate to be chosen as the male in the trio even though I had never personally executed a step of Spanish dancing. The opera directors idealistically scheduled only two rehearsals in which we were to learn and perfect the Spanish flavor of the dance. Felisa Conde, a former dancer in the Weidman Company, had assisted Charles in choreographing the work. Felisa met with us for the first rehearsal as she was better able to teach us the actual steps of the dance than was Charles. One of the women as well as myself, were completely new to the dance making Felisa's task not exactly easy. Charles took charge of the second rehearsal and tried to instill a little Spanish spirit into our souls along with our beating feet.

Two rehearsals did not prove enough to whip the dance into performance shape either technically or qualitatively. In desperation, we arranged with each other, Charles and the accompanist to meet one more time. The first performance of *Carmen* was to be on a Saturday matinee, so to save time we set our extra rehearsal for two hours before the afternoon performance would begin.

We were practicing in an upstairs studio when the stage director, José Rubens, wandered past the door of the room in which we were working. Seeing us in the process of rehearsing for his production, he ventured into the room to watch for a moment. When we had finished, he stated his satisfaction with the dancing that he had just observed. After a short pause, he then said that he now was looking forward to seeing both dances in performance that afternoon.

"B-b-both dances?" Charles questioned, his stuttering revealing his acute nervousness.

"Of course" stated the director in his thickly double accented voice. "The dance that takes place in the tavern and the other that is going on when the curtain rises."

Having clearly informed us of the facts, he turned abruptly and strode off. Charles was aghast. He had completely forgotten the dance at the beginning of the opera.

In the next few short minutes, Charles put his talents for the art of mime to good use. He quickly instructed the women to run around, holding out tambourines to the crowd of choristers and supers, begging to have them filled with silver pesos. I, meanwhile, was to entertain the crowd by pretending to play a guitar. Once everything had been clarified, Charles sent us to our dressing rooms to finish our make-up and to don our costumes. We hurried as fast as we could in order to get downstairs and develop some sense of spatial directions for the opening dance.

In a few minutes we were ready and on stage. Racing around the area, trying to make sense out of this last second madness, we attempted to finalize our spacing in relation to the rest of the cast. The overture had already begun when Director Rubens, noticing our frantic activities, strode angrily to us. His strongly accented English was becoming so dense that we could barely understand him when he attacked us with his question.

"What are you doing?"

We explained that this was our opening dance.

"That is no dance" he shot back. "I no like it. When the curtain goes up you be dancing or you are fired." With this, he stormed off the stage.

We looked at each other dumbfounded. It didn't occur to us that, in reality, he could never actually carry out his threat. The curtain was rising. I was stunned. I had no knowledge of any Spanish dancing except for the steps that I had learned for the tavern scene. Both women had at least studied a little Spanish movement, even if briefly. Taking authority on my broad shoulders quickly I placed each woman on either side of me and screamed, "Dance, damn it, dance!"

While the women improvised wild flamenco gyrations, I turned first to one and then the other, snapping my fingers, beating my heels and snarling, "Ole, Ole."

I was a monotonous participant, saved by the talents of my Spanish sisters. When we exited from the stage, we were all three nervous wrecks. Charles, much relieved, trailed close behind the director who rushed to greet us.

"Very good. Very good. That is just what I wanted."

Charles interjected, "K-k-k-eep it j-just that w-way. D-d-don't change it."

Because of the dance being totally improvised neither of them realized how difficult it would be for any of the three of us to be able to carry out their orders.

Even though an opera has already opened, all of the potential troubles that are involved in its presentation are not necessarily at an end. Soloists can still change from performance to performance. In *Carmen* the star role seemed to change with every new presentation and whatever the star wanted the star got. At one performance during my first season, the singer playing Carmen was responsible for changing part of my choreography without any help from the choreographer.

In the middle of the tavern scene dance I was supposed to jump onto the table and perform for a few minutes on top of it. At this performance, the dance followed its normal pattern without incident, but when I moved to the table at the proper moment, I discovered that our very well known and aging Carmen had already taken possession of it. I edged as near to her as I could and whispered to her innocently, "I'm supposed to dance on the table now."

To which our venerable mezzo-soprano answered under her breath with great determination, "Honey, I'm Carmen and I'm on the table!"

Needless to say I made no further protest and for that performance my feet remained securely placed on the stage floor.

The only actual film with which I was involved during my performing career was Martha Graham's *Dancer's World*. The film was shot in 1957 a couple of years after I first joined the Graham company, and was sponsored by WQED, a Pittsburgh, Pennsylvania television station.

Although *Dancer's World* presently is viewed mainly by means of video tape, it was originally created on film and most of its first showings were in art cinema theaters throughout the country. It was also shown at a great many international film festivals where it won an assortment of prizes.

The making of the film really had little to do with the procedures that are used on the Hollywood sound stages; however, some elements inevitably did remain the same. Martha had choreographed the main body of the movements for *Dancer's World* before the filming began. Still there were hundreds of retakes of phrases of movements and continuous repetition of whole sections of the dance. These were done again and again until Peter Glushanok, the film director, was completely satisfied with what he had recorded. Another of the similarities was the horribly long hours from early in the morning, for make-up, until late at night, for retakes. This made the ritual of filming the movie a singularly absorbing task. We not only danced for endless hours each day with all of the other members of the company, but we literally lived with each other as well, for we seldom were allowed to leave the confines of the studio. This was made bearable only by the constant in-house entertainment of invaluable performers such as Miriam Cole whose constant banter managed to keep full the reservoirs of our good humor.

But with all of the difficulties, there were marvelous realizations. We were all amazed to discover Martha to be so immediately adaptable to a new medium. Her major field of interest previous to the filming had always been in relation to a live audience, the power of the instant.

Now, in order to keep a controlling hand on her creative work, which she was always prone to do, Martha had to adapt to a completely new approach to the art of the dance. She was forced to learn the basics of a new and fascinating method. Martha quickly became the master of the eye of the camera. After one of our first days of filming, Peter Glushanok exclaimed to all that he had never known anyone to have developed such an expertise with the camera in so short of a time.

Another fascinating learning process lay in watching the development of the actual structure of the film. After all the dance shots had been accomplished, the filming of Martha's talks began. In each segment, as the dancers exited out the double doors of the large studio, Martha was supposed to enter into the studio and expound at great length on the various aspects of the training of the dancer. The film directors, Martha and Leroy Leatherman who was the writer of the script, tried this approach twice. Both times it was a complete failure. Martha could never memorize the clever lines that Lee Leatherman wrote for her and she also was terribly self-conscious when she came face to face with the camera.

In desperation the prominent director/actor John Houseman was brought onto the scene. Knowing Martha and all of her usable assets quite well he quickly suggested that a variation of Martha's own well devised method of flashbacks be used. Martha was to be placed at her make up table readying herself for a performance. Lee would not write a total script, but rather would assign Martha a different topic upon which she could ad lib freely for each section of the film. The make-up table was a place with which Martha could easily identify. It was a place in whose aura she felt completely comfortable. The make-up table also gave her a myriad of objects with which to occupy herself whenever she lost track of what she was saying.

It is easily observed in the film that Martha is saved by the act of applying her mascara when she loses her train of thought concerning the years that it takes to become a dancer. The Noguchi designed jewel, which was always worn on the front of her costumes, saves her a second time during her well known discourse on Nijinsky's famous leap. Having the freedom of an escape route, Martha could now face the camera directly. If she became too uncomfortable to sustain it, she could change the situation easily and view the camera through the medium of her make-up mirror. With little confusion, Martha easily made her choice for the role for which she was preparing. It was, of course, to be her long standing favorite, Jocasta.

At the end of the film, after all of her preparations and speeches are finished, Martha and her dancers are seen being funneled through the backstage corridors and onto the scene ready to perform *Night Journey*. With the performance comes that moment of truth for which all the preparations had been directed. John Houseman's insight both into the needs of the film and into using Martha's various strengths bordered on genius. He is surely to be given every credit for the success of the film.

The methods of rehearsing for concert dance have as many variations as there are individual choreographers. At one terminus is the choreographer who utilizes total improvisation for his creative stimulation. At the other terminus is the choreographer who comes to every rehearsal totally prepared by pre-designing each movement of the dance. Dancers soon determine the choreographers with whom they can best work. Once this discovery occurs, the dancers make a great effort to inveigle their way into their chosen choreographer's companies.

Other than my few rehearsals with Nina Fonaroff in the Spring of 1949, I had very little experience as a dancer when I left for Colorado the summer of 1949 to study with Hanya Holm at the Colorado College Summer Dance Festival. Upon arrival in Colorado Springs I was tremendously excited to discover that Hanya was to choreograph both a reworking of the *Ionization* section of her great work of the thirties, *Trend*, as well as the complete *L'Histoire du Soldat* of Igor Stravinsky. Alwin Nikolais' *Extrados* was to complete the dance portion of the program.

I auditioned for everything possible and with good luck I was selected to perform in all three pieces. Hanya used as many people as she could for *Ionization*. Thirty nine dancers, mostly women, were massed together on a maze of boxes that were constructed for the piece, all of us trying to make sense out of the difficult score by Edgar Varèse.

During all of the rehearsals for *Ionization*, Hanya choreographed from the front while Nik would stand on one side of the room and Oliver Kostok, Hanya's other assistant from New York, stood on the opposite side. The assistants fed us the arbitrary counts for the piece so that we could create at least some semblance of a unity of action.

In the rehearsal studio, Nik and Ollie could see each other easily and could follow each others constant beat, but the performances were a much more difficult matter. Standing in the wings of the stage, the two became blinded by the lighting and it became almost impossible for them to see what the other person was beating. The counts often were at great variance with one another especially as the piece progressed. We exited from one side of the stage to one assistant's count and then reentered with a completely different set from the assistant on the opposite side. On stage there were whispered questions frantically asked among us, "Which count are you on?"

The answer was always a different one. By some miracle the piece held together for both performances. It was received with such acclaim that we had to dance an encore each time that it was performed.

In *L'Histoire du Soldat*, Hanya cast me in the role of the devil. I had read the synopsis of the story so I knew that, by type at least, I was exactly right for the part, but never in my imagination did I take seriously the idea that I might be selected for the role. The day after the audition for the various dances, I scanned the casting lists nervously. There was my name in bold print for the part of the devil.

Rehearsals didn't start immediately. Hanya, for a few days, left all of us alone to begin to settle into our daily routines, to adjust our breathing to the lack of oxygen caused by the high altitude of the Rocky Mountains, and just to have a chance to absorb into our spirits the magnificence of Colorado with all of its luxuriant beauty. Coming from New York City with its eternal concrete walls and ways, we devoured the glistening green vegetation and radiant blue skies filled with billowing clouds with an insatiable hunger.

It wasn't until the middle of the second week that Hanya finally gave me notice of my first rehearsal. The devil had a relatively short but active solo which occurred in the middle of the work. This was obviously to be choreographed apart from the rest of the cast in order to prevent any waste of other people's time. The rehearsal was scheduled for nine A.M. in the smaller downstairs studio.

I was in a constant flush of anticipation the entire evening preceding the event. At times I was overcome by the fear that Hanya would find me totally inept. This panic alternated with an absolute exhilaration. Sleeping that night was an impossibility. Here was my first rehearsal with one of the leaders of the modern dance world and a brand new solo was to be created for me. I was sure that if I did manage to attain slumber, I would oversleep and miss the rehearsal completely. The clock ticked at a lethargic pace as the night slowly unwound. The hour and minute hands crept around the circle of time seemingly taking twice as long as usual. I watched their progress through the darkness with weary eyes.

Finally at seven a.m. I leapt out of bed, took a cold shower that left my body totally numb and threw a warming bathrobe over my nakedness. Breakfast was out of the question. If I ate anything, I was sure that I would be sick to my stomach. I paced up and down the corridors of the dormitory to pass the rest of the time. Back in my room, I put on my dance clothes militantly as if gearing for battle: the dance belt first, then leotard and finally tights. At 8:50 a.m. with my pulse rate constantly increasing, I started my walk to the lower studio, arriving punctually on the stroke of 9:00.

I slowly opened the door to the studio, peeking warily through the enlarging crack hoping to see Hanya sitting there waiting for me. The room was totally empty. The chamber was cold and smelled of dank and stale air from having been closed and left without heat all night. I had sneaked inside and closed the door behind me before I noticed the phonograph sitting in the center of the room. Lying on top of it was a record of *L'Histoire du Soldat*. On top of the record lay a note.

David, Here is the record. See what you can come up with. I will be back at 11:00 to check on what you have done.

Hanya

I just sat there quietly for quite a length of time. The excitement that I had felt for the last twenty-four hours slowly drained from me. My entire body trembled from its disappointment. I felt deserted and betrayed. In my entire dance career this was probably my most devastating moment.

When Hanya arrived I was still sitting there with nothing to show her. She didn't seem to mind which made me feel even worse. It was as if she had no care or involvement with me or the dance whatsoever. In time, the dance was completed and performed. Had I known what to expect from that first rehearsal, I'm sure that my disappointment would have been less devastating and I could have faced the situation more constructively.

Rehearsing with José Limón and rehearsing with Doris Humphrey created the possibility of making a clear study in the contrasting styles that were formulated by these two prominent, interrelated choreographers. Their methods of contributing each to the other lay in completely opposite directions, but the assistance which each gave was always presented with a sensitivity. The strengths of one seemed to compliment the weaknesses of the other.

Doris possessed a strong kinesthetic imagery that she had developed through her many years of performing. She could describe in strong clear terms whatever she held in her fertile imagination. José, with an intuition gained from years of working closely with her, could quickly penetrate her thoughts and translate immediately into physical action what Doris had only been able to intellectualize and indicate by gesture.

Not having worked with Doris before her hip ailment ended her dancing career, I have no way of knowing how affective she was as a choreographer previous to the disability. The damage to her hip and the pain caused by it forced her to verbalize her choreographic desires instead of using her obviously strong physicality. The presentation of her ideas was always cool and carefully directed and at all times devoid of passion. Even the quality and tone of her voice had a certain dryness about it which lent to analytical assessment rather than any intense emotional involvement.

The one piece that I rehearsed with Doris while she was in the process of choreographing it in 1953 was *Ritmo Jondo*, to music of Carlos Surinach. The dance was in three sections: the first portion was created for the men alone; the second for the women; and in the third section the men and women were paired together. The leading male figure in the dance was, of course, José. Doris selected Crandall Diehl, Ray Harrison, and me to perform as José's macho colleagues on the prowl. The women were Betty Jones, Ruth Currier, and Lavina Nielsen, with Pauline Koner as the central female figure.

The most successful section of the dance seemed to me to be the more contained second section in which the women moved with a quiet lyricism. In the choreography for this section, there was a compelling assurity of direction combined with an austerity of movement which all of the original women members of the cast managed to dance beautifully.

José provided the greatest assistance to Doris in the first section of the dance. In this section, not only did he have to help create his own role as the leader of the band of men, but he had to interpret physically all of Doris' intentions for the rest of us. The men's movements had a slick, overly masculine quality and utilized jumping combinations almost exclusively. In later years, watching performances of the dance from the audience, I was surprised at how little of the wildly expended energy of the men's first section projected across the footlights.

Doris' method of choreography for the third section was truly remarkable for its academic approach. Her pyramidal structuring of the movement was fascinating. Whether this device arose out of her inability to move or whether it was a process which she often used, I have no way of knowing. In this case however the method proved affective. First she established the pattern which the group made throughout each part of the third section. Then we put the foot rhythms, which she described to us, to that pattern. Following that the body with all of its convolutions was added and finally, the arms. This method allowed for an intricacy of movement which might not have been obtainable otherwise, but it did seem that it totally removed all spontaneous organic movement.

Doris believed that *Ritmo Jondo* was a sexually impassioned work. She felt that it would totally surprise her critics. She was well aware, by this time, of being categorized as a dance intellectual, cool and removed, a choreographer who worked in abstract conceptualizations of humanity with seemingly little care for or interest in the human individual. With this dance she hoped to erase some, if not all, of these images.

José, throughout the choreographing of the entire work, remained at Doris' side constantly ready to assist her. He was the physicalization of all of her intellectual ideas. Never once did he give the appearance of being exhausted or misused, but he always remained magnanimous and gracious in aiding his long standing mentor.

Choreographically, José's major talents fell at the opposite end of the spectrum from those of Doris. José found it easy to communicate his compassion for the human individual's needs. This natural ability drew him toward a more directly communicative approach in composition than Doris had usually used, and placed the emphasis of his choreography on the individual. However, because of his long association with Doris he became well versed in the choric approach also and could expertly handle massive amounts of dancers in sweeping phrases of movements. This gave José a wide range of possibilities to use in his choreography.

The only work of José's in which I danced was called *El Grito*. José had choreographed the dance on a group of Mexican dancers during his sojourn in Mexico in 1951. In 1952 he transferred the dance to his own company which was augmented by an additional group of dancers. It was performed at the Juilliard School then located in upper Manhattan. I think the only person who was in both the original performance of the work in Mexico and the showing in the United States was Beatriz Flores, a beautiful Mexican dancer who had followed José north to study with him.

Although *El Grito* was created relatively early in José's choreographic career, with it he already began to show his ability for texturing the strong thread of the individual against the fabric of a more complex society. José worked with a great passion. This made each rehearsal an event which one anticipated with enthusiasm. I was cast with Ruth Currier to dance a short but lively little duet. Later, I was also given the turning duet with Betty Jones, as the male dancer assigned to perform it could not accomplish the required turns.

We rehearsed on the stage and throughout the rehearsals Doris sat stoically in a chair at the very edge of the apron. She was so close that one slip and she would have disappeared backward into the orchestra pit. Although José was his usual gracious self during the working process, it was easy to detect an underlying rancor when Doris too often interrupted the flow of his thoughts or the process of his staging.

Doris' criticisms usually dealt with the overall structure of the piece or its dramatic line rather than any specific movements. She had an uncanny ability for connecting isolated segments into a continuous totality. Still, with Doris, one always had the feeling of an artistic watch dog at work. José, in his acute wisdom, kept his supposed irritation under control and made good use of Doris' all seeing eyes. The two together worked with an unspoken realization of the tremendous benefits that each gained from the other.

Some dancers never do develop an affinity for rehearsing. They may not mind directing others in rehearsal, but when it comes to their own practicing, they will do almost anything to escape it. Louis Horst, Martha Graham's musical director and for a time her personal companion, told many wild stories about the Graham–Horst violent conflicts that took place in the rehearsal arena. Such physical acts as breaking down locked doors in order to reach Martha and dragging her into the rehearsal studio to practice, seemed gross exaggerations at the time. Martha, on her part, told stories that Louis hit her and demanded that she work when she was not physically or emotionally able. Hearing both sides separately, I was prone to believe that each of their stories was nothing more than the product of a fertile imagination.

Some twenty years later, long after their personal relationship had ceased, both Martha and Louis taught for many summers at the American Dance Festival in Connecticut. Louis was teaching for the full six weeks session, but Martha taught just the first week of classes. That first week of each summer, Louis and Martha, as a ritual, had breakfast together every morning. Because I was demonstrating for Martha that week at Connecticut, I joined them whenever I managed to arise on time. It was then that I first began to realize that the relationship of which they had been previously speaking was real, based on actual fact.

By this time, in the mid 1950's, these two major modern dance figures had grown comfortable with one another. Game playing had become a major component of their existence. Martha teased Louis constantly, displaying her fragile femininity in order to heighten his characterization of a macho Don Juan. Louis, on the other hand, played to Martha's ego, constantly centering the focus of attention on her activities, past, present, and future.

A typical conversation at the Connecticut breakfast table was:

Louis, grumpily stating over his orange juice, "Martha, why did you always hate to rehearse so much?"

Martha, answering in astonishment with eyes held wide open, "Louis, you know that's not true. I loved to rehearse – sometimes."

Louis after wiping crumbs from the corner of his mouth, "You remember that time when you locked yourself in your dressing room and wouldn't come out? I had to break down the door."

Martha, batting her eyes rapidly, "Louis, you were terrible. You were hurting me."

Louis smiling slightly, "Oh, Martha, It was just a pat."

Martha, being her most feminine, "Louis, you were mean."

In return, Louis drawled, "Martha, you just needed to get to work."

They both laughed over the conversation. Their remembrance proved to be a pleasant experience for them both rather than something that was resented and painful. I sat there between the two. It was true. Everything that they had said separately about each other was real. Their tempestuous relationship had miraculously survived Martha's resistance to rehearsing and Louis' stubborn enforcement of its constancy. It had become a catalyst for a whole new style of dance movements and choreography.

If during her early career, Martha, herself, disliked rehearsing, she did not transfer that attitude to her group when she was working with them in the 1930's. According to those early company members, Martha was a tireless and an exacting task master. I was given an opportunity to speak with some of the company members of that period during the rehearsals for the revival of *Primitive Mysteries*. This was one of the pieces scheduled to be performed on the Louis Horst Memorial at Connecticut College in the summer of 1964, during the American Dance Festival.

Right from the first rehearsals, it was obvious that those original dancers remembered the piece with an amazing exactness. Thirty odd years had done little to diminish their capacity for memory. Most of them had almost total recall of many of the sections of the dance. This they credited to the long hours of Martha's demanding rehearsals, rather than any extraordinary powers of retention.

In order to try to reconstruct the dance for Louis' Memorial, I had gathered together, with Martha's permission, an array of women who had performed in the piece over years past. Gertrude Shurr, Elizabeth Halpern, Helen Priest Rogers, Kathleen Slagle, Ailes Gilmore, Dorothy Bird, Bonnie Bird, May O'Donnell, Nina Fonaroff, Marjorie Mazia, Sophie Maslow, Jane Dudley, and Yuriko were among the women who gathered together on the chosen day for our first meeting.

When I called each of them to ask if they would be willing to participate in the reconstruction, their responses were touching in their immediate enthusiasm. Nina Fonaroff was the only one from whom there was any feeling of reticence. She honestly felt that a revival of the work was not a good idea; however, she proved to be very cooperative and agreed to help in the rehearsals despite her feelings.

When I called Marjorie Mazia, she explained to me that she was getting married on the day that was set for the first meeting. Marjorie was perhaps the dancer who was most in favor of the project. She promised that if her wedding went well, she would be able to make the scheduled night rehearsal. If there were complications, she might have to miss our first meeting. The night of the initial gathering, Marjorie arrived at the studio exactly on time.

Many of the women had not seen each other for nearly thirty years so the beginning of the first rehearsal resembled a sentimental sorority house reunion. Once that the ladies turned their attention to the dancing, the passion and dedication with which they approached the choreography of *Primitive Mysteries* became evident. Every nuance of movement and gesture was made meticulously clear. The paces through which Martha had put her dancers thirty years earlier had been so thorough that the dance had made a lasting imprint on their minds.

By the end of the initial rehearsal, the entire first section had been pieced together. Before we stopped for the evening, the original dancers unanimously expressed the desire to perform that section from the beginning to the end. The ladies made the initial striding entrance onto the scene with the strength of women thirty to forty years younger than they themselves were. When they began to dance the major portion of that section their eyes glistened and their muscles moved with a revitalized power. They even danced the difficult continuous contraction leaps that came at the section's end with an amazing endurance.

When they finished, they were panting for breath. Their faces were flushed and perspiration trickled down their foreheads. These ladies for a few brief hours had rekindled the flame of an old romance. All of us who watched the rehearsal were greatly moved by the ingenuous dedication.

We met together once a week to try to complete the reconstruction of the rest of the dance. The other two sections took longer to rework, not because the women remembered the sections less well, but because the second and third sections were more complex choreographically.

Sophie Maslow remembered Martha's part. This made it possible to construct Martha's role completely and for Sophie to teach it to Yuriko who was to perform it on the Memorial. Martha was in Israel during this time and so was of no help. I am not sure that she would have aided the project anyway as she expressed major reservations concerning the revivals. Martha was participating mainly out of respect for Louis' memory rather than any desire to reconstruct the planned dances.

An augmented company of young dancers was selected to perform *Primitive Mysteries* and once they were chosen they attended every rehearsal. The process of recall was helped by the notes that were written into the music score describing the formations and movements of the dance. Marni and I also got in touch with Barbara Morgan who had photographed the dance in its entirety. She was most gracious in helping. She allowed us to spend long afternoons at her home going over every print of the dance that she had in her possession. Marni drew stick figure diagrams of each photograph. By the time that we finished the task, we had almost achieved a continuous pictorial representation of the work.

In spite of all of these aids and clear thinking minds, there still was one small part of the third section which could not fit together. This one element of the puzzle evaded all of us. Everyone's answer to the problem was to locate Ethel Butler and to ask her if she could solve the enigma. Ethel had been a featured member of Martha's company for many years. By 1964 she had moved to Washington, D.C., where she had formed her own company and dance school. I called her, explained our situation, and asked her if she would be willing to fly to New York to help us. She agreed without hesitation.

At the rehearsal, it took Ethel only a few moments before she had correctly realigned all of the conflicting elements. The women's remembrances, the notes in the piano score and Marni's diagrams taken from Barbara Morgan's photographs suddenly fit together like an intricate jigsaw puzzle.

As the reconstruction progressed, Yuriko and I, at separate rehearsals from the rest, taught the augmented company the various sections of the dance. The previous company members had passionately taken possession of the work and danced it continuously at all of their rehearsals. *Primitive Mysteries* belonged to them. It exemplified their youth and their idealistic passions of an almost forgotten era. This made it very difficult when the inevitable time for change from one cast to the other occurred. The rehearsal finally arrived when Yuriko and I were forced to tell these marvelous women that they must now sit and let the dancers of today take their place. It was a moment filled with emotion. For a brief second reality shattered all dreams. Then their magnanimity took command and the change occurred.

In thinking back, it is hard to analyze which seemed to be of greater importance to these women, their dedication toward *Primitive Mysteries* or their dedication toward Martha. Probably for most, the question was of no significance. To them, Martha was the dance and the dance was Martha. Gertrude Shurr expressed the feelings clearly in a letter that she wrote to me following the performances of the memorial. "For me, at that particular time in my life, the Mysteries became my religion, my way of life, and my belief in Martha that has never, never wavered, and in endeavoring to recreate the Mysteries. I hope that others may capture a little bit of this wonderful and meaningful period of Martha's creativity."

Personally, the only pressure during a rehearsal that I ever felt from Martha was during the first company season that I danced with her. Bethsabee de Rothschild was sponsoring a week of performances for the Graham Company at the Alvin Theater in the Spring of 1953. The performance week followed directly on the heels of Bethsabee's just completed Festival of American Dance. Now, in addition to dancing in Martha's *Letter To The World* as I had done in the festival, I was to have the opportunity to dance in *Diversion of Angels* and *Dark Meadow*.

After the first spacing rehearsal in the theater for *Diversion of Angels*, Martha approached me and threatened that if my cartwheels didn't improve, she would have to take me out of the work altogether and perform it with three instead of four men. She wasn't angry. She was very matter of fact, but there was no doubt in my mind but that she meant what she said.

Desperately, I looked all over the theater for a place to practice the cartwheels. The lobby was locked. The aisles were too slanted. The backstage was too small. Finally, I found the ideal spot. It was in the stagehands locker room that was located one level below the stage floor. The lockers were placed in such a way that half of them were braced against one of the walls of the room. The other half stood directly opposite to them and were free standing. This created a narrow corridor of approximately three feet wide. My observations told me that in order to complete a cartwheel successfully, I would have to be in a perfect vertical upside down alignment. My mind understood the challenge but my body didn't cooperate physically.

On my first attempt at a cartwheel, I hit the free standing lockers and with a deafening roar, the lockers and I crashed to the ground. The locker doors flew open and all of the contents came tumbling onto the floor. To my chagrin, everyone in the theater except Martha came running downstairs. The stagehands were unperturbed by the mess and treated me quite kindly. They stood the lockers back onto their legs, made sure that I was all right and left me to stew in my own embarrassment.

Martha never threatened me again about the cartwheels. By the next stage rehearsal they were evidently good enough to pass muster. I hoped that Martha's acceptance of the cartwheels was because I danced them with at least a slightly improved physical correctness, but I could not help wondering if Martha feared that if she threatened me one more time, I might demolish the entire theater.

Martha Graham in her later years was more devious about avoiding rehearsals than any other dancer I have ever known. Over the years she developed a bag full of tricks and constantly made use of them all. Her repertoire was large and seldom repeated. She tried everything: failing to come to the rehearsals at all; phoning in to the studio to give some wildly concocted excuse; arriving late and then gossiping non-stop until it was too late to start the rehearsal.

Martha couldn't stand to come into the studio and see a rehearsal already in progress. As rehearsal director, I always assigned a second dance that could be worked in case Martha didn't appear at the scheduled times. Someone had to be given the task of watching for her approach at the door. If Martha entered the building, we stopped practicing immediately. Everyone in the company was under strict instructions not to sit when she came into the room. If Martha felt that she could captivate her audience, she would never cease her prattle. Sitting dancers made much easier targets than did standing dancers. Future plans, the day's events, dreams, phone calls from Washington, D.C., and taxi drivers, it didn't matter about what she was speaking, for as long as she spoke, she didn't have to rehearse.

Because of the difficulties with Martha, I would usually get the dances together before I even tried to bring her into the rehearsals. Sometimes, if she had duets, she would work on them separately during the day, especially if they were with Bertram Ross who was her favorite partner and sounding board. The most conniving that I remember her was at a *Clytemnestra* rehearsal for the 1961 season. She was so purposefully clever that one could only stand back and marvel at her devastating ingenuity.

This rehearsal occurred after *Clytemnestra* had already been performed for two seasons. The third time around, Martha was always much less interested in her works. I finally had gotten the piece pulled together. All that it needed was to add the choreographer into the context in order to complete the work. She had already missed two rehearsals and I held little hope that she would keep her commitment for the third.

From the minute that she came into the room, I could tell that this was going to be a difficult evening. Martha was dressed for rehearsing in her usual black attire. The rehearsal was immediately blocked as Martha never ceased talking. She parried with her rapier like tongue, weaving in and out of various subject matter until she finally discovered her opening.

"Akiko (Kanda), what are you doing here? I told you not to rehearse until your knee is perfectly healed. I don't want you here. Go home. Go home."

Akiko mumbled under her breath, "I'm really all right." She had strained her knee slightly in a previous rehearsal.

"No, you are not. It is too dangerous. Now go."

Akiko left.

Martha continued her random diatribe. Finally she picked on Dan Wagoner.

"Dan, don't you dance with Akiko?"

Dan did partner her in the "Rape of Troy" section of the dance and admitted it. Anticipating a free evening he failed to mention all the other sections in which he performed.

"Well then it's silly for you to stay. You might as well go", Martha exclaimed.

Dan left. More variegated diatribe ensued.

"Dick (Kuch), you and Dan work together. If he isn't here, there is no reason for you to stay. Go. Go."

Dick exited.

Interspersed with discourse on any subject that came to mind, Martha, in this manner, slowly eliminated all nineteen dancers in the cast of *Clytemnestra* one by one. Finally only Martha, Bertram Ross, and myself were left sitting on the benches by the mirrors.

Martha spoke to her erstwhile partner, "Bert, we could run through our duets, but I don't think that it is necessary. We already know them well. It's better that you go home and get some rest."

Bert wandered into the dressing room to change his clothes.

Martha turned and looked at me, with the look of a champion. She had met a challenge head on and had won. In the back of her eyes lay a purposeful mischievous glint.

"Well, David, it looks as if there's no one left so you won't be able to rehearse *Clytemnestra* tonight. Maybe you can schedule it another time next week."

I didn't really mind the failure to rehearse. I was too fascinated by the cleverness with which Martha had worked her majestic plan. The subtleties by which Martha dealt with the matter were a lesson in themselves. What the lesson was I never could clearly discern, but certainly when wills were in evidence no one could ever contend successfully with Martha.

In a contest of wills, Martha Graham and Leonide Massine must have been nearly equal. Their collaboration or confrontation during the choreographing of Massine's version of Igor Stravinsky's *Sacre du Printemps* created many violent flying sparks.

In June of 1954 after the Graham European tour had been completed in Vienna, I took off for Venice to fulfill a childhood dream. As a young boy Venice had seemed to me to be a magical mirage which could only be conjured up by the use of some mystical incantation. Upon my arrival in that city, everything that I had imagined proved to be true. Instead of continuing my travels through the rest of Italy as I had planned, I remained in Venice for two weeks and explored every inch of it.

On one of the last few days that I was there, I took a boat from the Piazza San Marco across the lagoon to the isle of San Giorgio Maggiore. I wandered all over the island during the morning, finally arriving at the opposite side of it. There, it was obvious that an amphitheater was being dug out of the hillside. It was a beautiful, open, performing space which looked over the calm blue waters of the bay. I sat there for a bit basking in the sun and watching the workmen labor at their individual tasks. When it neared midday and the heat became too great, I headed back to find a cooler space to spend the afternoon.

On the return walk, I passed a low standing building. Out of it emanated music and the metered counting uno, due, tres over and over again. To a dancer, it was obvious that a rehearsal of some sort was being held in the unadorned confines of the structure. I questioned a couple of women as they exited from the building. They informed me that it was a dance rehearsal for a religious spectacle that was to open the amphitheater that I had just seen at the edge of the island. They assured me that no one would mind if I stuck my head through the door.

I did just that. It was over two weeks since I had been involved in anything related to dance and I was pulled toward it as if I had the need to satisfy a healthy addiction. When I stepped inside the door, a young man approached me to see what I might want. I explained that I was a dancer and had just finished a tour of Europe with Martha Graham. The man was exceedingly congenial. He told me that he was Canadian and was an assistant to Leonide Massine for this production. Massine was creating a religious spectacle on the life of Christ. Sure enough, I recognized Massine at work in the middle of the studio with a large group of performers around him.

With the Canadian's permission, I stayed and watched for an hour or so until the rehearsal broke for lunch. I cannot explicitly remember what I saw except thinking that this little dark man was almost completely submerged within the masses of dancers with whom he was working. When the rehearsal was finished, my new friend took me to Massine and introduced me to him, explaining who I was.

Massine was obviously in a hurry and not overly interested, but when Martha's name was mentioned he stopped for a moment. With deep introspection, he spoke slowly and deliberately, "Martha Graham is a very strong woman, but she's no real dancer."

He then hurriedly went on his way. Since that time Massine has written very highly of Martha and her work and Martha has certainly proved, despite Massine's statement of that moment, that she was one of the great dancers of the century.

In 1959 Martha Graham was asked to collaborate with George Balanchine on a dance work for the New York City Ballet Company. They were both to use the symphonic music of Anton Webern. It was arranged that Martha would choreograph her part of the work using her own company and then transfer it to members of the New York City Ballet. Without conferring with each other both Balanchine and Graham developed their own ideas and followed their own directions.

When Balanchine came to the Graham studio to observe what Martha had choreographed, he decided that with the allotted rehearsal time that was left, his dancers would not be able to do justice to the modern choreography. Instead, a few of the ballet dancers (mainly Sally Wilson as Elizabeth I) were incorporated into Martha's part of the work and one dancer from the Graham Company (Paul Taylor) danced a solo in Balanchine's section. Both pieces came under the umbrella title of *Episodes*.

I had missed performing in the dance the first season that the Graham Company participated in the collaboration. Marni and I were still enjoying our extended working honeymoon in Mexico, but we returned to New York before the season was finished and were able to see one of the last performances.

Before the second season of *Episodes* took place, Gene McDonald, a Graham Company member, dropped out of Martha's section of the dance. She then asked me to perform in his place. Martha's section was based on the story of Mary, Queen of Scots, at the moment of her beheading. It was a highly stylized, regal, and powerfully passionate dance.

On the day of the first performance of the second season, we spent the time at the City Center Theater checking everything that was essential for the production and idly passing the hours until we were called on stage for our spacing rehearsal. Being backstage with the New York City Ballet presented a clear view into a completely different working atmosphere. Because the ballet company was an organization of vast size, there seemed to be much more activity, confusion, and overt excitement connected with it than there was with the modern concerts of the Graham Company. Involvement with the latter seemed to be almost the consummate religious experience.

On the same program with *Episodes*, George Balanchine's one act version of *Swan Lake* was scheduled to be performed. The principal dancers in the ballet were Erik Bruhn and Maria Tallchief. I had met Bruhn, formerly a danseur noble with the Royal Danish Ballet, when I was on tour with the Graham Company in Copenhagen, Denmark. Maria Tallchief, long a prima ballerina with the New York City Ballet, had for years been my all time favorite ballet dancer, next to my sister, Barbara, of course. The two stars, Bruhn and Tallchief, had never before danced the Balanchine work together nor had they ever performed together at any time previous to this occasion.

When we arrived at the theater early in the morning, the two had already begun to rehearse. Completely on their own, all through the day, they continued their practice sessions together. Slowly they began to familiarize themselves with the individuality of the other's approach. Wherever they could find a space in which to work, they further clarified their relationship within the dance and their interrelated timing.

During the day, I spotted them practicing in the lobby, in the auditorium, in the dressing rooms, and up and down the corridors of the theater. Once I even saw them practicing in the backstage elevator when it descended to the ground floor. Their sense of responsibility to the performance was highly evident. Also evident was their responsibility toward themselves. Each of the two projected a positive pride which, as a professional dancer, would not let them perform in any manner other than at their absolute best.

That evening I pushed into the wings to watch their performance. Rarely have I have seen two people dance with such accord and sensitivity to one another. When this radiant ballet performance was finished, the response of the audience was overwhelming.

The next day Walter Terry wrote of the performance in the *New York Herald Tribune*, "Miss Tallchief, dark and beautiful and Mr. Bruhn, fair and handsome not only looked like the ideal princess and prince from your favorite storybook, but they danced as if they had been moving together all their lives."

7

ON TOURING

A large part of a performing dancers life is spent traveling from one city to another, from one performance venue to the next. This provides the dancer with the maximum number of performances over a set period of time. The ability to adapt to this unique demand of the dancer's profession depends on the individual's openness to and excitement about new acquaintances, and new situations. For some dancers the actual act of traveling from one place to the next is nothing more than an enervating necessity, but for the rest it is a time which can be used for relaxation and contemplation. For these dancers, it is a respite, when both the mind and the body can find pleasure in pulling back from the intense physical and mental activities of performing.

Company members spend the time during these trips from theater to theater in a myriad of different ways: some are avid readers; some knit constantly, needles clacking away; postcards and letters are written in profusion; conversationalists are in great evidence; card players become addicts for playing both solitaire and poker; stereo ear phones are in abundance. Some dancers spend the entire time from the beginning of the trip to the end, sleeping, totally obliterating the sojourn; certain other dancers nervously pace the aisles of the plane or train during the journey, anxious to get from one hotel room to the next as fast as possible. Each person finds his own way or combination of ways for putting the time of travel to the best possible use for relaxation.

To truly enjoy touring, one must be able to anticipate with relish the sense of the unknown. It does not matter how many times one performs in Paris, France, or Ames, Iowa, no two times are ever identical. Hotels, theaters, times of year, and the people whom one meets vary with each visit.

Home seasons are few in number and are usually of short duration. The majority of performances are mainly to be found on the road. These tours, if the companies are lucky, last usually from six weeks to four months at a time. Each scheduled stop takes from a minimum of one day to a couple of weeks at most. Just as one begins to find tranquillity in a new hotel room, empties one's suitcase, finds cheap but nourishing nearby places to eat and does one's laundry, it is time again to pack the bags and move on to the next dot on the map.

It takes a certain type of individual to sustain a love for this life style year after year. Inevitably, for most performers no matter how dedicated they are, the years of touring take their toll and the dancers eventually become disenchanted with this transient existence.

There are a few dancers who upon arrival at a new destination head immediately to their hotel rooms and never leave them except for the necessary rehearsals and performances. For these dancers touring is an anathema, and they attempt to perpetuate a secure constancy of existence within an unstructured and temporal situation. For myself, on arrival at every city, I immediately dropped my belongings into my room and headed for a long walk no matter how late our arrival. I could never sleep until I investigated my new surroundings and had staked out the territory.

The means of transportation that a company uses during their travels varies greatly in relation to the size of the group, the distance that must be covered, and the amount of time that is available between performances. The greatest change in touring over the past few decades has occurred with the advent of the airplane.

Trains were the essential means of touring until the 50's when air travel supplanted them because of cost and convenience. The tremendous saving of time has now made flying indispensable. Fast, fairly accurate in schedule, relatively inexpensive, often with cheap group rates, flying has easily become the major mode of transportation for the touring dancer. In Europe, however, trains still provide an immense charm and ease of travel as well as being a bit cheaper than most flights.

Until the 50's there was no other way for intercontinental tours to occur than by ship. If the dancer did not become too seasick and the voyage was not too rough, ships provided an excellent means of transportation. For the five to ten days of the trips duration one has no choice but to totally relax. Stretching and limited exercising are possible in order to keep the body in condition, but little else.

Quite a few years ago, station wagon tours were a prevalent mode of travel among young dance companies. The various companies would travel across the country from one coast to the other stopping in each city to arrange "on the spot" performances.

The dancers would gather together their costumes and props (sets were too cumbersome for this type of venture) and head off into the hinterlands to gain experience from any kind of exposure that could be made available.

The Joffrey Ballet Company came into existence using staton wagons. Gathering together mainly students from his classes at the New York High School for the Performing Arts, Robert Joffrey, began the kind of barn storming tours of the United States which only the youthful idealists of dance could survive. Such newly formed groups could not expect to draw an audience more than for a single performance in each town, and so they were constantly on the move. Money acquired from one performance was used by the group for survival until the next paid performance came along.

These companies could seldom afford technicians of any kind. The dancers were assigned the necessary tasks and responsibilities that were required for the performances. Each dancer had his own company piece of luggage to unload and unpack and after the performance to repack and reload. For the performance one dancer might be in charge of wardrobe, another lights while another called the cues or pulled the curtain. Because of their diverse occupations, it would seem that the dancers would have little time to concentrate on the task of dancing, but this was not the case. Every group that I saw which operated in this manner was bright and lively and showed no obvious ill effects from their hard and many faceted labors.

Very little of my touring experience was involved with transportation by car. Marni and I did have one experience during the summer of 1960 when we were forced to use our car to transport scenery from the American Dance Festival at Connecticut College, New London, Connecticut, to the Jacob's Pillow Festival in Lee, Massachusetts. The distance was not long; it took only a few hours.

Marni and I were teaching our usual stint of Graham technique at New London. Martha, as always, opened the festival with her stimulating Monday night lecture. That year she decided to present, in addition to the lecture, a performance of *Errand Into The Maze* with Helen McGeehee and Bertram Ross dancing the minotaur and the woman. Arrangements had also been made with Ted Shawn, the head of Jacob's Pillow, to present the same program the following weekend at the Pillow. It was easy enough to find a car to rent in order to transport the three participants, Martha, Helen, and Bert from New London to Lee, but for some reason there was not a truck or even a large station wagon available in order to transport the set for the dance. The difficult part to carry was the large Noguchi depiction of a female pelvis which consisted of two huge beams that protruded upward to a formidable height.

Marni, for her graduation from Sarah Lawrence College had received a little Volkswagen as her reward. The tiny bug became our family car. The one luxury which accompanied the Volkswagen's simplicities was a lovely breezy sun roof which opened out the confinement of that small compact auto into the spaciousness of the skies overhead.

Our Volkswagen proved to be the savior of the day. With the sun roof open we drove alongside the loading dock of Palmer Auditorium at Connecticut College and the stage hands, with great care, slowly lowered the Noguchi pelvis into the car from above. The base of the set piece nestled cozily into the automobile in back of the driver's seat, and then protruded through the sun roof seemingly miles into the air above the car. With no little trepidation concerning the legality of our endeavor we slowly backed the car away from the loading dock. The cheers of encouragement directed at us by the stagehands helped to build our fortitude. We began our journey northward hoping that we wouldn't be stopped by any police along the highway or be followed by any curious barking dogs.

Although we weren't chased by dogs or the police, we were followed on our path by curious fellow travelers with honking horns and shouts of derision. Some comments were even inexcusably vulgar. Our Volkswagen had taken on the shape of a modernistic mobile sculpture and for all anyone knew we might be the central figures in a performance art production.

The town squares of the small New England villages became immobilized with curiosity as we drove past, cleaving the air with our protruding bones. Birds found the set piece to be a marvelous place on which to perch and hitch a free ride for themselves. They showed no respect for Noguchi's artistry by excreting their droppings onto it as a way of making it their own. Insects found the sculpture difficult to avoid and by the time that we arrived at The Pillow, there was a collection of summer's bugs imbedded into the leading side of the pelvis. A flurry of butterflies that appeared out of the vegetation as we crossed an open field gave their lives for art without care or concern. It was necessary to stop at all low wire crossings and low underpasses to make sure that the top of the sculpture was not unknowingly lopped off as we passed underneath.

After a few hours, we arrived at our destination with some relief. With great difficulty the pelvis was lifted out of the sun roof, and *Errand Into The Maze* was performed once again. From that time on I viewed our little Volkswagen through different eyes.

The various bus trips always seemed to happen following a performance late at night or extremely early in the morning just as the cock crowed. Either time allowed the dancers to arrive at a new venue, take a class and have a rehearsal before beginning preparations for the performance. Because of this, touring by bus could be highly conducive to creating tensions and unpleasant relations among the dancers. Simply put, it brought out the worst traits of everyone.

The two bus tours of the Graham Company that took place during the 1949–50 season were notorious. These tours were so difficult for the dancers that there was almost a complete turnover of the Graham Company after each of the two trips.

Somewhere in the middle of the second six week tour, the company had finished yet another performance, packed up its belongings one more time, and boarded the bus for yet another late night journey. That night, as the bus began its travels, the usual din of voices raised in general uproar and complaint filled the air. Then as ennui and weariness settled onto the group, quiet descended. Not a sound was heard except for an occasional cough or soft snore. Coming from some unknown darkened space on the bus, these isolated sounds seemed to shatter violently the complete stillness. The oppressiveness of the silence seemed laden with dire portents.

The bus plied its path over rolling hills and through the backroads of small towns trying to avoid traffic. After a few hours it continued its journey on a road which divided an old graveyard directly down the middle. The tombstones and monuments gleamed brightly on either side of the bus, caught in the polarized reflection of the moonlight. From the deep blackness of the back of the vehicle, her thoughts relating the actual dead of the graveyard with the near dead dancers of the bus, Helen McGeehee's rasping voice came cutting through the dense air. "Look at all those lucky people!", she moaned gazing out of the window at the gravestones with tired eyes.

I myself didn't mind the late night trips nearly as much as those of the early morning. Since I was by nature a night person, the encompassing darkness gave me a chance to slip back into isolation, letting my mind freely wander over the plain of human experience.

Some trips were actually beautiful at night. On one tour with the Dudley-Maslow-Bales Trio, we drove through southeastern Pennsylvania where the steel industry with its belching furnaces were in evidence. At night the long stacks released their fires into the air. The shooting flames glowed sharply against the night's darkness. At one juncture there were so many furnaces in operation simultaneously that the impression was of being caught in Hades with no known route of escape. By daylight this illusion was lost. All that remained were a series of gray furnaces with endlessly tall chimneys releasing spirals of smoke into the polluted air.

No matter how beautiful or restful the late night trip had been, it was always a great relief to see the lights of the destined city appear on the horizon. As we drew nearer to the city, the lights began to appear as bright scattered dots. Then as the vehicle began to move through the edge of the city, the lights gradually grew in number. Here or there was an all night gas station or a twenty-four hour super market. In the few houses, one could almost see the mother or father bending over their crying child in an attempt to coax it to sleep. Little by little the illumination increased until the center of the city was reached.

The buses' inhabitants emitted groans when the overhead lights were turned on so that shoes and any other articles of apparel that had been cast off could be found. The transport pulled up in front of some strange hotel; another trip was concluded. The bus rapidly funneled its population of dancers into the strange lodging's immediately consuming beds. Within moments everyone was effortfully caught in slumber, grasping desperately at a few minutes rest in order to be able to meet the rigors of the oncoming day.

The early morning bus trips, from my point of view, were much more debilitating. On a typical morning, the hour for departure caught most of the performers unaware. It didn't matter what hour was actually set for leaving as no one ever arrived downstairs on time. To be punctual in the morning was, in reality, considered to be morally inexcusable.

Shortly after the scheduled departure time, the first dancers began to make their appearance. These were the morning people. These early risers looked at the rest of the company with disdain. Following the morning people, the remaining company members began to gather. They exited from the hotel onto the street singly, emanating great resentment against the world and all of its inhabitants. Each person would locate an empty doorway or other shelter where they could isolate themselves and eliminate all necessity for communication. Turned up collars were essential as were hats that were pulled down over the head as much as possible. The greatest necessities were the dark glasses or "shades" which were a definite protection from all of the evils of the world. Sun glasses seem to be today's version of the ostrich's buried head in the sand.

Inevitably by this hour, the bus was pulled up in front of the hotel. Being aware through experience of the late arrival of the dancers, the bus driver would have disappeared for his morning coffee into the hotel food shop and the bus would be locked tightly against entry, making the situation even more incendiary.

Always one dancer or roomful of dancers would have overslept. They had to be tracked down and awakened. By now the bus driver had returned, usually with take out coffee in hand. Somehow the sullen attitude of the dancers only made the driver seem brighter and more cheery. With the bus finally unlocked, the dancers disdainfully boarded it, murmuring endless complaints about the hour, the bus driver, the weather, and their colleagues. They picked out their usual seat on the bus while irritably grousing about the thoughtlessness of the oversleepers.

After a time the stragglers finally emerged from the hotel. With a false sense of bravado and an uncaring attitude, they pushed their suitcases into the luggage compartment located underneath the bus and then stepped into the vehicle to face a sea of dark glasses behind which were a sea of disapproving eyes. Without apology they slipped into whatever vacant seats could be found and drew the window curtains tightly across the windows cutting off the outside world and its sunlight. Now at last, a half hour late, the bus pulled angrily away from the curb and began its journey to the next performance.

In contrast to those agonizing early morning bus trips were the bus journeys of the Graham Company on the European tour in 1954. Following our highly unsuccessful few weeks in London's Saville Theater, we traveled to the Netherlands taking a boat from Harwich, England, to The Hook, Holland. As we stepped off our ship we were met by the Dutch management. We were transported immediately to The Hague. This capital city of Holland was a charming European town that was neither too large for convenience or too small for familiarity.

After we had completed three or four performances in The Hague, we were booked into many of the smaller cities throughout the country: Utrecht, Delft, Rotterdam, and Enschede were all one day performance stops on our dancing tour of the Netherlands. The distances that we traveled from The Hague to each of these places, were short. There was, thus, no demand for early morning departures. After traveling to each city often there was enough extra time for a little sightseeing or shopping before we were called to the theater for class or rehearsal. The return trips following the performances gave us just enough time to unwind before we were released back into the charm of The Hague.

The best part of each trip was traveling through the Dutch countryside. All of the trite conceptions which one had gained from picture books, travelogues, and reading material became a reality as we progressed each mile through the country's rural area. The beautiful canals that wandered ribbon-like over the landscape and the dikes that held the ocean's power at bay, revealed themselves. Best of all were the endless windmills with their many sails constantly rotating in the light breeze that rolled over the flat green land. In those days one could even see a few Dutch people dressed in traditional attire, wooden shoes and all. Each of these trips was a leisurely and beautiful sightseeing tour. This was one of the few times that I have ever known the Graham Company to travel in complete accord.

In Warsaw, Poland, on the Graham European tour of 1962, the company hotel was located geographically far from the space in which we were scheduled to perform. Our theater existed in a huge mausoleum-like structure of unbelievable size. It contained various other theaters as well as ours. It also had puppet theaters, movie cinemas, sports arenas, and bowling alleys. It was conceived as a total complex made to fit the diverse tastes of all of the Polish proletariat. We were informed that the Russians had built the edifice as a gift for the Poles, but had left them with the struggle of meeting the huge overhead required to maintain it.

Walking back and forth to the performances was a possibility, but in actuality it was a highly impractical solution for the dancers. The Polish sponsors provided the company with a large bus. It proved to be a great convenience as taxis to and from each performance were exorbitantly expensive and impossible to find. There was not too much to be seen in Warsaw at that time and certainly there was little shopping. Most of the dancers remained in the hotel and made Warsaw a break in the middle of a rather exhausting tour.

Everyday, however, there were a few of the company who went off by themselves on some adventure or other without informing any of the rest of us. When it became time for the bus to depart we were forced into a guessing game: did the missing dancers intend to take the bus to the theater or did they intend to make their way to the performance on their own?

No one was put in charge of the arrangements and our management completely side stepped the issue, not wanting to become involved, in a very sticky situation. During that tour I was already acting as company rehearsal director. The onus of finding a solution for this mess and enforcing it upon an unwilling company fell automatically onto my shoulders, although it had nothing to do with my actual job.

I posted a daily list downstairs in the hotel which was to be signed by each person who did not intend to go to the theater on the bus. Most dancers remembered to sign the list if they weren't returning, but there were always those few who forgot. As a result the loud harangues continued and antagonisms grew stronger and stronger. I faced every trip to the theater with hopeless dread.

If the bus trips to the theater were filled with tensions, the rides back to the hotel following the performances were even worse. Fifteen minutes following the final curtain, the female dancers were always on the bus ready for the return trip. The males were just beginning to remove their make up, following which they intended to take a leisurely shower. The dynamic energy of male and female dancers couldn't be more diverse.

Each night, anticipating the difficulty, I would hasten downstairs to try to placate the women while they were forced to wait for a half hour to an hour, and every ten minutes or so I returned to the men's dressing room to try to prod them into moving a bit faster.

I was totally unsuccessful as I could neither appease the women nor speed up the men. One of the last nights, tired of the interminable harangue, I told the bus driver to take the women to the hotel and then return for the men. I knew the men would have to wait a few minutes, but at that moment I couldn't care. If the men weren't able to cooperate a little they would have to suffer the consequences. After delivering the women at the hotel, I returned with the bus to pick up the men.

They had to wait no more than ten minutes but their rage was unlimited. Tirades of scorn were heaped upon me in a continuous flow. Somehow their wrath passed right over me. I was glad it was dark that night or the men might have seen the smile of satisfaction that covered my face.

Of all the different modes of transportation which are used for touring, traveling by train seems to elicit stronger emotional reactions in people (dancers and non-dancers) than any other of the methods. Maybe that is why people still maintain a close link with trains long after their utility has greatly diminished.

Cars and planes have a more immediate usefulness. The utilitarian automobile, with its door to door capability, elicits little emotional reaction. Planes are the symbol of the modern age. They are a magic carpet. Like a vacuum they suck the passengers into their entrails at the point of departure and unfeelingly spew them out at their destination. Boats and ships, once transportation's major source of romantic involvement, often become idle times of desperation for those on board. Trains, from their conception, have carried the burden of changing times with constant integrity.

After the Graham Company's 1954 European tour had been completed, I took off on my own to see another part of the world. My travels took me finally to Barcelona, Spain. From there I planned to catch a train to Madrid. At that time in Spain one had to petition the Spanish National Transportation System in order to purchase a ticket.

Not knowing the governmental protocol, I went directly to the railway station. At the last minute one of the passengers on my desired train failed to show and a kind conductor sold me the unused ticket. I'm sure that he then pocketed the money. Luckily the ticket was for a second class compartment so there were only four people jammed into either side of our small cubicle instead of the infinite numbers of people, chickens, cats and dogs that composed the third class compartments.

The train crept across the barren land of Spain, seeming to create more movement by its lateral motion than it did forward.

Crammed into my compartment along with the rest was a Spanish banderillero whose bright personality made the trip palatable. He was on his way to a bullfight in Madrid. Because of his previous experience with Spanish trains, he came well prepared with both food and drink. Shortly after the trip began, he pulled his picnic out of a basket. It was wrapped in a light tan and black, dirty looking rag. He was most generous in offering the food and drink to the rest of us in the compartment. One glance at the evil looking sausage from which he was cutting hefty slices and everyone graciously refused except for a little round gray haired lady who looked as if she had never turned down a crumb in her life.

The great gift of the banderillero lay in his method of drinking wine. He had two jugs, one of water and one of wine. He hooked each over a shoulder and then by lifting his elbows, gradually tilted them so that the wine and water poured in two streams that met and resolved into one rushing torrent of mixed liquid just before it reached his mouth. Nary a drop was spilt despite the trains jerky motion.

I had no idea that the trip took from eight p.m. until about ten a.m. the next day. I had brought no food with me and there was no restaurant car on the train. By the time that we arrived in Madrid my taste in food had greatly altered and I was partaking of the evil looking sausage with relish and washing it down with a little wine. I never did try my talent at mixing wine and water banderillero style despite his encouragement to do so.

The most beautiful trip by train may be the crossing of the Alps from Switzerland to Austria. A constant breathtaking view greets passengers as they gaze out of the windows literally making one gasp at the wonders of nature. Despite Martha Graham's constant pacing back and forth along the aisles of the train, nothing could detract from the beauty of the trip and the humility felt on viewing those majestic mountains.

Personally, ships have always held a special place in my life. By joining the navy in World War II, I not only escaped the hot breath of the selective service draft, but I managed to enter a branch of the service in which I could find adventure. My fervor wasn't even diminished when, upon reporting for duty to the light cruiser, the U.S.S. Philadelphia, I found the ship to be in dry-dock in the Philadelphia Navy yard rather than in the Mediterranean Sea as I had so delightfully imagined. My ardor persisted even though I was put in "hack" (confined to my room) for a week as punishment for my horrible misdeeds. The Philadelphia was acting as the flag ship for President Harry S. Truman's journey to the Potsdam Conference. During this trip I had piped the head of the British navy, the Admiral of the Renown, over the side of the ship without his boat being in attendance. The admiral erroneously assuming that everything was in place had climbed, without looking down, directly into the water below and with drenched pant legs was forced to climb all the way back up again. This event proved to be one of the highlights of my short navy career.

Nine years later I found myself crossing the Atlantic Ocean once again. This time the winter storms were less violent and the circumstances had a much greater ambiance. Martha Graham was making a second attempt at conquering Europe. Bethsabee de Rothschild was the sponsor of the tour and the full company was in tow. The prospect of a European trip was exciting with all of the new and unknown countries to visit, but to travel there on the Queen Elizabeth was the crowning glory.

Our departure was celebrated with great festivities and much champagne. The knowledge that we were being sent second class rather than third added to the excitement of the trip. As usual Bethsabee was much more financially gracious than she needed to have been. Since it was a mid-winter crossing we had the ship mostly to ourselves. Bob Cohan and I were the only two people in a huge four bed stateroom. It wasn't an outside cabin, but we didn't care as we seldom spent anytime in it.

For exercise the company walked the decks or swam in the ship's pool. For entertainment we played cards or went to the evening movies. Even though the weather wasn't terribly unpleasant, it was still too rough to try to hold any kind of formal class. We stayed up most of the night partying in the lounge and then slept late in the mornings, usually missing breakfast. Fortunately the trip lasted only five days or it would have taken us weeks to rid ourselves of our "sea legs" and get back into shape ready to perform.

For the return trip I cashed in my second class ticket for a third class one to gain some extra money for my trip following the end of the tour in Vienna. My stateroom on the return voyage was one sixth the size of my second class stateroom, and I shared it with an elderly Italian. He was a nice man who spoke very little English but had obviously not bathed in months.

In the confinement of that unventilated stateroom I found it impossible to sleep because of the smell. The first night that we were underway, in desperation, I went up to the third class sports deck, found a deck chair, and breathing fresh air, curled up in peace. It was magnificent lying there in the light cool breeze with the moon shimmering on the glassy water as the ship cut a triangle through it. The ship's engines, from below decks, throbbed just enough to create a sleep inducing lullaby. Each night of the voyage I camped out there in the open air, alone and unfettered. By the time that I arrived in New York I was well rested and ready to attack my career with renewed energy.

As much as I loved the ocean travel, I could only manage one other major journey by ship during my active dancing career. Marni and I were going to Stockholm, Sweden, for our first teaching session with Lia Schubert at Balettakademien.

After a hectic summer of new parenting (Marina, our eldest daughter was five months old) and teaching, we felt the boat trip would provide us with a few, much needed, relaxed days before we had to start back to work.

It was a lovely trip filled with delicious Swedish food, Schnapps, and sparkling blue-green water all around us. We even discovered other dancer friends on board. Robert and Maggie Moulton with their two children were also making a journey to Stockholm. Their son, Charlie, now a grown man, has become an excellent performer with Merce Cunningham, and an innovative choreographer.

There have been, in addition, many short boat trips over the years: Germany and Denmark to Sweden; Norway to England; France to Spain; traveling through the beautiful countryside of Sweden from Stockholm to Göteborg on one of the charming boats that ply Göta Canal. Every chance that I get even today I travel by ship, but sadly the chances are fewer and fewer as time passes.

By its very nature the media of the airplane readily lends itself to anecdotes. Crowded conditions, weather difficulties, schedule changes, and missed connections create endless circumstances that give company managers heart failure. There are two flights that stand out in my mind, one because of its difficulties and the other because of its terrifying beauty.

Following our decision to marry during the Israeli tour of 1958, Marni and I flew to Berlin to see her sister Emma Lewis Thomas, who was in Germany studying with Mary Wigman. That gave us the opportunity to visit Wigman's classes and also to watch Wigman rehearse her performing group. We then spent a few lovely days in Paris wandering leisurely through all the scenic areas of that unbelievable city.

From Paris we had planned to fly to New York on El Al Airlines. We had originally flown to Israel on El Al with the company. Because of all the Graham sets that had to be flown from New York to Israel and back for the performances, El Al refused to let any one of us change from their flights to another airline. We were free to rebook our flights for anytime that met our needs but not to switch from the Israeli airline. Marni and I had flown at our own expense from Tel Aviv to Germany and then on to France, but because of finances, for crossing the Atlantic we were forced once again to take El Al.

The two of us were to depart from Orly Airport for New York City one early afternoon, but we received word at the hotel that the plane would be delayed for approximately six hours. This meant nothing more to us than a little additional enjoyable time in Paris. The airplane, Marni, and I finally arrived at Orly Airport and without too much delay the plane was loaded with bags and people. Once everyone was on board, the vehicle slowly worked its way up the line of departing planes. At last the plane started full speed down the runway.

The wheels of the vehicle were just lifting from the ground when thick black smoke began pouring from the engines, sweeping back past us along the fuselage. Everything on the plane was suddenly put into reverse to slow its forward progress. The entire plane began to reverberate as if it were going to disintegrate completely.

Racing through my mind were the headlines that had reported a recent accident in which an entire tour group from Atlanta was killed at the same airport in exactly the same situation. The pilot of that plane was unable to abort the take off and had careened over the end of the airfield. The plane was ripped apart killing all on board.

I tightened my seat belt in anticipation of the worst, but still tried to keep my mind filled with positive thoughts. We hurtled down the last yards of the runway, and just at the final second the pilot in a desperate attempt to prevent the plane from shooting over the end, swerved to the right. Amid the screams of the passengers, the plane turned over onto its wing and then rocked wildly from one side to the other. Immediately soothing music poured out of the loudspeakers. In seconds fire trucks, ambulances, and police appeared alongside. We were herded out of the plane as quickly as possible. I didn't realize how closely we had come to total disaster until friends in Paris sent us newspaper articles proclaiming the pilot to be a hero for the quick actions which saved all of our lives.

Because of the restriction on our tickets, El Al refused to let Marni and me transfer to another airline, despite the traumatic event that we had just been through. We were made to sit and wait for many hours while the airline flew in another plane from Israel. They provided us with couches on which we could try to get a little sleep, but it was hard for us to relax enough to get any beneficial rest.

Finally the next plane arrived and once again we were loaded on board. This time we took off without incident. We flew for what seemed endless time. Then it was announced that the plane was making an unscheduled landing at Gander, Newfoundland, for emergency repairs. Once on the ground we were directed into Gander's small barren airport. It was closed at that early morning hour, but the authorities managed to open a coffee stall for us. After two cups of coffee and two unexpected hours of delay, the repairs finally were made, and we boarded. By now Marni and I had lost complete faith with airplanes in general.

Once more we flew for what seemed many hours. At last we were told to prepare for landing. All of the passengers were sure that by this time we had arrived at our destination in New York, and that the awful trip had finally ended. Once on the ground, however, the pilot informed us that we had arrived at Toronto, Canada, and immigration regulations there prevented any of us from leaving the plane. Strong headwinds had evidently slowed the plane to such a degree that we were forced to land in order to refuel. On receiving this information, the passengers en mass stood. Shouting a chorus of hoots and boos, they threatened to rip the inside of the plane into bits. Soothing music did nothing to calm the riotous conditions.

After another hour's delay we rose into the air a third time in an effort finally to complete our flight into New York. By the time that we arrived at our destination we were twenty-two hours late on what was definitely the worst flight that I have ever taken.

All of the transportation on the Graham Company's Asian tour of 1955–56 was done by airplane, and almost all of the flights were memorable for one reason or another. Sometimes it was because of the turbulent atmosphere which bounced the plane around like a rubber ball, upsetting both our minds and our stomachs. Usually it was because of the beauty of a sunrise or a sunset which we would discover etched against the horizon of a small airport that had been dropped onto a desolate plain in some exotic country.

During the tour we usually used two chartered planes. One was allocated mainly for technical equipment, sets, and costumes. The other was reserved for the company. This gave us an entire plane for our personal use. As we traveled from one performance venue to the next, the planes seemed to become smaller and flimsier with each separate journey. Our last official stops on the State Department tour before Bethsabee de Rothschild took us to Israel were in Iran. There, we performed first in Abadan and then in Teheran.

Abadan was a city that oozed in oil. In 1956 there was so much inflammable gas in the air that it was prohibited to light a match while out of doors traveling through its oil fields.

The trip from Abadan to Teheran provided the company with the most difficult but the most exciting flight of the entire tour. Extremely high and dangerous mountains lay between the two cities. In order to get from one city to the other these mountains needed to be traversed. The only alternate route was to pass through a canyon that lay between two of the mountains. The canyon was very narrow and often was closed in by inclement weather. The conditions were especially bad in early morning fog.

By the time our performances were completed in Abadan, the weather had prevented any flights from leaving its airport for a few days. Because the weather became increasingly menacing as each day progressed the only chance to get a flight out was to depart extremely early in the morning.

For our first effort to cross the mountains, we were roused before dawn and were at the airport by seven a.m.. It was already too late; the airport was closed in by fog. There was nothing more for us to do but to return to the guest house and wait for another chance the next morning. Fortunately our performances in Teheran were a few days later.

The following morning we started an hour earlier, hoping that we could get into the air before the weather became too difficult. By six a.m. we were at the airfield and everything looked positive for a take off. We had a small, two engine, pressurized plane (it was in our contract that we could only fly in pressurized planes), and the weather continued to look fairly good. The difficulty was that we had to fly through the canyon pass rather than over the mountains, since the plane did not have the power to climb to the altitudes that were necessary for crossing into Teheran.

In good spirits, anxious to get on with the trip and get out of Abadan, we eagerly boarded the plane. The pilot immediately took off and our singular stewardess did her best to make us feel comfortable and secure.

The scenery as we entered the canyon pass was unbelievably beautiful. One could look directly out of the windows on either side of the plane and see the jagged mountains, pitted with snow, ruggedly rising into the open skies.

We were only about a half hour into the pass when, without warning, all hell broke loose. The previously peaceful weather conditions suddenly shifted. Winds came thundering down upon the plane knocking it about as if it were a child's toy made of balsa wood. The air currents roared through the canyon smashing back and forth off of the mountain's walls with a rage that could only be equated with the wrath of the Gods themselves.

The plane was lifted forcibly by an unseen hand placed underneath its belly. It soared up along one of the sides of the canyon where it was suspended for interminable seconds. Then with no notice, the air gave way from underneath it and the plane came rapidly crashing downward. At the last minute at the bottom of the air pocket, the plane was caught. It shuddered desperately as if trying to free itself from some unknown horror and then immediately was swept up the opposite side of the canyon at full speed. At the top of the air shaft the plane hung once more almost upside down before it descended helplessly only to repeat the whole process.

Loose objects were flying wildly all over the cabin. The stewardess was not belted into her seat because she was trying to help all of us. She came close to being knocked out as she stumbled around the cabin of the plane.

The dancers sat as if they were frozen in their seats, not daring or wanting to make a sound. Martha was sitting all the way back in the plane in a right rear seat. Her arms were crossed on her breasts. Her eyes were not closed, but were cast down, completely introverted. Only the ashen color of her skin gave any indication of her inner emotions.

It is hard to say how long we were buffeted around the pass in this manner. As the plane swept up one side of the mountain, its wings seemed nearly to brush the sheer edge of it. The plane's suspension at the peak of the curve only anticipated the chilling descent that was to come.

I had been a fan of Antoine de Saint-Exupéry since I was a boy, and had read all of his books, especially, *Wind, Sand, and Stars,* over and over again. I felt that at that moment, we were experiencing one of his flights. We were caught in an impossible battle with the powers of nature. Here man was not the determining factor, but had to accept his existence in proper relation to the elements. In that acceptance, he could then discover a unique selflessness and beauty, a powerful unity with nature.

Both ends of the pass had closed so there was no way out. Nothing could be done except to allow the elements to take their course. In the end, the Gods finally smiled on us and the Abadan end of the pass opened for a few moments. The pilot quickly reversed his direction and returned to the Abadan Airport. It wasn't until the wheels of the plane touched earth again that any of us finally felt safe. Stunned by the experience, the dancers slowly descended from the aircraft. I was directly behind Martha as we climbed down the stairs that had been pushed up to the plane.

The stewardess stood at the foot of the stairway, a little blood running down her cheek from a cut over her left eye. She smiled and helped each of us as we passed. As Martha reached the bottom of the stairs, the stewardess said, "Oh, Miss Graham, I am so sorry that it was such a dreadful flight, but if you go into the waiting room for a short time, I'm sure that the weather will improve and we can try one more time".

Martha visibly shaken but without anger slowly looked the woman directly in the eyes and in her most severe voice stated, "My dear, I may spend the rest of my life in Abadan, Iran, but I will never fly in that plane again".

With a swift authoritative throw of her head, she descended the last step and returned once more to the guest house.

Martha, however, did not have to spend more than one more night in Abadan, Iran. The next morning at five a.m., on a large but unpressurized plane, the company, plus a few extra Iranians, flew over the mountains and into Teheran. With one oxygen mask available to be shared among all of us we were soon in a state of euphoria. A drunken-like condition caused by lack of oxygen, infected us. We were a haggard but definitely carefree group of dancers who finally arrived in Teheran and were met at the airport by the officials of both the Iranian and American governments. These officials must certainly have been greatly astonished to see the company's condition upon our arrival.

Maria Tallchief and Eric Bruhn in *Swan Lake*. Photographer: Jack Mitchell.

Xavier Francis, Guillermina Bravo, and David Wood teaching in Mexico, 1959. Photo credit: Wood Collection.

David Wood and Miriam Cole aboard the *Queen Elizabeth* on the 1954 European Tour of the Martha Graham Dance Company. Photo credit: Wood Collection.

The Martha Graham Dance Company at the Taj Mahal, Agra, India, on the Asian Tour, 1955–6. Photo credit: Wood Collection.

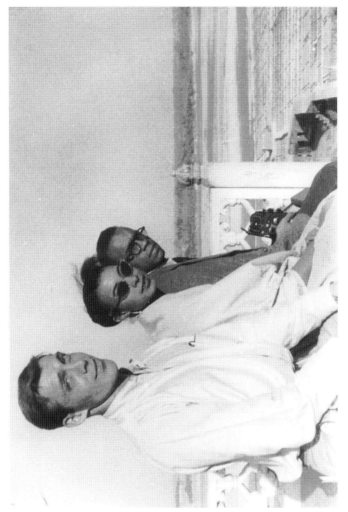

Paul Taylor, Matt Turney, and Donald McKayle at the Red Fort, Delhi, India, on the Asian Tour with Martha Graham in 1955–6. Photo credit: Wood Collection.

8

ON CONTRIBUTING PERSONALITIES

No one art form can continuously exist in isolation. Even an individual artist who unrealistically wishes to withdraw from the "outside" world, finds that the world's reality constantly creeps into his awareness. Some artistic media, such as writing and painting, are structured in a manner which allow the artists to remove themselves somewhat from society. Often these individuals may demand isolation, for the sake of complete concentration. Nevertheless, all writers and painters, as human beings whether isolated or not, must allow objective as well as subjective memory to invade their minds. Both literature and painting, even if partially abstracted, have their greatest significance when they occur in relation to the existing "real" world.

In drama and music, the basic artistic creations of a playwright or a composer must deal with interpretation. In drama, the play is analyzed by the director in order to determine by what approach he can best bring the script to life. In turn he translates this to his cast. They, then, as individuals, may exercise their prerogative to develop their own inter- pretations, trying to balance their characterizations carefully between the overall context of the play and the director's perceptions. An exact parallel can be drawn in relation to music. The composer's compositions must bear the interpretive weight of the conductor, the instrumentalists and/or singers.

From initial creation to performance, the creative works of these art forms usually pass through numerous, sometimes traumatic, transfor- mations. In order to actuate their ideas, even constructivist architects are reliant on other men's technical abilities, as well as their individual interpretations, in order to complete the creator's original conceptions.

Dance is the only classical art form in which the initial creativity must make use of human beings in order to accomplish its purpose. Choreography is, by definition, an arrangement of human movement whether it be structured or unstructured.

Dance exists basically as a collaborative activity. Music, scenography, costume and lighting design work in easy interplay with the dance production. One of the major collaborative efforts in this century occurred with the Diaghilev Ballets Russes. Between 1910 and 1925 prominent composers such as Darius Milhaud, Igor Stravinsky, Claude

Debussy, Erik Satie, and Francis Poulenc were commissioned to write new musical compositions for the Diaghilev produced ballets. Great visual artists such as Nicholas Roerich, Leon Bakst, Alexandre Benois, Jean Maria Sert, Natalia Gontcharova, Andre Derain, and Pablo Picasso created both scenography and costumes for these same productions. It was Diaghilev's vision which was the initial force for his artistic collaborations. Instead of camouflaging the production elements of dance, he used them to enrich the movement values of the choreography itself.

In *L'Après-midi d'un Faune*, the new and innovative choreography of Vaslav Nijinsky was enhanced by the haunting, sensuous music of Claude Debussy and the revolutionary designs for set and costume by Leon Bakst. The three creators worked within the parameters of an impressionistic reality, contributing an artistic aesthetic which introduced an atmosphere of open sensuality.

In the modern era, Martha Graham utilized the varied talents of other artists to enlarge the scope of her diverse conceptions. From the 1930's through the rest of her career, Martha not only collaborated with a wide variety of contemporary creators but she also discovered much new and untried talent. Alan Hovhaness, Aaron Copland, Carlos Chavez, William Schuman, and Robert Starer were commissioned to write musical scores for her. Arch Lauterer, Isamu Noguchi along with Alexander Calder, Ruben Ter-Arutunian, and Ming Cho Lee physicalized the complexities of Martha's psychological dances.

Dancer/choreographer Merce Cunningham has, almost alone, revolutionized the act of artistic collaboration in choreography. Without any concerted effort to create an individual approach, but rather, following his rapidly developing aesthetics concerning dance and the making of dances, Merce pared away the decorative aspects that had accumulated around the art form during the previous decades. These elements occurred in the collaborative workings where the music and the design factors were thought at times by Merce to overpower the movement itself. Imposed emotional intent and specific meanings, as seen through his eyes, were equally decorative distractions.

The Cunningham choreographic collaborations are much more a gathering of artists under an umbrella of Merce's different creations than they are an interweaving of artistic ideas toward a common productive goal. Such renowned artists as Robert Rauschenberg, Jasper Johns, and Andy Warhol along with composers John Cage, Christian Wolff, Conlon Nancarrow, and Morton Feldman are only a few names of creators who have been associated with the Cunningham individualistic approach. Each singular artist and his work stand as a distinct unit alongside those of the other artists within the collective of each of his works.

Merce's dance form, stripped of all nonessentials, reaches back to the fundamental importance of movement as a unique entity, similar to the dance that existed in primitive times. The passion of the choreography lies in the intensity of its presentation. Internal rhythms and structured movement hold prominence in his creativity. Cunningham movement as presented in his choreographic works exists within its own virtuosity, not demanding any form of structured sound. Its only accompaniment could easily be the hard and labored breathing of the exhausted dancers, the harsh slap of their feet against the performance surface, and the brush of their bodies as they dance in close contact while moving through his complex choreographic structures.

The strong emphasis upon the movement, of necessity, changed the physical shape of the performers whom Merce chose for his company. Carolyn Brown will always remain the quintessential Cunningham dancer: long-legged, with a lean body extending upward along a fluid spine, and ending in a regal swan-like neck. A coolness in performance, allowed Carolyn's personality to permeate the movement just enough to place a stamp of individuality upon it without destroying Merce's creativity by falsely superimposing her own personal style. At present time, similarly shaped dancers seem to be a requirement for acceptance into the Cunningham Dance Company. They may very well be a necessity for the proper execution of Merce's movement theories.

The world of dance has a multitude of methods and approaches which fulfill the beliefs of the various dance artists, but the changes with regard to collaboration which have been wrought by Merce Cunningham have created a world of movement filled with artistic integrity. Merce's discoveries have vastly broadened the entire range of creativity in dance for those who wish to take advantage of it.

Besides the artistic collaborators who are involved in the various productions of a dance company, there are other individuals who make their major contributions behind the scenes, unacclaimed by the viewing audience. The complex world of government and private funding, and the scheduling of performance dates, require handling by specialized personnel. These specialists must work in tandem with the choreographer or director of the dance group.

When rehearsing with Martha Graham, we dancers were never made overly aware of the composers with whom she chose to work. Martha had great respect for the artistic integrity of every individual who collaborated with her. Because she fought against having her own integrity compromised, she treated the creativity of other artists with the same respect that she demanded for herself. Once Martha received the score, from the composer, whether it was in sections or was a completely finished work, she never asked for it to be altered in any manner. Thus there was very seldom any need for a composer to be present at rehearsals. Martha did often complain that the music was driving her to distraction, but the statement was made more as an expression of choreographic frustration than anything else.

In later years, once she had selected the composer, the procedure always remained the same. For the benefit of the musician. Martha would write at length all of her ideas concerning the proposed work. These writings contained: the basic sequence of the various sections of the dance; informative material which she felt would help to clarify the work for the composer; Martha's own personal images in relation to the choreography; a basic estimate of the time to be allotted for each section. None of these ideas were presented with rigidity, but were left open and flexible enough to allow the composer artistic freedom for his own creation.

Martha never began choreographing until she had the music in hand. Once in possession of a piano reduction of the score, she would disappear into the studio with the pianist where she would spend hours working, in an attempt to fully understand the music. Often, upon hearing the score, Martha would throw out her entire prior structure, only retaining her basic concepts. She would let the music lead the choreography in new and previously unthought of directions. Only then was the company brought in for rehearsals and the process of choreographing a new dance begun.

On occasion certain composers appeared to understand Martha's ideas better than any of the rest of us did, perhaps even better than Martha. The composer for *Acrobats of God*, Carlos Surinach, who was a very amiable and distinguished gentleman, must have been made aware of the lighter, comic elements of Martha's intentions for the piece long before any of the rest of us were. The on-stage use of the three mandolin players, although limiting the dancing area, yielded a delightfully direct interplay between music and dance. The different sections of the work accented the playful quality of the dance throughout. The charming drollness of Martha's first solo and the archly accented music of the bolero section for three couples, are obviously conceived musically as being comic. The same is true of the wildly hilarious final explosion of group revelry.

The company had no knowledge of the comic intent of *Acrobats*. During the rehearsals, Martha said little more than that the work was her own personal comment on dance technique. On stage, opening night, just before the curtain rose, Martha instructed us to perform the work in a straightforward manner. We began the premier performance as Martha had advised and continued in our seriousness until we arrived at the point at which Martha teetered to the barre during her first solo, and to the accompaniment of a crash in the orchestra, did her simple but dedicated tendus. The audience immediately erupted in hysterical laughter. When Martha came away from the barre, *Acrobats of God* was a comic work. It remained that way for the rest of its performance life.

Certainly Carlos Surinach either must have been informed of Martha's feeling about the comic elements of the work, or he intuitively interpreted the information that he was given by Martha much better than any of the rest of us did.

Although most of the time musicians, like all other artists, have pride in whatever they undertake, there are definite times when they overestimate their abilities in relation to what is demanded of them. Such was the case in Paris during the European tour of 1954. We had given the first performances of *Ardent Song* in London a few weeks previously. It was choreographed to the specially composed music of Alan Hovhaness. At the time Hovhaness was thought to be an outstanding avant garde composer whose works elicited sparse but exotic atmospheric qualities.

In London, the members of the orchestra, on first playing the work, were appalled by his composition and let the fact be known openly to everyone present. Martha talked to the orchestra members discreetly, convincing them of the beauty of the music and its effectiveness in relation to the choreography. We had brought only a few of the musicians from London along with us for the rest of the tour in Europe, so in France a large part of the orchestra was hired on the spot. At the afternoon rehearsal at the Théâtre Champs-Elysées, the difficulties that were experienced with the music of *Ardent Song* in England occurred again. Martha exercised the same tactics that she had previously used in London and after a short explanation, everything was clarified. By the end of the rehearsal the orchestra was playing *Ardent Song*, if not beautifully, at least intelligibly.

The music for the evening performance, however, was an entirely different story. There was hardly a note that was recognizable. We struggled through the performance, wandering in a complex maze of unintelligible sound. It wasn't until after the performance was finished that we learned that the French musicians who were playing the evening performance were completely different from those who were present at the afternoon rehearsal. This was the first time that we were made aware of the French system which allowed the members of the orchestra to hire substitutes for the rehearsals. For the performances, the originally hired orchestra members appeared and played.

For the Hovhaness work this created a complete disaster as there was no possible way that the musicians could sight-read such a difficult score. Under those circumstances the resulting massacre of *Ardent Song* was both an inevitable and a needless waste.

A positive collaboration with a musician, either a composer or a performer, can be an exciting and stimulating event. The best experience that I ever had, in this regard, was with Michael Senturia, a member of the music faculty of the University of California, Berkeley. Michael was the conductor of the University Symphony Orchestra as well as the major advocate for performance activities in a highly academic university department.

Our initial collaboration was with a performance of the Kurt Weill-Bertolt Brecht opera, *Rise and Fall of the City of Mahagonny*. The production was directed by Jean Bernard Bucky who had worked with both Michael and myself previously. I was asked to choreograph two dances. My instincts told me that the dances didn't belong in the opera; nevertheless, the idea of working with the two men was so intriguing that I agreed. The opera was a great success and we each vowed to work together again.

A few years later Michael contacted me. This time the idea was to create a full scale dance concert with the University Symphony playing each of the works. For the dancers, the situation could not have been more idyllic. Michael and I had to agree on the pieces to be done, but that created no difficulties. I compromised on one piece, Debussy's *Jeux*. Although I liked the music, it wasn't the type with which I preferred to work; however, Michael very much wanted the orchestra to have a chance to perform it. The compromise turned out to be a fascinating challenge.

Before this occasion, Michael had never worked with a choreographer during the process of creating the movement for the dance. I choreographed *Jeux* over Christmas break so that Marni, Julie Brown and Richard Peck, (the three dancers in the work), Michael and myself were free from classes. Michael came to almost every rehearsal. He displayed an open, almost childlike, curiosity about the process of the choreography and the relationship of the music to it. He sat on the floor with the score resting on his lap for hours, watching and absorbing as much as he could.

Following this production, Michael and I collaborated over the years many times. Some concerts were not only with full orchestra, but with full chorus as well. Because of these collaborations, I was given the opportunity to work with live music, which is difficult to achieve. The students were presented with a richness in performance which, because of cost factors, can seldom be realized except in such a university situation. With each collaboration new ideas were explored and new challenges met. Michael constantly visited rehearsals. Every time that he walked into the room to see how a dance was progressing, he brought with him a radiance of positive energy. This permeated the studio with a special enthusiasm that affected everyone present.

Scenography in dance production has progressed from the realism of the romantic period of ballet, with its imposing representational sets, to the sometimes improvisational, clearly abstracted decor of certain contemporary dances. This move in scenic design from attempted reality to visual suggestion, provides the audience with a more spacious and undelineated background. The viewers of today are better able to perceive the linear and curved lines of the dancers' moving bodies.

With this concept in mind, it was inevitable that Isamu Noguchi and Martha Graham would be drawn together as collaborators in her dance theater. Martha, as a choreographer, never placed Noguchi in the position of being an isolated set designer. Rather, his sets remained as living sculptures within the context of her works. The designs were presented as equal participants along with each of the human characters in the dances. Noguchi understood the primitive ritualism that lay below the surface of most of Martha's compositions. This manifestation of the collective unconscious was easily translatable for him. It was a simple step from his knowledge and interest in Noh Theater to Martha's sparse but richly symbolic approach to mythic drama.

Their first collaboration began with Martha's Americana solo, *Frontier* which was choreographed in 1935 and ended, except for one later collaboration, with *Cortege of Eagles*, in 1967. During those thirty-two years, Martha employed few other scenic designers. A close bond of communication developed between the two artists. Theirs became an established relationship in which Martha felt completely comfortable.

Martha's procedure in working with set designers grew to be as routine as was her working procedure with composers. When Martha was about to commence choreographing a new dance, she would summon Noguchi and discuss the proposed work with him, conveying her ideas through qualitative imagery. The two would agree on certain basic physical concepts. This gave Martha enough information to begin to work. Noguchi then departed the scene, leaving Martha to start her choreography. He was fully aware that before his return some of their ideas would be greatly altered during her working process.

As Martha started rehearsing, she put together a mock up of the set from among the materials that were to be found in the vicinity. At times the surrounding chairs, tables, screens, etc. would feed her imagination and lead her creative thoughts in new directions.

Once the dance was nearing completion and the scenic concepts were fairly well established, Noguchi would come to the studio to watch a rehearsal. He was then able to ascertain the changes which Martha might have made since their original conversation. With the intelligence thus gained, Noguchi completed his design and constructed a model of the set. This had to satisfy his own creativity as well as Martha's, by now, well defined scenic requirements. After the model was approved by Martha, construction was begun on the actual set for the dance. The pieces were scheduled to be completed early enough so that they could be brought into the studio. We then were able to work with the set before it was necessary to transport it to the theater.

In the Noguchi finished work, there were always surprises which Martha and the rest of us had not anticipated. It was Noguchi's way of asserting his own artistic individuality. Martha never complained, but instead rechoreographed whatever part of the piece that she felt was necessary in order to make the dance and the set work together.

I can remember only two occasions when the actual set that was created from Noguchi's final design proved unusable. The entire set for, *Diversion of Angels* which was in reality more of a backdrop, remained in the storeroom of the warehouse after the first few performances and was never used again. Also there was a reworking of one of the *Phaedre* set pieces. For *Phaedre*, Noguchi had designed two homing areas, one female and one male. The female piece was basically for the provocative Aphrodite, although Phaedre also used it extensively. It was an obvious representation of the female vagina. The sculpture opened and closed at will, hiding or revealing the goddess of love in the process. The male piece was designed for the young and virile Hippolytus and clearly depicted an erect penis. The design was such that apertures placed along the length of it could be moved to beguilingly reveal different areas of Hippolytus' anatomy.

The myth of Phaedre is explicitly sexual in content and both Martha and Noguchi made full use of it. The graphic pubic hair on the Noguchi male set piece was a slash of realism which journeyed far beyond the boundary of suggestion. A few days after the set arrived in the studio, the male phallus was taken away. It returned one day later without pubic hair. We all breathed a sigh of relief and wondered how Martha had managed to solve the difficult situation with Noguchi.

Sometimes, for financial reasons, the set from one work previously dropped from the repertory, was dragged out of the warehouse and used for another dance. The set from *Voyage* or *Theater For a Voyage* quite successfully made the transition to the Olympian world of *Circe*. Not as successful was the translation of the additional set pieces from the film of *Night Journey* to the Greek tragedy of *Alcestis*.

At other times Noguchi's busy schedule called him away to previously arranged artistic commitments before he could complete any changes which might become necessary on one of his new sets. Martha's *Clytemnestra* required considerable alterations. The original gold net was too cumbersome to be handled easily and was changed to the gold streamers that the furies manipulated. Clytemnestra's red cloak which changed into a bloody pathway for Agamemnon to follow to his death also needed major alteration. The blue set piece was a necessary and completely new addition to Noguchi's set design. Charlie Hyman, husband of Ethel Winter, was always a great aid in these emergency situations, but seldom received enough credit for his efforts.

Don McDonagh states in his *Martha Graham, A Biography* that as the Messenger of Death, I first appeared in *Clytemnestra* carrying a Noguchi designed staff. Quite to the contrary, Noguchi had already withdrawn his presence by the time that Martha created that role for me. Instead of a Noguchi designed staff, Martha handed me a pole to use and suggested that it be decorated in some manner. Following her orders and anticipating her desires, I created a staff which I thought would be serviceable for the ominous figure of death.

Many of the Noguchi designed structures were very difficult to work with. They were constructed with strange angles and odd shapes which pitched the body weight in unexpected directions. Everyone had to use them with conscious care. Part of the reason for using the scenery in this manner was the visual effect that it created such as happened on the raked stages of the past. At first I thought that Noguchi's sets were created as mischievous perversions. In retrospect I realize how thoroughly Isamu Noguchi understood the dance theater of Martha Graham.

Martha's choreography was not usually fluent in entrances and exits. We often remained on stage throughout the work. When not moving we were considered to be stationary participants and we were never allowed to drop our energy for a second. Noguchi designed his sets with this concept of performance in mind.

In *Appalachian Spring* the rock for the Revivalist is steeply canted toward the audience which forces whoever portrays the character to press his weight deeply against it in order to maintain his balance. The bench for the four girls is sloped so that they can never relax without slipping off. For the long periods that the four of them sit, they must lift their backs and press into the heels of their feet. Even the rocking chair used by the Bride and the Pioneer Woman is structured so that it is impossible to sit on in a normal manner.

In *Seraphic Dialogue* except for the period during their solos, the three Joans sit on a small brass tubing. If they drop their weight in the least, the tubing slowly cuts into their hips. The two female saints on either side of Saint Michael must stand on the same tubing for long periods, making them lift their weight out of their legs. In all of these situations Noguchi has consciously forced the dancers to remain internally alive and energized while outwardly quiet. In the theater Noguchi was not just a sculptor who abstractly dealt only with his own art form, but was a sensitive and observant collaborator who made a vital contribution to the dance.

By the time of *Cortege of Eagles*, Martha and Noguchi had arrived at diverging points in their personal and professional lives. Noguchi by the late 1960's, was emerging as one of the world's most celebrated sculptors. His interests, in that decade, centered on large outdoor creations and sculptured gardens. He was climbing the peak of his career and, for him, age contributed to a deepening of values and personal concepts.

On the other hand, Martha's progressing age took its toll not only physically on her body but also with her creative process. It was during *Cortege of Eagles* that I heard Martha bemoan the fact that, in addition to the reality of physical deterioration, her creative abilities were also beginning to disintegrate. "I can't create a thing anymore", she wailed during one evening rehearsal.

As her artistic frustrations and personal loneliness increased so did Martha's persistent reliance on alcohol. Noguchi, realizing the difficulties that Martha was undergoing, stepped into the rehearsals and began to choreograph the dance. The finished set for *Cortege of Eagles* had been delivered to the studio earlier than usual, and upon first viewing, it failed to arouse any feeling of excitement. The pieces were big, heavy, and cumbersome to manipulate. The set seemed more related to the monumental sculpture that Noguchi was involved in creating at that time rather than the marvelously suggestive pieces that he had previously designed for Martha's theater.

Martha, although she said nothing, was disappointed in and frustrated by the set. Receiving little stimulation from the various sculptures that Noguchi created for the work, Martha left them basically in a static state. Noguchi became more and more upset because Martha did not make full use of the set pieces. Martha found herself trying to move sets rather than choreographing the dance. Noguchi found himself being forced to choreograph in order to overcome ineptness in the use of his set. Both of their antagonisms grew to the breaking point. Martha violently objected to Noguchi's overstepping of previously unstated boundaries by moving into her private realm of choreography.

As Charon, the boatman on the river Styx, I began the dance by slithering onto the stage on all fours. I slowly pushed myself from the downstage right wing toward a plain white flat upstage center. When I arrived at the flat, I did a back bend on my knees and by using my mouth picked up a mask which Noguchi had created for the character. Martha and Noguchi were at odds on this matter. Martha wanted me to take the mask from off of the white flat. Noguchi wanted the flat left pure and untouched and for me to pick up the mask from the floor just in front of it.

The matter never was settled. On opening night, it became a focus of attention. William Batcheldor, our stage manager, was totally confused. Martha would come onto the stage and instruct him to place the mask on the flat. Then Noguchi would come onto the scene, see the mask on the flat, and tell him to remove it. This interplay went back and forth between the two many times. Finally, totally perplexed, Batch asked me what I thought he should do to solve the situation. My prejudiced suggestion was that it was Martha's dance and her wishes should be respected.

Batch waited until Noguchi went into the audience to see the performance and then, for the last time he placed the mask on the flat where it could be clearly seen when the curtain rose. Noguchi never came backstage that night after the performance as was his usual custom. I doubt if this incident directly caused the rift between the two artists, but rather it was just the final act in an inevitable drama.

Personally, Noguchi appeared to build a thick wall around himself when he was in the studio. Except for one or two of the young women, especially Akiko Kanda and Takako Asakawa, he seemed to be unaware that any of the rest of us existed. He was a complete blend of east and west, combining an eastern contemplative demeanor with a western drive for immediate success.

Noguchi was at his most charming the few days that he intercepted the Graham company in Karachi, Pakistan during the Asian tour of 1956. We were performing there and he was very curious to see first hand the reaction of the Asians to Martha's choreography. On one of our free days a few of us along with Noguchi accepted an invitation from the wife of one of the U.S.I.S. officers for an afternoon on the beach followed by a steak dinner. She had rented a little hut a short distance from the shoreline where we left all of our supplies and clothes while we alternately basked in the sun and cooled ourselves in the lightly breaking waves of the glistening ocean.

While we were totally occupied with our sun-filled pleasures, a roving pack of wild dogs sneaked up to the hut and raced away with all of the food including the steaks. Rather than end the party in disaster, Noguchi went up the beach a short distance and found a lobster fisherman who sold him more than enough food for all of us. Noguchi was the only one in the party who knew how to handle and cook the lobsters. He was not only resourceful but he turned out to be a superb chef. I had always had great respect for his artistry, but after he had satisfied my acute hunger that evening with an epicurean meal, my personal respect for him immensely increased.

An outstanding scenic designer with whom I worked was Henry May, a professor in the Theater Department at the University of California,

Berkeley. Before coming to the university, Henry had designed the sets for the Omnibus productions that were seen on early television. From that diverse experience, he acquired a clear sensitivity toward dance and a thorough knowledge of how best to design for it. We collaborated on many productions; the most memorable of them for me was that of Debussy's *Jeux*.

In constructing *Jeux*, I had followed the notes that Nijinsky had written in the score, in an attempt to keep the same relationship between the trio of dancers (one man and two women) as had existed in the original production. My major structural departure from the Nijinsky version was that I substituted a chess game for the Nijinsky conceived tennis match. Henry constructed three gigantic but elegant chess pieces that were patterned after early Swedish originals. The structures were translucent so that the dancing figures behind them could be clearly observed if they were properly lit.

While choreographing the dance, Nijinsky had expressed the desire to have a plane crash occur on stage. I, myself, didn't really want a plane crash, but I was intrigued by the conscious or unconscious idea that lay in the back of Nijinsky's mind. I finally came to the logical conclusion that Nijinsky wanted a violent and complete change of scenery which would provide an explosive climax for the building sexual tensions of the dance's trio of lovers. Near the end of the work, there was a point at which the tennis ball rolled onto the stage for the second time. I told Henry that I wanted a disintegrating background that, at the prescribed moment, would destroy itself. Henry looked at me questioningly and asked if I would give him the music so that he could listen to it carefully that night.

The next day Henry voiced the opinion that no matter what Nijinsky wanted, Debussy had not written any violence into the score. He suggested that we use china silk which could be released to ripple slowly down the back curtain. Though the movement of the china silk intrigued me, I felt that the solution was too gentle, and that it also failed to create the change of visual landscape that I greatly wanted. He then suggested releasing the china silk so that it would float menacingly downward over the entire stage at the end of the dance, completely covering the scene. I suggested using another full piece of silk at the beginning which would lift from the set, revealing the chess pieces and chess board.

By the give and take of a constant flow of ideas, we arrived at what I felt to be a beautifully effective set which worked in perfect accord with the dance. Without that reciprocal interplay, I doubt that, we would ever have arrived at such a solution. Henry had a marvelous ability constantly to feed out his ideas and in return to comprehend and absorb the ideas that he received from others.

The demands placed upon costume designers for dance are much more complex than those placed on regular clothes designers or even costume designers for other theatrical forms. In dance whether one reveals or conceals the body and the means by which it is accomplished must be approached with sensitive perception of each choreographic work. Color, texture, weight of material, even the transparency of the fabrics are all elements to which a designer must give some thought. The movement of the materials that are used must be in accord with the movement requirements of the dance. Some fabrics are immobile while others move with such easy fluidity that they become a distraction rather than an asset to the movement of the dancer. Because the emphasis in present day dance is placed upon a clear perception of movement above all else, unitards with a few brush strokes painted across the body are prevalent. Also, the natural, blousy and sometimes shabby clothing of everyday attire is used by designers to show a forced lack of concern.

Costume design for dance, at its most effective, calls for an abstraction of realism. Pauline Lawrence, the wife of José Limón, was a master at using realism in costuming but placing it within an ambiguous context. As did many Denishawn descendants, Pauline developed a feeling for the weight and flow of materials in relation to the dancer's bodies. The costumes that she designed for José Limón's *Moor's Pavane* are a case in point. The three characters, Othello, Iago, and Emelia, wear classically and elegantly designed attire which are rich in texture and heavily weighted in both feel and look. The diaphanous, flowing purity of Desdemona's white costume sets her distinctly apart from the other three. By costuming, Desdemona is established as a separate element before we are ever made aware of her plight choreographically. With the further handling of her white handkerchief, which appears as an extension of both her costume and herself, we can immediately divine her eventual victimization. Although *Moor's Pavane* is a choreographic masterwork in itself, Pauline Lawrence's costumes help to enhance its world of intrigue.

Along with Pauline, Martha Graham had developed the Denishawn touch for handling materials. Although toward the beginning and at the end of her career Martha used other designers for her costuming, during the major part of her creative life she designed nearly all of the costumes. Martha's designs were never done on paper, but were always developed on the bodies of her dancers.

The first time that I became involved with Martha in the area of costuming was while I was in my first year at the Neighborhood Playhouse. A few of the beginning students were chosen as dancers for a Playhouse production of an early Roman comedy, Menander's *The Arbitration*. Sanford Meisner was to direct and Nina Fonaroff was to do the choreography. Rita Morganthau, who was administrative head of the

Playhouse at the time, asked Martha if she would help them by creating the costumes for the production. Martha agreed, and one male and one female dancer were chosen on whom she was to try to work her wondrous deeds. Lucy Vines and I were the chosen victims and we were called in for a costuming session with Martha on a cold winter's eve.

I arrived for the appointment punctually. When I came into the room, I was met not only by Martha, of whom I was already petrified, but also by her younger sister, Georgia Graham Sargeant (Geordie). The whole costuming event from the beginning to the end grew into a surrealistic nightmare. Later, I was to discover that each of the ladies was difficult enough on her own, but put together, the two sisters became a Machiavellian tandem of an extremely diabolical nature. They seemed to speak a special language of which, at most times, only the two of them were knowledgeable. The intensity of their ridicule built in constant progression during the session. As my part of the costuming proceeded, I felt like Alice in Wonderland growing smaller and smaller, while in my mind the two women loomed like huge ogres rising above me with great glee. They placed one ridiculous article of clothing after another on me. With each new addition to the costume, they stepped back to better view their handiwork and then broke into gales of hilarious laughter.

I can't remember exactly what the finalized costume was, but I think that I was partially bare cheasted and wore a strangely draped skirt over my loins. The piece de resistance was a green snood which drooped jauntily from the top of my head.

Martha and Geordie stepped back one last time to look at their creation. I turned slowly in front of them so that they could view me from all sides. Nothing could staunch their uproarious laughter and their raunchy remarks. With their backs against the wall, they slid slowly down to the floor in uncontrolled hysteria. I finally was excused from my torture and raced, much relieved, from that chamber of horrors.

Following the Asian tour of 1956, Martha took over all of the designing of the costumes, except for a few that were created by Helen McGehee for specific dances. Ursula Reed executed Martha's often difficult designs with great expertise. We all stood for hours while Martha folded and draped material around us, under us, and over us, and at the same time, stuck pins methodically into our bodies, arms, and legs. She could seldom get herself to cut the material, thus she usually presented Ursula with wads of fabric which Ursula, with an exceptional talent, cut and sewed into the exact shape that Martha wanted.

The men's costumes were usually very simple. We were stripped to fundamental bikini briefs with a cape added here or there for effect. The women's costumes seemed more complicated. They usually were draped in flowing swirls of material with elaborate designs. The fabrics were often woven of real gold and silver threads. The expense never seemed to be a factor for Martha. In Martha's group work *Legend of Judith*, Martha created a cape for me as Nebuchadnezzer, the tyrant. It was divided into four sections; each section was of a richer gold or silver material than the next. I have no idea what the total cost of the cape was, but when dancing in it, I felt wildly debauched.

By her use of costume design, Martha could create unbelievable illusions. Her preference for tall male dancers for her company was well known, and as a result of her prejudice, I felt at a distinct disadvantage when dancing with her. Even though she created the character of the Messenger of Death in *Clytemnestra* specifically for me, I knew that she held in her mind's eye the image that the figure should be one of imposing height.

Before she could begin to choreograph the role, it was necessary for her, to build the image of the character for herself in some manner. Martha and I met two or three times a week for what were officially called rehearsals. During these times Martha tried numerous ways to elongate the look of my body in order to gain the illusion that she wanted. By the third week desperation had settled in. At one session we walked into the large studio to work on the project. Sitting innocently on the piano was a tall pile of gold cords. Martha picked them up in one piece and placed them in a wad on the top of my head. She then stepped back, took a clear look, and broke out laughing at the sight of the golden ropes dripping down across my face. I began to hear echoes of my first costuming session with her at The Neighborhood Playhouse. At least Martha seemed not to have lost her sense of humor over the years.

At our next meeting, Martha arrived with a tube of purple stretch wool jersey and a bald rubber head piece. She plopped the rubber onto my head and told me to take off my tights and put on the tube of material. Once it was on, she attached the jersey to the back of my dance belt and drew the extra cloth through to the front so that the fabric wrapped around my legs in the back but left a full skirt in the forward part of the costume. It was the opposite of the women's *Diversion of Angels* costume that Martha had designed earlier. She then took all of the material that was wadded in front, tucked it into my dance belt and began to pull the material and dance belt lower and lower and lower. At the moment of extreme danger, I grabbed Martha's hands to stop her as there was but an inch to spare before a full revelation would have occurred. The front of the costume followed the line of my groin downward, but clung to the top of my hips in back. The tube was too long and lay under my feet, but Martha refused to cut it.

"That will make you seem taller", she said with a touch of pride.

Martha had finally achieved her goal. By the use of the rubber head piece and the purple tubing, she had created the appearance of great length. I was one bare line of skin from the top of my head to my groin with a long serpentine purple train that fell from my hips and trailed off under my feet. Through Martha's talent in costuming, I gained the illusion of height that she had so much wanted for the character.

Except for the use of artificial lighting, obviously nothing in the proscenium stage theater would be visible. Without the element of illumination created by man, dancers with their costumes and sets could not be seen by any audience. The use of artificial lighting allows the designer to create the illusion by which he can guide the eyes and the perceptions of the audience. For theater productions, the importance lies not only in the actual visibility of the performances, but it lies in how that visibility is created. Lights which color the stage also color the perceptive intelligence of the audience. Illumination, when used creatively, can have such a tactile feel to it that it rightfully takes it's place as an integral part of the performance along with the other design elements.

Although involvement in lighting design was at first the exclusive province of the male gender, lately women have moved into the area of technical theater and have gained prominence as lighting designers. Jennifer Tipton, Thereon Musser, Beverly Emmons, Peg Clark, Carol Rubenstein, Doris Einstein Siegel, and Louise Guthman are all accomplished designers who have made a name for themselves. Many of them began their careers as dancers. All have developed into highly regarded artists in lighting design. The reason that women have gained importance in this field is a matter of conjecture, but a great deal of the impetus probably comes from the leadership and inspiration of Jean Rosenthal who was one of the great innovators in the field.

Jean Rosenthal, to all who knew her, was a very special lady. Her untimely death in 1969 cut short a brilliant career. Fortunately, she was involved in lighting design for the theater over a long enough period of time, allowing her to make a major contribution in that field, especially in relation to dance. Jean was one of the most dedicated people that I have ever seen at work. Small of stature, with large friendly absorbing eyes, she was one of the most confident of designers, yet without in any way, seeming overbearing or falsely imposing.

Jean Rosenthal was devoted to Martha Graham. She began her lighting designs for Martha and because of the intensity of her feelings for her, it was fitting that her last lighting design was also created for Martha. She appreciated Martha's dedication toward her own unique vision and the clarity and strength of her direction toward fulfilling it. Even more she felt in tune with Martha's spirituality. She sensed the strong underlying religious fervor which existed in most of Martha's works. One evening during the time that we were performing at the 54th Street Theater, Jean appeared on stage just before the performance began. American Ballet Theater· was performing in New York at the same time, and as·she had designed the lighting for some of their ballets, she stopped at their theater before joining us.

"It's bedlam over there.", she declared. "It is so different here. It's so quiet and concentrated, almost like a religious service."

Whenever Martha premiered a new dance, Jean was there. Her presence created an aura of assurance for everyone. No matter how chaotic the situation had been, leading up to the dress rehearsals, with the arrival of Jean, things seemed to take a peaceful turn. Martha always discussed her new works with Jean, but in the process of creation, left her completely to her own devices. Martha had total faith in Jean's artistic abilities.

The only place that Jean seemed adverse to going, even to light a new dance for Martha, was to a university campus. She was definitely suspicious of academia. Once, when she had come to Connecticut College to work on the premier performance of *Secular Games*, I asked her if she was enjoying being out of New York in the summer for a few days.

She answered, "I love getting out of the city for a bit, but I can certainly think of better places to go than a college campus."

Her professionalism seemed more at home in a Broadway theater than anywhere else. It was in a Broadway theater, the 54th Street Theater that Jean provided me with new insights into the machinations of working with Martha Graham.

That season *Alcestis* was being premiered and it was definitely running into a great deal of trouble. For the set, Martha had used the additional sculpture pieces that Noguchi had designed for the filming of *Night Journey*. The pieces worked well in the school's big studio despite their large size. Martha turned and tumbled them at will. But when they were confined to the space that existed on the stage between the wings, they became a menace. The pieces banged into one another and blocked the dancers' entrances and exits. Martha had used the entire company in the dance, and as a result, there were too many people on stage at one time. The music was another major problem. Vivian Fine had written a very complex score and from the piano reduction which had been used in rehearsals, not much could be clearly discerned to help in understanding the orchestrated version.

We had already started to perform by the time that we had the first of our two scheduled dress rehearsals for *Alcestis*. During the rehearsal, chaos reigned as the sets banged into the dancers, the dancers had no space in which to move, the costumes split and fell off and nobody could recognize a note that the orchestra was playing. Martha was stunned.

It was one of the two times that I had ever seen her cry. She insisted that after the evening's performance we had to have an emergency rehearsal of *Alcestis*. Craig Barton, the director of the de Rothschild Foundation, which was sponsoring the season, vetoed the idea as the cost would have been prohibitive. Instead a 9:00 a.m. stage call was made for the next day, followed by a full rehearsal with orchestra at 1:00 P.M. On that same evening's performance we were to present the first viewing of *Alcestis*. Martha was placated for the time being.

Dancers, stagehands, and the accompanist all gathered at the theater promptly at 9:00 in the morning, ready to work. Martha, however, was missing. We waited for her for a half an hour and still Martha did not come. As rehearsal director, I decided that we should go ahead and try to solve the seemingly unsolvable problems of *Alcestis*. Everyone cooperated. We shifted the placement of the sets so that they could be moved without bumping into each other. I stood in the wings like a traffic officer at a busy intersection and guided the people who were turning the sets so that they would just miss each other. Some of the dancers were taken out of certain sections so that there was room for the others to move. By noon we had almost finished. Most everyone took a break for lunch, but Bert Ross and Helen McGehee stayed with me to finish working out a few remaining rough spots.

At 1:00 p.m. everyone returned. The dancers stretched their muscles readying themselves to dance. The orchestra began warming up their instruments readying themselves to play. The stagehands put the sets in place. On the dot of one, Martha arrived fully prepared and completely serene. She gave no apology or excuse for her absence from that morning's rehearsal. The stagehands asked if the spike marks for the replacing of the sets should be made permanent. I told Martha that I had made certain changes and the stagehands wanted to know whether the marks should be left altered or not.

"How do I know until we do it?" she haughtily answered.

We ran through the piece. Everything went smoothly. The sets turned, missing each other with ease. The dancers had room to move. The costumes stayed on everyone from beginning to end. And the sound of the orchestra was discernible at last. When it was over, I asked Martha again if the changes were all right and if the new spike marks should be used.

"Of course they were all right. Why shouldn't they be?" she shouted at me.

Martha swept off the stage and disappeared into her dressing room.

I told the stage hands to make the spike marks permanent and then, disillusioned by the rebuff from Martha, I left the stage and went into the audience area. Jean was working on the lights trying, without complaint, to keep up with all of the changes that had been made. Drawn like a moth to her light, I sat in the row behind her. Jean had seen the entire event that took place on stage. She turned around sympathetically and patted me on the knee.

"I just don't understand Martha. The longer that I am here the less I can fathom her.", I complained.

"Darling.", Jean placated with a comforting smile. "You should know by now that Martha has her special ways. She always picks the best person for the task that she can, and then relies on them to carry out their job. She has such an ego herself that she thinks everyone else has the same ego, and they will do whatever the task that she has assigned to them to the best of their ability." Jean paused as she thought a moment. "And you know", she revealed, "she's right."

Jean Rosenthal had an exceptional way of seeing and comprehending an entire scope of events in one sweep. This made her a marvelous collaborator on every production with which she became involved and allowed her to light those productions with beautiful insight.

A dance company's compliment of administrators often changes with such rapidity that it is hard for their personalities to make any lasting imprint on the groups with whom they have worked. Even the company's Board members are usually transient and bear little relation to the strongly felt presence of the financial benefactors of previous years such as Bethsabee de Rothschild.

Bethsabee de Rothschild is one of the major financial contributors toward the development of dance in contemporary times. Beginning with the financing of Martha Graham's first European tour in 1950, Bethsabee provided the backing for a great many New York seasons for Martha plus additional tours to Europe and Israel. She also provided Martha Graham with an entire building in which to work, undisturbed by outside forces. While her major contributions were directed toward Martha, she also commissioned new works by many other dancer/choreographers. She produced three Festivals of American Dance on Broadway in New York. Upon her move to Israel she created and sponsored two dance companies, first the Bathsheva Dance Company and then, in conjunction with Jeanette Ordman, the Bat Dor Dance Company.

Bethsabee's involvement in dance was not that of an outside benefactress whose financial contributions created a dividing line between herself and the artists. Rather, she assumed an integral role within management wherein she could knowledgeably participate as an artistic observer. Bethsabee was very clear about how her money was to be spent. Her role as patroness of the arts was carried out with intelligence and care. Constant emphasis was placed on never interfering in the artistic creations of any of the dancers to whom she contributed. I was not studying at the Graham 5th Avenue studio when Bethsabee first arrived there to take classes, but many rumored stories circulated later around the studio concerning her timidity and lack of style. There were even rampant rumors that she bought all or most of her clothes at Klein's Bargain Basement on Union Square. Whether there was truth to the rumors or not, Martha evidently took Bethsabee in hand, gave her renewed confidence and even provided her with an elegance in grooming. Bethsabee was extremely grateful, and slowly the friendship between the two women grew. Over the years each acknowledged a debt to the other and each easily and without regret honored that debt.

Bethsabee continued her classes for a short time after the shift was made to the 63rd Street studios. I clearly remember her in class, dressed in regulation leotard and tights, bravely trying to physicalize the pretzel like movement of Graham technique on her small, frail, and somewhat unformed body. Finally her terpsichorean attempts ceased and she relegated herself to the inevitable position of an involved observer of dance.

Bethsabee was very friendly to all of us, bright and outspoken. She often squinted in relation to the depth of her thoughts as she spoke. She had a lovely smile and a strongly accented voice, an accent which no one was able to clearly identify. At times, when she was excited and spoke too fast, it was impossible to understand what she was saying, so we all just smiled in agreement and nodded our heads. Bethsabee was never considered an outsider by Martha's Company, but was accepted with warmth and respect. On the European trip of 1954, Bethsabee refused to go to Germany because of the treatment of the Jews. As Bethsabee was sponsoring the tour, Martha, in turn, refused to perform in Germany. Out of loyalty, Martha did not wish to dance anywhere that Bethsabee would not go.

Bethsabee wanted to join us on the State Department sponsored Asian tour of 1955–1956. Although she could well afford to make the trip by paying her own way, she didn't want to go as a hanger-on without purpose, but wished to have some official involvement. Martha had an inspiration and offered her the job of wardrobe mistress. Bethsabee accepted. She was certainly not the most outstanding wardrobe lady, but she did consistently work at the job. By the end of the tour, there were many costumes burnt from the heat of Bethsabee's iron and much relaxed and drooping elastic from Bethsabee's over-boiled laundry.

Our State Department tour ended in Teheran, Iran. From there Bethsabee took us for our first trip to Israel where we performed at the renowned Habimah Theatre. In front of the theater were large posters which read:

The B de Rothschild Foundation

presents

Martha Graham Dance Company

The dancers were then listed in large print followed by a listing of the technical crew in smaller print. At the bottom of the list was the acknowledgment –

Wardrobe Mistress … B. de Rothschild

I think that series of performances in Israel is the only time in theatrical history that a major dance company has been presented anywhere by its wardrobe mistress.

The qualities that surrounded the generosity of Robin Howard, Martha's English benefactor, are difficult to catalogue, for Robin, like the Biblical Joseph, wore a coat of many colors. He was the renegade son of a distinguished English family. He was a simple man of great distinction, who radiated an aura of earthy nobility. He was a 20th century missionary who had a talent for converting those against into those for. He gave freely both spiritually and monetarily. He was frugal in analysis. He was a man who reflected the basic instincts of an artist, wrapped in a humble, proletarian intellect. No one of these descriptions would be accurate enough by itself, taken together they begin to create the image of a powerful and deeply dedicated human being. Robin's physical difficulties and my first meeting with him have already been described in Chapter Three. Despite his loss of legs, Robin could easily have been an imposing figure on the theatrical stage as an actor. His voice rang sonorously and his great height as well as his excellent sense of theatricality could have made him fair competition if not for Laurence Olivier certainly for Maurice Evans or John Gielgud.

In the year immediately following the first meeting at the Gore Hotel, none of us had any further contact with Robin. One of the last performances of the 1962 Graham European tour took place in the Netherlands. Peggy Harper, who had originally introduced us to Robin, appeared at the theater. She had flown over from England just to see the Graham Company dance. Backstage afterward, she voiced the complaint that we hadn't appeared in London, thus forcing her to travel all of the way across the channel to see us. We explained that the State Department, which was our sponsor, approved performances only in those countries where the United States felt that it needed to build better relations. This did not include England. Peggy suggested that we should have asked Robin Howard to sponsor us in London. He definitely would have jumped at the opportunity. As with all such nebulous suggestions, we smiled weakly, and said that we would remember next time. Bob and I did mention the suggestion to Craig Barton just in case the information might be useful at a future juncture. It was.

In 1963 the Graham Company was invited to perform at the Edinburgh Festival in Scotland. The fee for performing was small so that the brunt of the basic costs for transportation, etc. had to be carried by the company. Martha's management seemed unable to locate any readily available funding for the venture thus it appeared as if the engagement would have to be declined. Craig Barton remembered the information that Bob Cohan and I had given him concerning Robin and asked us if he should attempt that route.

"What can you lose by trying?", we chorused.

Craig contacted Robin immediately in England as the deadline for acceptance was very near. True to Peggy Harper's word, Robin was overjoyed. Not only would he partially sponsor us at Edinburgh, but if he could book a theater, he wanted to present us in London as well. Robin was a gracious and generous host and Martha became deeply affected by his devotion as well as his generosity. It was the opening that Robin wanted. He had for some time dreamed of establishing a Graham based school of dance in England. With Martha's approval, he began to send British students to the Graham school with a guarantee on their part that they would return and teach in his London establishment.

The school that Robin founded began on a miniature scale in a small building in Berners Place just off of Oxford Street. Over the years, Robin sometimes came to New York taking over the managing of Martha for short periods of time when Martha's official managers were absent. He also brought the whole Graham Company to perform for a second time in London. Slowly the London Contemporary School outgrew its confines and moved into a much larger complex on Dukes Road called The Place. It flourishes now in London, acting as a magnet for students from all over Europe who flock there because of the school's diverse teachings. Bob Cohan stayed in England and became the director of the school and its resident company, working actively both as teacher and choreographer. He has become highly respected as one of the leading figures in modern dance in England.

Robin Howard's premature death in Poland cut short an outstanding career in dance administration, but it didn't lessen the major contribution that he made in the dance field for England and much of Europe.

If the criterion for the relationship which a dancer/choreographer develops with critics in general is difficult to construe, the criterion for the alliance with a singular critic is even more querulous. What limits should be set concerning the propriety of currying the critic's favor or, at the other end of the spectrum, creating a demeanor of complete indifference are matters which run into conflicting opinions. In relation to associating with critics, the path of discretion is long and narrow, and any misstep may court disaster.

Although I have known numerous critics over the years, I have actually written to a reviewer only twice during my career in the dance profession. Neither time was it in retaliation to a critical appraisal. Once I wrote to correct an error of omission, and the second time I wrote because of a personally humorous situation which had developed concerning the review. Both times, whether by coincidence or not, in the very next reviews by these critics, I was given highly favorable mentions.

A few years ago, the *San Francisco Chronicle* employed as one of its major critics a man by the name of Heuwell Tircuit. He was the type of reviewer who was somewhat irrational. As time progressed, Mr. Tircuit became well known in the San Francisco Bay Area as a critic whom the *Chronicle* often had a great deal of difficulty in controlling.

Mr. Tircuit had attended a concert at the university in which I had created two dances, *Pre-Amble* and *Today and Tomorrow*. Both of the dances were presentably choreographed, but, in all honesty, neither was of a caliber that would create a major change in the future course of dance composition. In each of the two works, the dancers were required to speak. Mr. Tircuit objected to this most violently.

The evening following the publishing of the review, my family was sitting around the dinner table as was our usual habit, Marni and I were reading the article, laughing over some of its misperceptions and not really digesting it with any degree of seriousness. Sardonic comments flew from one end of the table to the other.

"Who does that man think he is?"

"What does he know about dramatic theater?"

"He couldn't tell a proscenium arch from his you know what."

We easily digressed from the review to the reviewer. The conversation began to take on an obscene tone with occasional interjections of ribald humor.

Ellis, our youngest daughter, was about eight years old at the time. She sat at the table intently listening to us carry on about the review, her already big oval eyes growing larger and larger by the minute. It was soon her bed time. She kissed us all goodnight and then in a hesitant voice, asked me if she could take the review to bed with her to read. Receiving permission, she clutched it scornfully in her hand making sure that there would be no question of the great disdain that she felt for it. She then disappeared down the hall into her room and closed the door behind her.

Later that night, as I was going to bed myself, I noticed slivers of light slipping out from underneath the closed door to her room. I opened the door very quietly in order not to wake her if she were asleep. She was lying peacefully on her bed breathing heavily in a state of deep slumber. Her body, in its relaxed position was not under the covers but was curled loosely around the odious review so that she seemed to be slowly crushing it. Beneath the review was a piece of paper. The article in question was placed at an angle across the page in such a manner that most of its pure white surface was visible. On the paper, in heavy black ink, Ellis had boldly emblazoned:

"HEUWELL TIRCUIT MUST DIE".

Never has a man spawned such a protective and revenging seed. For the good of the world, such progeny should be the reproductive result of the coupling of all parents.

Whether the dancer seeks to establish connections with reviewers or not, occasionally within a social context, there are accidental meetings. In 1984 Marni and I plus two other directors, Carol Egan and Carol Murota, were touring England and Scotland with our group the Bay Area Repertory Dance Company from the University of California, Berkeley. The last stop on the tour, after we performed in London and the festivals at Buxton and Aberdeen, was the Edinburgh Fringe Festival. Being too old for youth hostels, but having been worn out by staying in a continuous series of them during the tour, Marni and I decided to splurge and get a room at the Roxburghe Hotel on Charlotte Square. It was a way to enjoy a relaxing week in that graceful city and not be inundated by student dancers.

The first morning at the hotel, we luxuriated by sleeping very late, managing to arrive for breakfast just before the doors to the dining room closed. Eating in a hurry, we failed to take serious notice of a little man who kept ominously circling our table. The man finally became aware that we were now watching him and, using our attention as an invitation, he boldly approached our table. He apologized for disturbing us, but revealed that we looked exactly like another couple that he knew.

"…A dancer and her husband, so I'm sure you wouldn't know who they are."

He announced this information with just a touch of superiority.

"We might. Try us."

I was growing a bit defensive.

"Oh, she's a ballerina with the Royal Ballet. Her husband is a business man, I think, or a doctor or something like that. My, but I've never ever seen two people who look so much like two other people. I've seen one but never two."

He paused, gasping for breath.

"Which one of us looks like the ballerina?" I asked, winking at Marni.

The man didn't seem to pick up on my obtuse joke. He was rather short and evidently very earnest in all matters. He wasn't overly old, but age had sketched its imprint upon him with small lines on his forehead and broken veins on his nose. He smelled and looked of old tweed, a little shabby and unkempt. He reminded me of an excited gnome who had just peeked out from under a toadstool after a rainstorm to see the sun brightly shining.

"What is this ballerina's name?" Now I was really becoming curious.

"Merle Park. Have you ever heard of her?"

"Sure. I know who she is. I'm not acquainted with her personally, but I've seen her dance."

By now the little man was radiating. His lonely breakfast was beginning to bear fruit.

"Then you're dance enthusiasts?"

"You might say so."

Our little gnome practically levitated.

I felt that we had better go through the formality of introductions before we involved ourselves further.

I went right to the point.

"What's your name?"

"Oh, you wouldn't know me. I'm a dance critic for the *London Daily Telegraph*, Fernau Hall."

"I know who you are. We have a couple of your books in our dance library at home."

That we knew who he was pleased him tremendously and his small chest seemed to grow ever the least bit larger. He immediately drew up a chair to our table and settled into it as if expecting to spend the rest of the morning in conversation.

After many more exclamations over his discovery of the similarities in appearance between family Merle Park and family us, Fernau Hall finally asked, "What do you do for a living?"

"We're in dance."

"I knew it. I knew it." He was actually bubbling. "You have that look. You can always spot a dancer. What are your names?"

"Marni Thomas and David Wood."

"David Wood. I've seen you dance many times." He was literally bouncing up and down in his chair. "With Martha Graham."

Now it was my turn, and my chest grew ever the least bit larger.

At every breakfast that week, we were joined by Mr. Fernau Hall, author and critic. We heard the entire story of his life and learned about his genuine love for all types of dance. He came to the performances of our company in Edinburgh and wrote an outstanding review about the production in the *London Daily Telegraph*. I hope he wrote it because of his honest feelings about the level of our performance and not because we had become friends. I am sure though that without meeting us at the hotel, he would never have found his way to our performances.

Fernau was a great help in giving us advice and introductions to various dancers when Marni and I made our trek through Asia in 1985–1986. We remained friends by correspondence and occasional meetings a few more years until his death.

In the first years that I lived in New York, whatever money that I had was spent on the absolute essentials for existence. I had little to squander on entertainment or pleasures of any kind. For diversion I had to ferret out activities which were either free or close to it.

One of my favorite diversions, especially on a rainy Saturday afternoon, was to wander down to lower 4th Avenue where New York's second hand bookstores were located. I could spend the whole afternoon roaming from store to store, browsing through stacks of old editions which were filled with flaking, yellow pages and musty smells. These books sometimes sold for as little as one or two dollars each. From these excursions, I began building an entire library of tattered classics. The short stories of Poe, poems of Millay, novels of Hemingway, Tolstoy and Hardy, and the chronicles of St. Exupery began to enrich my reading hours and to fill the newly made orange-crate bookshelves. Because of my background and interest in dance, books on that subject also caught my eye. They were not plentiful in the 1940's, but once in awhile I would come across a rare find. On one of those many browsing excursions, I ran across a book called, *Looking At The Dance* by Edwin Denby. It sold for the magnificent price of two dollars and it was greatly to affect my future.

The main body of Edwin Denby's book dealt with his reviews written for various newspapers and magazines. They concerned performances of ballet, modern and ethnic dance styles that had taken place in New York City in the early 1940's. The articles were created with vivid reality utilizing the poetry of Mr. Denby's writing. I discovered new insight to my existing meager knowledge of dance. From the darkness of ignorance a glimmer of enlightenment began to emerge. Although Mr. Denby showed an open preference for classical ballet, his explanations of the modern dance made that form the most intriguing of all the styles for me. The dances of Martha Graham were interpreted in a manner which partially unraveled the complexity of her originality. Mr. Denby's means of criticism, rather than using negativism, was to express his ideas and theories through perceptive revelation. Dance for me now, rather than being an ephemeral art form, seemed to take on real substance and with it the direction of my theatrical career began to take a slow but definite turn.

But who was this man, Edwin Denby? How did he develop his genius for peering into and analyzing the art of dance? I became fascinated, trying to discover the man inside the book, the man inside the poetic dance critic. The most that I could discover was that Edwin Denby had been the critic for the *New York Herald Tribune* during the years of World War II while Walter Terry, the regular *Tribune* dance critic, was serving in the armed forces. Upon the return of Walter Terry, Edwin Denby left the *Tribune* and for the five or six years following, nothing more had been heard of him by the reading public. I also discovered that I was not alone in my appreciation of his talents. Edwin Denby had become nearly a cult figure within the dance world, loved and appreciated in anonymity.

Over the next few years, I would ask all of the dancers whom I met if they had heard anything of this man, but no one seemed to be able to offer more information. The mystery of Edwin Denby was much more intriguing to me than his reality could ever actually become. It wove around the man a mystique which was impenetrable. His discovery became an obsession.

Martha Graham's Asian tour of 1955–1956 terminated in Israel. Because I had been surrounded by so many people for such a length of time, I decided to go off by myself, divorced from the familiar faces of the rest of the company. We were all given our paid return tickets back to the United States, but we were allowed to alter them in whatever manner that we wanted. Never having been to Greece, and because of its proximity to Israel, I had arranged to go directly to Athens. The Greek plays of Aeschylus, Sophocles, and Euripides, an interest in Greek mythology, and Martha Graham's dances of her Greek period, all stimulated my desire to visit that exceptional country. My finances were very limited so I found inexpensive lodging, ate simply and rarely, and walked everywhere.

I would have loved to have seen all of Greece, but Athens was the most that my money could cover. I could not bear the thought of leaving however, without at least visiting Delphi with its oracle, and making an attempt to solve the mysteries of Eleusis. While cashing travelers checks at the American Express office, I discovered that there was an overnight tour to exactly these two ancient attractions. The tour traveled to Delphi early in the morning, visiting the site of the oracle that afternoon. The tour then stayed overnight at a newly built hotel in that city, with each person having a private room. The next day the group was to tour the Delphi museum with its unbelievably exquisite Charioteer, and then stop at Eleusis on the way back to Athens. It was a perfect two day excursion at little expense.

Everything worked as advertised except for the hotel which had booked its rooms before it had finished building them. One entire wing had not been completed so the members of the tour were forced to double up. For me, this wasn't too bad as it meant that some of my money was to be returned. My roommate was an older, rather distinguished looking, and seemingly very quiet man.

The day could not have been more delicate, a mixture of sun one moment and snow the next. The early blooming trees had a slightly embarrassed and mystified look as the light snow brushed their newly formed pink-lined buds.

After dinner that night, there was a huge fire blazing in the grate of the oversized fireplace to help heat the large reception room where everyone had congregated. All of the members of the American Express tour gathered around the hearth and began to recite who they were and in what manner fate had participated in bringing them on the tour. My assigned roommate sat a little way apart from the rest, divorcing himself from the group, but watching and listening with some amusement. When my turn came to confess my sins, I told my story of dancing with Martha Graham on an Asian tour and how I was now completing the trip around the world on my own.

Tired from the day's journey and the questioning of the oracle, the conversation and the fire burned to glowing embers at the same time. Having an early morning call, we all drifted off to our rooms. My roommate was already in our quarters by the time that I got there. We exchanged a few pleasantries and then he somewhat shyly stated, "I was interested in what you had to say about dancing with Martha Graham in Asia."

There was a short pause and then he continued, "I knew her slightly at one time."

It was like a flash of inspiration – a light bulb of illumination over the head of a character in a comic strip. There was no doubt. After all of these years. Here in Delphi, Greece, I was sharing a room with Edwin Denby.

He seemed a little embarrassed as I effusively burst forth with the exclamation, "You're Edwin Denby!"

We stayed up most of the night talking hungrily. He asked me to tell him all about the Asian tour. I wanted to know all about Edwin Denby. He lived in New York with his cats directly behind my 23rd Street loft. He didn't like to write reviews under the demand of a deadline. He wanted to write, only about those dance events that interested him. He was a generous, unprejudiced, understanding, and gracious man. Like the poetry of his writing, he created a sense of poetry in his life. I had been wrong. Edwin Denby was a far more fascinating person in actuality than he ever was in the mystery of my imagination.

The subject of dance contributors cannot be completed without mentioning an extraordinary group of people who have made a lasting imprint on all of the dance world. They are known as Dance Educators, and their influence has been felt both by artists and audiences alike. Without their unselfish involvement, modern dance could never have arrived at the position which it occupies today. They established a rising level of consciousness throughout the dance field for contemporary practices.

These revolutionaries were, in almost all cases, women who were driven by an unbridled passion for dance. They were logical, dedicated and sometimes violently stubborn. Because of their tenacity and overt determination, I approached them with extreme caution, but upon meeting them I became immediately convinced of their energy and integrity. They created a feeling of respect and deep admiration. They fed dancers into the New York performance cauldrons, to fill out the companies of the modernists. They convinced university and college physical education departments to fund performances of known and unknown modern companies. They provided audiences for the performances through their own personal enthusiasm. These audiences, if not appreciative at first, were at least stunned enough to return for a second performance. These women were not always pleasant, nor easy to work with, but they always had purpose to their actions and accomplished their goals with zest and flair.

They were the blood and the guts of the dance world. They were the actual sustenance of life for the early days of the modern dance revolution. Sometimes that sustenance took the frightful shape of tea and cookies instead of meat and potatoes. This was especially devastating when the dancers were starving after a performance.

They mostly were American but there were a few who were located in foreign countries. These women often had the most difficult time of all in establishing their idealistic aims: Guillermina Bravo of Mexico, who single-handedly made modern dance an artistic commodity in her country; Takani Hirai of Nara, Japan who is just beginning to create inroads for modern dance; Lia Schubert of Sweden, who created opportunities for performers in all forms of dance: ballet, modern, and jazz, against all odds; Hassia Levi in Israel, who bravely fought her battle of acceptance for many years.

In the United States, most of these women were or are associated with colleges, but, one, Steffi Nossen established her own school. She provided a direction for many of the wealthy young women of Westchester County in New York who were wandering without purpose through a vital part of their lives.

Margaret H'Doubler of the University of Wisconsin was the initiator for all of the Dance Education in the United States and inspired many of the other leaders in the field: Martha Hill of Bennington College,

New York University, and Juilliard; Teddy Weisner of Brooklyn College; Bessie Schoenberg of Sarah Lawrence College; Helen Alkire of Ohio State University; Margaret Erlanger of the University of Illinois; Virginia Tanner who was associated with the University of Utah; Ruth Bloomer of Connecticut College; and Alma Hawkins of the University of California, Los Angeles.

They have as a group pressured university administrators to accept dance as a valid field of study within academia, and have stimulated, each in her unique way, the philosophy that dance in all of its manifestations is an exciting art form.

Teaching at the American Dance Festival, Connecticut College, New London, Connecticut in 1959: Marni Thomas, Martha Graham, and David Wood, with pianist Robert Dunn. Photographer: Serge Silbey. Photo credit: Wood Collection.

Raegan, Marina, and Ellis Wood performing at the Temple of the Wings, Berkeley, California. Photographer: Margaretta Mitchell. Photo credit: Wood Collection.

Raegan, Marina, and Ellis Wood at the Temple of the Wings, Berkeley, California twenty years later. Photographer: Jon Marlowe. Photo credit: Wood Collection.

Marni Thomas, Richard Peck, and Julie Brown in David Wood's choreography of *Jeux*. Photo credit: Wood Collection.

Marni Thomas as Athena in Martha Graham's *Clytemnestra*. Photographer: Martha Swope. Photo credit: Wood Collection.

David Wood as the Messenger of Death in Martha Graham's *Clytemnestra*. Photographer: Martha Swope. Photo credit: Wood Collection.

9

ON MAJOR PERSONALITIES

What propelled the major modernists in the dance world of the 1930's through the 1970's; Hanya Holm, Helen Tamiris, Charles Weidman, Martha Graham, Doris Humphrey, José Limón and Alwin Nikolais to spend their lives in a profession which placed overwhelming demands upon them? Any acclaim that these artists might have acquired through their unique style of dance was minimal; the number of working hours was enormous; the financial rewards were minor if not completely lacking. Confronted by such major disadvantages, why were these twentieth century innovators driven to follow dance as a chosen profession?

Persistence alone can create a degree of achievement, but to make any kind of effective and lasting imprint, a greater contribution is required. Belief and vision are two key qualities that are demanded in the developmental process of any art form. Both involve an ego which holds the artist on a well directed path. When used creatively, the artist's ego is consumed by the ritual of fire. If, however, the ego fails to become transcendent, but is used only for personal gratification, it often stands as a barrier that isolates the artist.

The major area that these dance artists had in common was their intense need to express themselves in movement, combined with the tenacity to carry it out. This was the prime factor which permeated everything.

There was also one more element which every dancer shared. It was the food on which each performer fed. It was the desire for acceptance by the audience, physicalized in the form of applause. If the audience's reaction was one of acceptance it provided a unique elixir for the spirit of the artist. Applause is an actual, tangible manifestation that is carefully metered through the aural senses of the individual performer. It is a return for work accomplished.

Applause for fields other than performing does not carry the same importance. Those dancers who continued their careers in choreography seemed to feel out of place on stage when receiving their accolades. The illusionary covering of make-up and costume had been removed from them and they, for a brief moment, could be seen standing before their appreciative audiences as if they were caught completely naked in some bizarre dream. In addition, to compensate for the changes that occurred in their professional lives, these artists seemed personally to become less demanding and more social, attempting to fulfill their lives in a completely different manner.

But for one artist, the reverse procedure proved to be true. Martha Graham, as her life progressed, became more and more isolated. Louis Horst and Erick Hawkins had left the scene. With the departure of these two men went all possible serious romantic involvement. Martha even placed her sister Geordie at an increased distance. Bethsabee de Rothschild, her long-time friend, had moved to Israel.

Martha's only continuing relationship was with her captive audience whether it was appreciative or not. They were her needed friends, the only people on whom she could, without question, rely. The theater contained a special aura for Martha. It was an exciting, living world in which the real and the unreal were interwoven in a vivid tapestry. Once on stage, whether dancing or not, Martha was always performing, and the taking of a bow, even as a nonperforming artist, drew from her a performance which was the equal of her dancing days. Martha's theory on bowing was that of an iconoclast. She believed that for one second, as the performer lowered his upper body which contained his heart, mind and soul, he allowed the audience to be on the same level as his performing self. Then, following that acknowledgment, he would rise, and again take command of the stage.

Over the years, as Martha continued to dance, her range of friendships increased as she increased the size of her audiences. From the sparse number of people that watched her performances during her early cross-country tours, the audiences grew constantly. In Tel Aviv and Amsterdam there were lines that circled the theater waiting to buy tickets. In Yugoslavia and Japan the audiences stormed the stages, charging down the aisles, shouting and throwing flowers. In Lisbon, there were so many blossoms covering the steeply raked stage that Martha slipped on the petals and came perilously close to pitching off the edge of the platform. In Dhaka, there was the all male audience to captivate. In Paris, there were the controversial fights in the lobby at intermission. In Florence, Martha, in reaction to penny whistles and catcalls, turned her back to the audience and bowed upstage to her own company instead.

Martha's inner needs demanded that she prolong her performance life for as long as possible. They drew her personally away from concerned friends in order to conserve her energy and sustain her focus. Hers was a lonely existence, but that was by conscious choice, preferable to terminating her performing career. She was forced to feed herself from within. Although the audience was of a nebulous nature, Martha knew it well, and by the time she had finished a performance, the audience felt they knew her well. There wasn't an audience anywhere which, in Martha's own words, "Couldn't be had."

On my last tour of the United States with Martha, I stood backstage each evening and watched her take her bows. The reception was especially powerful in the large auditoriums of the mid-western universities. At the end of the dance, the company curtain calls were taken first, until the time that the applause began slightly to diminish. Then, as the clapping in anticipation of Martha's solo bow started to build expectantly with one last surge, Martha would instinctively move alone into the upstage left wing. She waited for exactly the correct moment and, riding the crest of adulation with expert timing, swept out in a huge arc that brought her by means of small mincing footsteps to down stage center. Then, as if caught unexpectedly and with great surprise, she greeted her friends, the audience. They rose to their feet with rapturous cheers to meet her. This was the moment of Martha's reality and these were the only real people with whom she could honestly communicate.

Just as one is able to gain a slight insight into the personality of Martha Graham by the way in which she reacted to an audience, so can one learn more about the other early modern dance pioneers by probing further into some of their various working activities. The manner in which they interacted with their colleagues, or how they dealt with their own company members is revealing. A look into the process by which they handled finances, touring, and rehearsing can help in constructing a more complete and in-depth picture of the different personalities of this period.

ON HANYA HOLM

Because of her striking personality, the image of Hanya Holm, has remained indelibly imprinted on the memory of all those who have ever met her. Small, agile, compact and clearly focused, Hanya was at all times well directed. Her tiny stature seemed to compress her energy, intensifying it until her vivacity literally exploded from within her.

Hanya's appearance had many distinctive elements, but nothing was more predominant than her sparkling eyes. Slightly oval and piercing, they openly revealed the thoughts that lay at the back of them. Her anger could burst from them with an intense fire, while in lighter more playful moments, her eyes radiated a warm glow. The plait of hair, which usually was worn circling her head or wrapped in a bun at the nape of her neck, was at rare times allowed to fall in a straight weighted line down her back. Its tightly constructed weave was a direct indication of the precision and exactness with which Hanya approached most of the activities of her well ordered life.

She was a perceptive and extremely intelligent woman whose mind raced at a pace that far out-distanced her feeling for physicality. From her early financial struggles, Hanya developed a necessary frugality and a calculated approach toward most of the conditions of her life. The tritely conceived Germanic quality of stubbornness proved to be an actuality with Hanya in most of her relationships. She was definitely a believer in the formula of master–disciple in all teaching situations. Her demand for respect and her separation from co-workers and students alike created a constant aura of impenetrability.

I had been studying at the studio for at least two weeks before I caught my first glimpse of Hanya. By the spring of 1949 when I began my studies with her, Hanya had already started her slow climb out of the relative obscurity of the modern dance world by choreographing a charming rendition of *The Eccentricities Of Davy Crockett* for the John Latouche, Jerome Moross production of *Ballet Ballads,* as well as the sparkling dances for *Kiss Me Kate.* Her life was active and full because of her creative work for the dazzling neon-lit world of Broadway. As a result of these activities, her focus on teaching began to retreat further and further from the center of her concerted interests.

My first class with Hanya was certainly not disappointing. Her vitality filled the room which was crowded with eager students. Although Hanya did not posses the overpowering mystique of a Martha Graham or the commanding austerity of a Doris Humphrey, she displayed a clear authority as a master teacher who had complete command of her subject. All that Hanya presented in class was conveyed with perceptive analysis. Although the hour and a half sessions that I took were purely directed toward technique, her theory classes, which always had been a part of her curriculum, aided her greatly in all of the analysis which she used. Her explanations inspired the movement and, the core of the movement was at times beautifully wrought and excitingly presented.

That first class moved constantly with an even flow of energy. Hanya obviously responded to the massive size of the class. As the first months of study with her passed, I was to find that the number of people in the room was a direct stimulation for her. If she had many receptive students, she responded to the occasion with enthusiasm, but when only a relatively few mediocre students were at hand, Hanya seemed bored and eager to finish with her labors. Following that first session with Hanya, her classes often were not up to standard. I could always recognize the potential in them, but felt frustrated by not being sufficiently challenged. Still, when the opportunity arose to try for a scholarship to the 1949 summer session at Colorado College in Colorado Springs, I took the dare.

Hanya, Alwin Nikolais, and Oliver Kostok were all teaching during the session. To be able to concentrate just on dancing, with no financial pressures such as I had constantly felt in New York, was a definite attraction.

Beside the benefits that I could gain from the professional aspect of training in Colorado Springs, I was anxious to get out of New York for a while. After two years of living in that pulsating intensity, I felt the need to escape from the city and to experience a complete change of scenery and friends.

Because I had studied dance seriously for only a few months, I approached the scholarship audition with much trepidation. In my naiveté, I had no idea how desperately in demand were all aspiring male dancers, good or bad. But without the benefit of supporting money, there was no way that I could possibly afford the tuition and living expenses for the summer at Colorado College. Nik gave the audition class, and Hanya watched with her eagle eyes and made the selections. There were many new and strange people auditioning. Some were students of Nik from Henry Street, and others were students from all over the east coast. It was my first audition of any kind. The scholarship I won increased my confidence in my future as a dancer.

The advantages of studying in Colorado with Hanya proved themselves immediately. Hanya's classes seemed infinitely more stimulating than they had in New York City. The lofty, green, pine studded slopes of the Rocky Mountains that interlaced with the angular red rocks of the landscape seemed to give a feeling of majesty to everything. In classes and rehearsals, working was concentrated and intense. As we relaxed we released ourselves with abandon.

The roster of attending students was amazing. In one summer it included Gladys Bailin, Billie Mahoney, Debbie Choate, Joan Jones Woodbury, Al Srnka, Murray Gitlin, Murray Louis (Fuchs) and Don Redlich. We were all struggling young dancers trying to learn more about everything that touched us in dance or in life. That summer course at Colorado was an example of the major benefits that can be gained from summer intensive courses. These courses allow novitiate dancers to place upon their own bodies the broad cloak of dance in order to test its fit and its weight. For some, it is the cloth to be worn for many years to come, but for others, its weight becomes an overbearing pressure, too cumbersome for continued wear.

The classes, the opportunities to perform, and the newly made friendships helped to create for me a dream-filled summer. The eight weeks were so positive that it was hard to think of returning to the grime and confusion of the New York scene and once again to begin the struggle for survival. Even after two years spent in New York, I had no ties or connections which drew me back to it with any enthusiasm. The major pull was an offer from Hanya. I had worked very well with her over the summer (she seemed to have a penchant for young men) and her promise to use me in her upcoming Broadway musical, *Out Of This World* was the major reason for my return to the big city.

Like all exciting things the weeks raced by rapidly and with the performance of the dance concert, the summer session came to an abrupt end. Al Srnka and I loaded our bags into Martha Howe's car and the three of us headed for Chicago. I had enough money left to catch a plane that, depending on my decision, would be directed either to New York or San Francisco, plus a few remaining pennies with which I could enjoy a couple of thrifty days in the windy city. I gave my destiny no thought, but enjoyed my purposelessness for forty-eight unconcerned hours. On the prescribed morning, I went to the airport and, without a second thought, bought a ticket for New York. There was no conscious choice made. It was inevitable.

Later that afternoon, I arrived at Teterboro Airport where all of the chartered planes seemed to land and depart. The terminal was lost in New Jersey somewhere. Because I had no money left for transportation into the city, I tried to hitch a ride. After a short wait, a van belonging to the Dainty Diaper Service pulled up alongside and gave me a lift all of the way into town. Sitting on a pile of dirty diapers with the sun slowly burying itself into the road behind me in a bright red-glowing last gesture, I made my inauspicious return to New York City.

Shortly after resettling, I learned that the musical, *Out Of This World*, had been postponed for a year; with that postponement, my vision of a financially profitable time of dancing went down the drain. I quickly obtained a job at the Presbyterian Hospital and instead of performing in a Broadway musical, settled for a year of concentrated dance study. The only classes that I had money enough to take were those at the Holm studio, and I had great difficulty gathering together enough cash even for them. This schedule of events continued for a few months and then my career took a definite sharp turn.

As I walked out of my intermediate class at Hanya's one day in the early winter, Elsa Reiner, the school secretary, met me at the door. Elsa had a charming clipped German accent which seemed to make my plain name of David dance with fascinating, strange rhythms whenever she used it.

"David, David, please help me. Ollie (Kostok) has hurt his back and can't teach the next class. Please could you teach it?" It never entered my mind to say no. Elsa had often saved my life during the past months, so I was personally obliged now to help her in return. The fact that I had only studied dance seriously for eight months and had little or nothing to teach anyone, didn't occur to me in my ego-ridden world.

"Of course I can", I affirmed.

The word "can" meant for Elsa that I had the free time to teach the class, but for me the word "can" meant that I felt that I had the knowledge and the ability to be able to teach it. The brazenness of youth was served.

That evening, Elsa called to tell me that Ollie's back was badly injured, and that he had to remain quiet for many months. She asked, with the approval of Hanya, if I would be able to teach all of his classes. This entailed instructing a beginning class in Holm technique everyday along with the Saturday morning general level class, plus classes at the Mill's School for Girls and Adelphi College. To teach that one class had been a premature blind reach into the unknown world of pedagogy, but as a continuing practice, I had grave doubts. Still the money that was offered allowed me a certain financial freedom which I had never had while living in New York. Without much thought, greed overcame integrity and I answered with a resounding, "Yes."

Very few people knew what little training I had had before I started to teach; nevertheless, I felt under great pressure with every class. The most surprising element was that Hanya never once spoke to me concerning the elements of teaching or came to observe any of my classes. Elsa watched once at Hanya's behest so that she could report on my progress as a teacher, but she gave me no advice whatsoever.

The situation lent itself to many embarrassing occurrences. One day I arrived to teach class and found a charming lady waiting to take it. On first sight she looked familiar to me, but not being able to place her, I gave her little thought and continued upstairs to change my clothes. On entering the studio to teach the class, I found the woman stretched out on the floor with a flexibility that could only be possessed by a professional dancer. I now immediately recognized her. She was my former ballet teacher, Dorothy Etheridge with a new-look, short haircut that had confused me. Panic set in. I was finally caught. Because of teaching me in ballet, Dorothy knew exactly how untrained I was.

Much embarrassed, I timidly approached her to say hello and passionately begged her to take the intermediate class that was being taught at the same hour. She refused, saying that as she had never studied modern dance, she wanted to learn the basics clearly and correctly. It was an admirable attitude on her part, but I was desperate and had no shame. I practically got down on my knees and pleaded with her to change her mind.

With determination, she still repeated, "No", reiterating her reasons.

After ten minutes of imploring, I gave up and in complete confusion began the class. When my ordeal of teaching finally ended, Dorothy approached me and stated appreciatively how much she had enjoyed the different way of moving.

She ended with the killing statement, "When you took ballet with me, I didn't know that you were a modern dancer. I just thought you couldn't dance."

While it was said in all innocence, the statement definitely hit its mark.

At the going rate of $5.00 per hour for teaching dance classes, I could just manage to eke out a slightly sub-par, poverty-level existence. Classes were always relatively expensive in New York, so one of the main benefits that I thought came along with teaching for Hanya was the privilege of taking free classes. To make certain that this was the case, I asked Elsa what the procedure was at the studio. She assured me that I would be allowed to take gratis as many classes as I wanted, but she would speak to Hanya about it.

One month and many classes later Elsa, with great embarrassment, informed me that she was very sorry but that Hanya had said that I must pay for all of the classes that I had taken. She quoted the staggering debt that I had accumulated over the month. Aghast, I told her that there was no possible way that I could come up with that amount of cash in order to pay for them.

"You can take it out of my salary until the amount I owe is covered, but when it is paid off, I'll stop teaching and go elsewhere."

Elsa looked soulfully at me, but knew that I was right.

In another week, after one more visit to Hanya, Elsa presented a second offer. Hanya would wipe out my past debt and in the future all of the classes that I took would be charged only at half price. By now I had checked at other studios and discovered that all of them gave their teachers free classes. I was building courage and bravado with every exchange.

"It's still unfair. If I am good enough to teach, I am good enough to get the same benefits as everyone else. I'm not going to take any more classes under these conditions."

Another week passed and Elsa returned to me with carte blanche. I had won my first battle of wits in the dance world and the valuable free classes were achieved. It is interesting to note that all communication was done through Elsa. Hanya had removed herself from the studio and was not teaching any classes at all. I had asked Elsa with each exchange if I could speak with Hanya directly in order to solve the matter, but was told that she was totally unavailable. After working with Hanya so well in Colorado this dispute was actually very upsetting.

Even though Hanya was not giving any concert performances at this time, she insisted that I not dance with other choreographers. She even overtly objected to my taking class and dancing with Alwin Nikolais who was still the major instructor at her studio.

With my wings clipped, I began to feel like the complete prisoner of a very stubborn and autocratic woman. The freedom to experiment in dance in every possible way seemed essential to my development. I was barely starting on my career and now I was inadvertently becoming

stifled by restrictions that I felt to be unfair. I didn't recognize the benefits gained from working with Hanya, the marvelous opportunities that
she had already given me over the brief period of one year. I was
a young, unbridled colt and the world was mine for the taking.

I made it clear to both Hanya and Elsa that I would finish my assignment of teaching through the spring semester, but then I would have to
leave. I needed exposure to other ways of moving and the limitations
placed on me, I felt, were too demanding. When the end of the semester
drew near, Elsa informed me that there was to be a teacher's meeting and
Hanya wanted me to attend. I explained once more to her that I intended
to leave, but Elsa implored again with begging eyes and fractured but
convincing accent. I finally gave in both because of Elsa's pleading and
my own curiosity concerning what Hanya had in mind for me.

We met in Hanya's tiny office in Michael's studios. After the proper
amount of idle conversation, Hanya got down to the reason for the
meeting, the teaching assignments for the coming year. Hanya left mine
for the last, and without any questioning, I was given a full quota of
classes. Hanya obviously hadn't believed a word that I had said to her.
The money that I was offered for teaching was much improved and
again avarice suddenly reared its ugly head, but I was too close to
freedom to turn back. As unappetizing as the thought of soda jerking
again at Whelan's Drug Store was, I needed to be free to dance wherever
and whenever I wanted. I carefully thanked Hanya for all that she had
done for me. I assured her that, although it must seem otherwise, I was
very grateful to her, but that now I wanted more than anything else to
dance. I had started my career later than most people and so wanted to
accomplish as much as I could as soon as possible. I had years ahead in
which I could teach. With that I rose from my chair and exited from the
room, closing my first door behind me.

I didn't leave without a feeling of regret. There was much to admire
about Hanya. Whether choreographing or dancing it was both comforting and challenging to be under her watchful eyes, for her powers
of observation were clearly honed. But I did not want it at the price of
losing my chance to try to dance by following my own directions.

During the fall of the next year *Out Of This World* finally went into
rehearsal. As an adventure, I went to the first audition and Hanya
graciously passed me through to the call back. I heard rumors through
the grapevine that Hanya had stated firmly that she had no intention of
using me. To save us both embarrassment, I didn't return for the final
audition.

Quite a few years later, I was rushing to the High School of Performing
Arts for an after school rehearsal when I literally bumped into Hanya on
the corner of Broadway and 47th Street. It was as if no time had passed

since I had studied with her and taught at her studio. By then I was dancing with Martha Graham. Hanya told me that she was still teaching her special classes and invited me to attend. I was greatly pleased and assured her that I would take them when I finished the new choreography that I was starting that very day.

"How marvelous to stand naked in the studio again", Hanya said, her eyes expressing a truly honest glow of excitement and understanding.

Hanya knew well the pleasure and anxiety of many new beginnings. Because of her explosive vitality and energy, she had already traveled along the path of constant change and continuous growth and as a result had achieved a reputation of tremendous value and worth in the dance world.

ON ALWIN NIKOLAIS

On reflection, I always picture Alwin Nikolais hopping across the floor as if a perpetual spring had been released inside of him. I cannot ever recall Nik in class or rehearsal using an easy flow of movement. Impulse was almost always the order of the day. No matter what movement he devised, Nik continuously bounded and rebounded through it, rejecting the floor with such rapidity that one had the feeling that the surface was so hot that his feet could only remain upon it for a few seconds.

Also, during most of the class, Nik smiled. His eyes sparkled, but the rest of his face reached upward in broad sweeping curves. Nik was one of the few people that I ever knew whose cheeks, the area that is commonly associated with smiling, truly radiated every time that his face lit up. When he accompanied a class on the piano or with drums, he always sat on the edge of his chair, alert and ready for whatever circumstances might prevail. He reminded me a bit of Helen Keller the one time that I saw her at Martha's studio, for he carried his spine strong and straight, never touching the rear of the seat with his back, as if it might cause the dulling of some needed vital vibration.

Alwin Nikolais has evoked both praise and condemnation for the use of his many-faceted talents. As far as his students were concerned, there was no question of the richness gained by Nik's in-depth knowledge of design and music along with his kinesthetic feel for movement. Whether it was in class or rehearsal, Nik could stimulate his students with spontaneous spurts of imagination, propelling them forward into their own creativity. Negative criticism was aimed at Nik by those few who felt that his multi-talents led to a lessening of the total intensity of his choreographic works.

The human crucible for creativity, some individuals believe, can only be filled to a certain level before it overflows and dissipates the energy.

If this is true, the question that occurs is whether the imagination is better used in the intensity of a single productive direction, or by covering a greater span to a lesser degree. In Nik's unique and original creativity, he builds a cumulative total which expands the imagination in every direction and which analysis cannot destroy. Like tightly woven threads, Nik's strength lies in the intensity by which he interweaves the elements of his vast talents.

Nik effused to everyone an easy warmth. It was first evident to me while I was studying with him in Colorado. After an evening's rehearsal, he sometimes would accompany a group of us to the local eatery to consume some well-earned calories. We spent the late hours interspersing the intake of food with endless esoteric discussions on the theories and the future of dance. Nik would fill us in on the history of the modern movement and the excitement that he had felt while participating in the Bennington years. He was full of fascinating anecdotes that were gleaned from his experiences during that earlier period.

In the classroom, Nik was highly conscious of his artistic beliefs and clearly projected them to his students. He was an actual dance isolationist, referring back to the days of the acolytes at the Bennington summer sessions. Once he had formed a performing nucleus at Henry Street, Nik attempted to construct an insular world around them. The geographic distance of the Henry Street Settlement House from the rest of the dance world made this an easy task.

We traveled uptown one weekend to perform with other groups on Trudy Goth's Choreographer's Workshop. The night before that event took place, Nik sat the group down and gave us a long lecture warning us not to have anything to do with the uptown dancers as they were jaded and wore spangles in their hair. I was surprised by his attitude, as I was basically an uptown dancer, at least during the daylight hours, and I hadn't noticed any spangles falling off of me.

Years later Nik and company were invited to teach and perform at the American Dance Festival at Connecticut College. I had already been teaching Graham Technique there for a few summers. I was honestly excited that Nik was to be in residence as I would be able to take a few more classes with him. On first running into him on the campus, I mentioned how nice it was to have the group there, and now, as a result, his company would get a chance to be in close association with other dancers.

Nik's answer was curt and to the point, "My company is sufficient unto itself. We don't really need anyone else".

In later years, out of necessity, Nik became more open to outside forces, but his preference was always to work in interaction with a close-knit group. It is doubtful that he ever could have developed his unique style of theater in any other manner. That first period when he and his company worked in isolation, proved to be a time of necessary incubation, experimentation, and development.

The sections involving improvisation were always one of the best parts of Nik's classes. He had a truly creative mind which worked better in conceptualization than in actual dance terms. Like so many choreographers whose kinesthetic sense of movement is not their most outstanding premise, Nik allowed his dancers to create certain movements within the confines of his creative structures. Using his highly developed artistic sense Nik would then shape and form the total work, combining it with other elements from his fertile imagination into a magical whole. Nik also had the luxury of the use of the Henry Street Theater in which to experiment and to bring, by trial and error, the fantasies of his imagination into actuality. When I left Henry Street, Nik was just at the beginning of working in this integral way. When I returned as an audience member to his theater I was amazed at the miracles he had created.

In 1985 when Marni and I were living in Tokyo for a few months, Nik came to Japan on tour with his company. He actually was there to open The Spiral Theater that had recently been built to house experimental productions. Marni and I attended two different performances which were enough for us to observe how completely in command of his various techniques Nik had become. After one of the shows, Marni and I had dinner with Nik in a neighborhood restaurant. The original warmth and ease that I had felt emanating from him previously in Colorado, still proved to be in evidence. Although the demands of his creativity ideally required an isolationist point of view, personally Nik was an open and gregarious human being. Time had passed, but the easy relationship remained.

Eve Gentry, a former Holm dancer, had come to Hanya's to watch me instruct one of my classes. She evidently liked what she saw as she invited me to teach part time at The New Dance Group where she was working.

The Group was located on 59th Street just off of 5th Avenue. It was a gathering of teachers who presented classes in about every type of dance that ever existed, classical ballet to Afro Haitian, but the emphasis was definitely placed on the various styles of modern dance. The original members of The Group were all politically conscious people gathered under the umbrella of social reform, but by the time that I began teaching there in the summer of 1950, this premise had been watered down.

What pleased me most about the school was its complete diversity. As I was allowed free classes, I could taste many different styles of dancing without having to commit myself in any one way. Another positive factor was that there were many different companies operating from within the school. This provided me with a host of opportunities to perform during those early years.

ON THE DUDLEY-MASLOW-BALES TRIO

The Dudley-Maslow-Bales Trio (Jane Dudley, Sophie Maslow and William Bales) worked under the belief that dance should be an artistic expression which existed basically for the betterment of society. Rumors were passed at the time that The Trio, as well as the entire New Dance Group were communistically oriented, but in the days of the late 1940's and early 1950's, McCarthyism was rampant and anything that was considered to be in the least bit liberal was seen as radical. The trio of dancers joined forces out of need and mutual respect, but often had broad disagreements concerning the overall direction that they should take.

To enlarge the scope of their choreographic activities, the Trio gathered around them a company of outstanding dancers: Billie Kirpich, Muriel Mannings, Lili Mann, Anneliese Widman, Rena Gluck, Ronnie Aul, Donald McKayle, Irving Burton, and Norman Maxon made up the nucleus of a constantly changing group. My own entry into the company was made when I was invited to audition in the fall of 1950.

Dancing for the Dudley-Maslow-Bales Trio exemplified the best and the worst in a working situation. The group of dancers that the trio assembled was highly volatile but extremely friendly; self-centered, but, in serious situations, deeply caring; intensely professional, but at times, childishly vindictive. I have come to believe whatever atmosphere is prevalent within a group of people, is a direct result of the attitude that is created by those in charge. As friendly as Jane, Sophie, and Bill were personally, once we arrived at the theater, their professional antagonisms rose to the surface. The serious tensions that existed among the three spread rapidly to the rest of the group, causing most of the rehearsals to be filled with unpleasantness. The long hours of rehearsing didn't help. All three of the trio believed in the old adage of rehearsing directly up to the time of the performance. This left everyone's nerves frazzled from exhaustion. Despite the difficulties, it was always amazing to me that most of the performances were enthusiastically received by the audiences. Bill Bales was more of a dance educator, administrator, organizer, and activist than he was an actual dancer or choreographer. Besides participating in directing The Trio, Bill taught choreography and technique at Bennington College in Vermont and later at the State University of New York in Purchase. Bill was always under pressure as his rehearsal time was limited by having to travel back and forth to Vermont every week. By the time that I joined the group, Bill had stopped choreo-graphing. In contrast to the choreography of Jane and Sophie, Bill's works had never been terribly well received. He seemed to feel much more comfortable teaching than he did choreographing. As a dancer, the tightness of Bill's body limited his range of movement. What he lacked in technique though, he made up in enthusiasm. He always danced with a sincere belief in what he was performing.

During stage rehearsals, Bill became the critical eye for the other two choreographers. He supervised all spacing and lighting, attempting to perfect it. He often would spend hours removing a nondescript shadow from the face of some exhausted dancer. Over a period of time, it became a struggle for Bill to maintain the artistic pace that his female partners set, but he administered the company excellently.

Jane Dudley was a tall, rangy, large-boned woman with a deep and commanding voice. She had an amazing control over her long limbs and body. She could use them in isolation to heighten the ludicrous aspects of comedy or integrate them within her total size to move with great power. She was a dancer's dancer. Her respect for movement also made her an excellent instructor. Her teaching was well conceived and well paced. One came away from her class having gained a great deal of knowledge concerning physicality and the use of space. In the creation of dances, Jane's movement device was better than her choreographic structure. Her choreography was always a pleasure to perform, but more for the doing of the movement itself than for its content or its form.

Sophie Maslow was artistically completely the opposite of Jane. She was soft and lyrical in movement, sweet and truly decent as a human being. Her lack of a sharp personal edge probably was what stood in the way of her receiving more acclaim for her work. Sophie's talent far outstripped any success that she gained as a choreographer. In creating dances she evinced an ability that was inventive in conception and eclectic in style, giving her a wide range of choreographic possibilities.

Folksay, a work done in Americana style, was one of the major factors which propelled me into the dance field. After seeing it, for the first time, I left the theater highly impressed by its power of communication and sense of simple human dignity. Unfortunately, I never got to perform in the work as the dance was not done during my tenure with the company. Instead I was put into *Champion*, Sophie's choreographic interpretation of the Ring Lardner story concerning the fast-paced world of boxing. My favorite dance of Sophie's was *The Village I Knew* which was taken from the stories of Sholem Aleichem. It was a passionate dance full of feeling and pathos, speckled with moments of humor throughout. Except for one of the reveling students in the male trio, over the years I danced every male role in the work. My favorite always remained my initial part of the rabbi. When I first performed it, I didn't even know that a rabbi was Jewish, but there was something openly vulnerable and exacting about the choreography which Sophie created for the character that made him a most appealing figure.

If there was a fault to be found, it was Sophie's lack of organization. She lost many dancers from the group because of their resentment over time wasted. Sophie was offered a few outside opportunities. She choreographed many Bonds For Israel performances during Chanukkah at the old Madison Square Garden on 8th Avenue. She came to the New York City Opera and choreographed, among others, a highly esteemed production of David Tamkin's *The Dybbuk*. She was an excellent rehearsal director for Martha Graham's reconstruction of *Primitive Mysteries* for the Louis Horst Memorial. She did the choreography for the musical *Groundhog* presented at the Phoenix Theater. Each of the opportunities, as successful as they were, and they all were successful, proved to be a dead end from which Sophie always had to retrench and start again. At times she seemed discouraged by the constant disappointments, but never gave up her struggle to choreograph. For her, creating dances wasn't a matter of choice, it was a need which she had to fulfill.

The only trouble with the classes at The New Dance Group was that all of the teaching was done second-hand. The three major modern techniques of Graham, Holm and Humphrey-Weidman were taught by former teachers, company members, or students of the original company members who had left the source and migrated across town to The Group. Like myself, some had taught or studied for only a short period of time with the master teachers and were vastly limited in the knowledge that could be communicated. Martha Graham objected bitterly and loudly over other people using her name and movement technique without her permission, but Hanya and Doris and Charles never voiced any obvious objections or felt any sense of misuse.

Still it seemed sensible to me that if I were going to learn something, I should experience it at the source of its development, providing that the spring of creativity was still available. The only classes that I continued to take at The Group after my first year there were those of Jane Dudley. Besides having a sonorous ring of authenticity to them, Jane's classes had a feel of original invention as well.

ON CHARLES WEIDMAN

By the time that I arrived on the doorstep of the Weidman studio on 16th Street in the fall of 1950, my desperation about the rapid passage of the years had increased considerably. Time in a dancer's life becomes a determining factor. It hangs ominously, ever present over the conscious vision of most performing individuals. If I were to make any mark as a dancer, I had immediately to start progressing forward at a much faster pace than I had recently been doing. Along with the pressure that I placed on myself, I felt a certain pressure from my family to show some progress that would prove to them the worthiness of my undertaking. Studying with Charles Weidman was a new area of learning for me. It was a definite expansion of my dance knowledge. Charles also was the major choreographer for the New York City Opera Company and the possibility of obtaining a paying dance job with him always lay at the back of my mind.

Charles was a lovely man, or probably it would be more accurate to say that he was a loveable man. As with most great artists, he was ego-oriented and all actions and activities were turned toward himself. This gave him, a certain air of pathos. Bound by his own self-image, Charles could never understand why he was not constantly struck by success. One of Charles' distinctive traits was his stutter. It was not one which made speaking impossible and the speaker mute, but rather a stutter which repeated the beginning of words many times over. When the tensions of rehearsals or performances increased, so did the stutter.

One can see from pictures that Charles was strikingly handsome as a young man. He must have cut a dashing figure as a matinee idol during the Denishawn days. He had a mobile face which, through distortion, could project any character or emotion of character. He used it expertly portraying roles as disparate as Abraham Lincoln in his *Lincoln Portrait* to a chipmunk in his Thurber's *Fables*.

In later years, his face took on a haggard somewhat ravaged look. I could never quite tell if this was a condition of normal aging, over-developed facial muscles, or a result of the excessive drinking of alcohol. Even as an older man, Charles provoked sympathy in his colleagues by conveying, when he was in difficult circumstances, the impression of being a little boy who had just been caught in a naughty act.

There was nothing of logic about Charles. He moved with the whim of the moment. If he had five dollars in his pocket that was designated for a haircut and he saw a beautiful piece of material, the hair would be left to grow longer while the urge to possess the material was satisfied. That evening the material, after one showing, probably would be shoved into a drawer never to be taken out again. Doris Humphrey revealed that once she brought Charles a beautiful hand-woven Indian rug from Canada as a gift. He wanted to use it immediately as a costume for a new dance and without thought or care, took his scissors to it and changed its purpose in life.

Charles loved to talk. He wasn't selective. Anyone who would give him attention became a ready victim. Many marvelous hours were spent in the Carnegie Tavern, which was located across the street from the stage door of the City Center Theater. We listened to Charles tell engrossing tales of past years of Doris, Martha, Louis, José, Miss Ruth and Ted.

Charles' 16th Street studio was one of the first multi-purpose dance spaces to be devised. It was an arrangement that fulfilled the needs of the Humphrey-Weidman Company in those early years, allowing them an excellent space for classes, rehearsals, and performances. In concept, it was far ahead of its time. The studio was situated behind a Chinese laundry. One entered through a narrow passageway into the school office. The most imposing object that the office contained was a distinctive bust of Doris Humphrey that had been sculpted by Isamu Noguchi. Even though Doris had removed herself from the premises a few years earlier, one felt that through that sculpture, she still dominated the activities that went on in the building. The small audience section and large dancing space lay beyond the office. Even when the audience section lay empty during class, it conveyed a feeling of professionalism. The idea of taking class in a theater lent a special quality: the sense of performance was vastly heightened.

Charles actually lived illegally in an apartment in the basement of the building. These lower depths were also stuffed with crates filled with costumes and sets from the old Humphrey-Weidman Company. The whole building was dark and eerie in quality and Edwardian in style.

By 1950, the expenses for the running of the 16th Street studio had grown extensively. Rents in the area were slowly rising and at the same time the enrollment in Charles' dance classes was rapidly diminishing. The building was also a firetrap, and in order to keep the studio operating, payoffs had to be made. A certain official from the fire department would appear unexpectedly every month seemingly materializing out of the mist and on having been given the required sum of money, quickly disappearing back into it.

One afternoon I was in the studio after having taken a class, when some of the students who had just left came running frantically back into the office, crying that the payoff man was coming down the street. Before I could turn around, Charles had disappeared. Immediately, everyone in the office assumed calm and unsuspicious poses. The official entered and requested to see Charles. He was quickly told that Charles was not in the studio at that moment and no one knew exactly when he would return. Suspecting that something was amiss, the man hung around the building for a long time before finally departing.

Once he was gone, I was sent down to the basement to ferret out Charles from the back of the costume crates where he had been hiding.

He didn't have enough cash on hand to make the payoff. When I found him, he was crouching like an animal, shaking in terror of being caught. The lack of funds that places such an established artist as was Charles Weidman in that kind of debasing situation is a tragic comment on the state of the arts in the United States.

On off-seasons of the opera, Charles would once more return to his studio and teach and work with his company. He had only a few performing dates and they were usually in the near vicinity. Sometimes, while the company took a day's journey out of town for a performance, and no one else was available, I was asked to teach Charles' classes. This was a very easy process as the patterns of movement were so set that I had only to decide what arrangement of them I wanted to make. While it left little room for error, it also left little room for creativity. Some teachers such as Peter Hamilton, Carl Morris, and Betty Osgood followed the set forms during the first part of the class, but then created their own material for the locomotor section. These were the most satisfying sessions.

Charles had a fertile and creative mind for choreography. *Lynchtown*, *Lincoln Portrait*, Thurber's *Fables* and *Flickers*. (I will always regret not having been able to see Charles dance in his *On My Mother's Side* and *Daddy Was A Fireman*), all showed the excellent range of his abilities from high drama to what might be deemed low comedy. Charles claimed that his own gift as a comedian lay in his sense of timing. His use of the double-take closely resembled the various types of *mie* which are a Japanese form that are used by the *aragoto* actors in the highly stylized Kabuki Theater of Japan. This was permeated by the little boy quality that he often used in everyday life and which gave him a special brand of innocence for the stage.

On one occasion in Burlington, Vermont, one of the male dancers became ill the night before the performance. Charles could cover most of the parts with the dancers at hand, but needed someone for short sections of *Lynchtown* and *Flickers*. Being a somewhat fast study, he asked me to fill in. It was my only opportunity to dance in Charles' company, but I pride myself on it. To perform in *Lynchtown* and *Flickers* two pieces that were so opposite in quality, was challenging and satisfying. The company members who knew the dances already, taught them to me. Not Charles. Charles was completely isolated the whole day and evening of the performance. He had enough to do at his age to raise his energy to a level at which he could perform, and to maintain a credibility that would meet the standard that he had established for himself in the past.

As a choreographer, Charles was a very easy taskmaster, perhaps a little too easy. By the time that I joined the City Center Opera Company, he had already choreographed successfully the dances for the repertory operas of *Carmen, Turandot,* Prokofiev's *Love of Three Oranges,* and several others. Except for those few of us who were new, the dancers already were familiar with the choreography, so again the major teaching was done by them rather than Charles. Charles' talents were reserved for honing and refining, as best he could, our varied abilities, trying to bring us into an effective, cohesive group.

Charles' choreographic powers began to wane as his addiction to alcohol increased. It didn't seem to diminish his energy for creativity, but rather the ability to analyze his own work accurately. The mind kept functioning with its familiar rapidity, but the sensitivity to that which took shape was deeply dulled.

During my last season, with the company, Charles was assigned a new Italian opera to choreograph, *The Three Ruffians* by Ermanno Wolf-Ferrari. It had a lovely, funny, Venetian, roof-top ballet within it which was just waiting to be created and we were all looking forward to working on it. When Charles started the dance, we immediately knew that it was not in the correct mood for the opera. At this point feeling inadequate, Charles had fallen back on his, up-to-now, sure fire and successful mime. Once he had completed the choreography for the new opera, we were brought downstairs onto the stage to show Laszlo Halasz, the opera company director, what we had done. Mr. Halasz was a most tactful man. After seeing the disaster which Charles had created, he praised him highly as to his general choreographic gifts. He then suggested subtly that the choreography was not in the correct style for the opera, but he was sure that Charles could create a much better dance than that which he had just seen. He then repeated to Charles the quality that he felt was necessary for the dance section and gave Charles two days in which to accomplish it.

Back to the studio we went to start anew. But instead of following Mr. Halasz' suggestions, Charles began to repeat exactly what he had just presented with only a few minor changes. We tried to persuade him to take a different tack, but to no avail. Two days later we again showed the ballet. This time Mr. Halasz was not so patient. He gave Charles an ultimatum that either by 1:00 P.M. the next day, Charles would show him the kind of dance that he wanted or he would use that section as a musical interlude. The final dress rehearsal would take place immediately following the showing at 2:00 P.M., and the premier performance was that night.

Early the next morning we all met in the upper rehearsal studio. It was now or never. Again Charles began his same pattern, seemingly eternally stuck in one train of thought. This time we tried much more forcefully to redirect him toward what Mr. Halasz had suggested. There was one woman among us, Bodil Genkel, who Charles respected greatly. She was a Danish dancer whose energy, and positive enthusiasm, were equally captivating. She had a strangely angular body and keenly perceptive mind and she managed with ease to make both of them accomplish whatever she wanted them to attain. Charles finally realizing that a new path had to be taken, put Bodil in charge and made her the central figure of the dance as a character entitled, "She who hangs laundry". The rest of us were the laundry in one form or another which made last minute costuming very easy.

Once the basic idea had been created, Charles excused himself, saying he would be right back, and left the room. At first we were at a loss, but knowing that time was running short, Bodil suggested that we go ahead and begin the dance as a communal effort, and when Charles returned, we would show him what we had done. We all agreed and proceeded to choreograph a beginning section. When Charles returned, we showed him what we had choreographed. He seemed neither surprised nor upset that we had begun without him. He made some suggestions; we ran through it a few times incorporating his ideas and then Charles stated again that he had to leave.

With Charles out of the room, we continued to create. He returned after about thirty minutes and asked us to start the dance from the beginning. We did, adding to it our newly created section. He commented, suggested and then left once more. This pattern was repeated several times before I spotted Charles from the window headed down the street and into the Carnegie Tavern. Each time on his return, Charles was a slight bit more inebriated. Little-by-little we, dancers, inched our way through the choreography, and by 12:00 noon we had it completed. A few run-throughs and we were ready for the showing.

We tremulously went downstairs as scheduled where we found the stage fully set for the dress rehearsal. Charles accompanied us on very unsteady legs. Rejection now would be a cruel blow, not only for us, but also for Charles whose ballet it was supposed to be. Our worries were groundless. Upon completion of the showing, Mr. Halasz applauded enthusiastically.

"Charles, I knew you could do it", he praised.

Charles smiled back through somewhat bleary eyes and said nothing. By the opening performance that night, Charles had acquired another successful opera. The *New York World Telegram*'s review the next day read, "One of the highlights of the new production is an underwear dance. Yes, in the second scene which takes place on a roof top, the red flannels and white lingerie climb down from the clothes line and come to life, claw at each other, crawl, spin, stretch, twist and tumble. It is first-rate comedy, it suits the music to a b.v.d. and is, like the whole production something you will undoubtedly want to see. It is the work of Charles Weidman."

After three seasons with the opera, I left, as I wanted to focus more directly on my concert dancing. I had very little contact with Charles thereafter. Every once in awhile I would return for a class or two in whatever studio he was teaching. Because of financial troubles, he had to give up the 16th Street studio. Charles' drinking increased a great deal. Finally he was brought to Bellevue Hospital because of being overcome by delirium tremens. A former student of Charles, hearing of the situation, went to the hospital, got custody of him, and took Charles into his own home. It was a grueling task for him to undertake for the recovery was long. To Charles' credit, his personality was such that it created a distinctive loyalty among his students.

Many years later after I had moved to California, I saw Charles once more in San Francisco. Marni and I had dinner with him in a traditional restaurant in Chinatown. He seemed once again his old self; clear, charming, lucid, humorous, and full of his many tales, some old and some new. Charles was able to return to his career and continued teaching and choreographing. He traveled throughout the country sharing his spirit and special talents with dancers all over the United States. One day after teaching a class in his New York studio, Charles lay down to rest. He slept never to awake. It was a rest well earned.

ON DORIS HUMPHREY

Of all of the American innovators in modern dance, Doris Humphrey probably is considered the most controversial. Critics are seldom dispassionate when discussing her, but rather express themselves violently on one side or the other. By one faction, Doris is described as a cool, calculated woman, acidly bitter because of never having achieved the acclaim which she honestly felt that she deserved. The other faction sees her as heroic and courageous, a gifted choreographer who was able to use dance in formulated ways that reflected the ideals of a utopian society. Both sides agree on the point of view that Doris was not known to be an easy person to work with. Personally there were only a few select people that she allowed to come within close range of her, and those individuals were carefully chosen.

For me, upon first meeting her in 1949, Doris seemed like a demanding and angry matriarch, one who was most difficult to please. Assuredly the agony that was caused by her arthritic hip and which made her increasingly immobile, was a major element in the expression of her personality. A great deal of what people felt to be anger must have been the projection of her physical pain.

Doris's strength of character and will power are legendary. Through sheer determination, she forced herself to continue to dance despite her physical infirmities. She never oppressed others with the magnitude of her disability, but internalized it which must have made the problem even more difficult to handle.

Through the use of chair choreography, Doris continued to create dances, relying on her highly trained kinesthetic sensitivity to fulfill her mentally constructed works. The spartan attributes which Doris exhibited gave to her personality the quality of a New England woman of puritanical background rather than an openly creative dancer/choreographer from the midwest, which she actually was.

Nevertheless, Doris's life was an organized plan which she carried out with great care. Her physical disabilities were not a part of that plan nor was the cancer which eventually ended her life at a relatively early age. The rest: her marriage, her child, her career, seemed to make up one of her better structured dances, but a dance which was completed by an unpredictable and sad ending.

The three women who led the modern dance movement in the 1930's were easily placed into ready-made categories by most dancers and critics of the time. Hanya was the pedagogue; Martha, the dancer/performer; Doris, to most, the choreographer.

I have always felt that Doris was underrated as a dancer. I was amazed by her commanding regal projection and excellent technical control. What seemed lacking in Doris was the passion of the instant. Regality took the place of emotion. Although Doris did not have the hypnotic power of Martha, in performance she had a powerful stature which drew the eye of the audience and held onto it. In a sense Doris, as a performer, was far ahead of her time. Long-legged, lean and dispassionate in approach, today, she would be right at home as an outstanding performing member of the Merce Cunningham Dance Company or some equally abstract modern group.

Doris's ability to organize material must have helped immensely in her choreography. She came to all rehearsals with every phrase of music well thought out and planned. This allowed her to develop outstanding structural dances that resembled the great classical works of architecture in their monumental proportions, but disallowed the probing and deepening which was always necessary for the growth of more emotional pieces.

Two works choreographed by Doris oppose this supposition. *Lament for Ignacio Sanchez Mejias*, based on the poem of Garcia Lorca, was an emotionally devised arrangement of the spoken word and dance movement. Doris could not have found a more excellent protagonist for the work than her favorite dancer, José Limón. She used his elegance and strength to present forcefully this epic tragedy, sensitively varying the tensions of the work in order to achieve the greatest effect. The haunting *Ruins and Visions* proved to be a large step forward for Doris. It opened the rigid framework that she had established for most of her pieces and ventured into a theatricality which had heretofore been alien to her choreography.

Doris was always the teacher. Her exactness in instruction established rigid parameters which, for students, always clarified the subject matter upon which they were working, but when used in choreography left little leeway for creativity in performance. Whether one agrees with the ideas that Doris expounds or not, her teachings on choreography have contributed vast amounts of material on the subject and have stimulated endless discussions.

My professional experiences with Doris over the years were not exactly pleasant. Where there were difficulties, the fault was my inability to fulfill the technical requirements that Doris demanded and my failure to complete the different personal commitments that I had made with her. The one time that we worked together amicably was the one time that each of us seemed to meet the professional needs of the other.

When I left the Neighborhood Playhouse in 1949 to begin my intense study of dance, along with Hanya's classes and classical ballet, I had also begun to study with José Limón. Men were at a premium and were often used before they were sufficiently trained. I got along with José and Pauline, his wife, very well so that when Doris found that she was shy one man for a revival of her *Variations and Conclusion from New Dance* which she was recreating with her repertory class, Pauline suggested to her that I might be available. The dance was to be performed at Adelphi College and the YM-YWHA on Lexington Avenue.

I was overwhelmed by the opportunity to dance for Doris. Even more, I was to perform José's original solo in the work. The entire dance consisted of a series of solos, ending in a trio and a finale of unison movement. José's solo was very difficult for me. It was extremely complex rhythmically, threes in movement against quarter notes and strongly accented syncopations. Danced in clusters of sevens, the movement consisted of sharp leg thrusts, off-centered turns, body pitches and wild jumps. For most dancers, it would be an exciting challenge, but for a novice of a few months of dancing, it grew into a horror. Accomplishment of the task nearly became impossible. I have never toiled over any part to the degree that I did for those two performances, but try as I might I could seldom be on the correct foot at the correct time. Doris, who was famous for always being in cool control of herself, came close to losing that control in her desperation with me. Instead she shot her vitriolic comments piercingly at my sensitive skin. The more Doris let loose her barbs, the more tense I became, and the more difficult the entire situation grew to be.

The Adelphi College performance was passable and I breathed a sigh of relief when it was over. We did the performance at the YM-YWHA and I danced no better but no worse. Following the last performance, I went up to Doris and thanked her for the chance that she had given me to dance in the piece. She was greeting her admirers on the stage and in response turned to me with the comment, "Well, I hope it hasn't been too much for you. It almost was for the rest of us," and turned around to continue her conversation.

Bad as I had been, her comment took me completely by surprise. It hung like a cloud over me for many of the following months.

The summer of 1952 I went to the American Dance Festival at Connecticut College as a part of the company of the Dudley-Maslow-Bales Trio. In the first week of the session, Doris asked me if I could dance in the *Variations and Conclusion* again as she was setting it on the Limón Company. This time I was to be a member of the trio that occurred at the end of the dance. 1952 was a few years and many technique classes past my earlier fiasco of working with Doris and by now, I was beginning to feel a little more in control of my body and legs and thus much more technically capable.

I asked and secured permission to perform in Doris's work from Dudley–Maslow–Bales. They assured me that all was well as long as there would be no conflict with their own rehearsals. The trio section of the dance was fast moving and exhilarating, so I thoroughly enjoyed the movement. Sweeping slides and bursts of elevation prevailed. The entire cast of the dance was outstanding. José and Pauline Koner performed the roles originally danced by Doris and Charles Weidman. Every performance at the beginning of the dance, I stood in the downstage-right corner of the stage with José and Pauline on either side of me. The banter that was exchanged between the two of them up to the last minute was enough to drive the dance totally out of my mind; nevertheless, I was delighted to be given another try at such a kinesthetically exciting work. Doris never did mention our previous working relationship, nor was it necessary. We were starting over with a fresh and new approach. The following fall I performed the dance again in The Limón season at The Juilliard School.

In 1953 Bethsabee de Rothschild conceived the idea for a second Festival of American Dance. She gathered under one banner most of the prominent modern dancers and choreographers in the United States. For the festival Bethsabee commissioned some newly choreographed works and sponsored some revivals. Among these was to be a new dance, *Ritmo Jondo* choreographed by Doris to the music of Carlos Surinach and a revival of Martha Graham's *Letter To The World*. José's company on whom Doris was to choreograph the new work did not have the large men's contingent that it later developed, so Doris was forced to select the three extra men that she needed. I was one of those that was chosen.

Doris, with her usual sense of thoroughness, started the dance a great deal ahead of time in order to forestall any last minute pressures. Rehearsals were at Dance Player's Studios and Doris moved ahead rapidly with the choreography. She was nearing the end of the third and final section of the work when through misuse and overuse while dancing, I developed water on the knee. The doctor's advice was to stop all physical activity until the inflammation had completely subsided which might be a matter of months. That wasn't the route that I desired to take.

Besides dancing in *Ritmo Jondo* on the festival, I was also scheduled to dance with Pearl Lang in one of her dances, *Rites*. Although, there was a lot of jumping in her choreography which would be difficult, the dance had already been performed, so rehearsing for it would be minimal.

At this moment, Martha Graham called. She needed one more man for her revival of *Letter To The World* and wondered if I would be available.

"I don't know if you have other commitments, but I would like you to work with us," she beguilingly purred.

I was fully aware that Martha knew exactly what my commitments were, but she obviously felt confident that it wouldn't make any difference.

She was right. Without any thought I said, "Yes."

I knew that I might never get another chance to work with her.

I was completely knowledgeable of the difficulties that would arise, the circumstances surrounding the situation, and the path that I would have to take in order to rearrange my priorities, but there was no question of my decision.

Doris and Martha had never been known for their friendliness toward one another. Even from their early days at Denishawn, they were strongly competitive. By 1953, the two were hardly speaking. There was no possible way that I could appear with both of their groups on the same festival. Pearl was a member of Martha's Company, so that presented no problem, but to appear both with Martha and Doris was an impossibility.

My knee gave me a way out of the situation. Being afraid to take action immediately, I continued attending Doris's rehearsals for a few more weeks. Finally, facing the inevitable, I picked up the telephone and called her.

"*Ritmo Jondo* is too difficult physically for my knee because of the jumping, and I feel I might injure myself permanently if I continue. I am going to dance in Pearl's *Rites* as I already know it, and can just do the performance."

I drew a long breath.

"I'm going to dance in Martha's *Letter To The World* as the movement is simpler and there is little elevation."

It all stumbled out of my mouth in jerky gasps. When I finished, there was a long pause on the other end of the phone. I could hardly breath in anticipation of Doris's reply.

Finally she responded, "I think if you don't do one dance, you shouldn't do any."

Another long pause as I gathered courage, "I am sorry, Doris, but I have made my decision."

I was growing more and more insecure by the second.

Doris slammed down the telephone.

I was totally in the wrong, and yet I believe that one time during most people's lives they choose to act against what they know to be morally and ethically right in order to gain some impossible goal. One has to consider the benefits and liabilities, and in the balance make the decision. This is one time that I did such a thing. I am not sorry that I did it, and I would do it again. But I have never lost a certain feeling of guilt because of my actions.

After that entanglement, Doris refused to speak to me for many years. José spoke, but sharply. Only Pauline Lawrence accepted my apology, saying she was sure that I would eventually return. I spent many summers at the American Dance Festival teaching Martha's technique. Each summer Doris was there and I tried in every way to make amends for my fall from grace. As often as I could, I would get her lunch at the snack bar, carrying her tray to her table. When I started to choreograph, I asked if she would criticize my dances. She did, most graciously and succinctly. My earlier betrayal was never again mentioned by either of us, but it was a handicap to our relationship which was never overcome.

The interaction between Doris and Martha was never a happy one, personally or professionally. In the early years, Doris sat in the catbird seat. She was the favorite of Miss Ruth while Martha was pushed away and given to Ted Shawn to train. In those years, Martha was made to observe Doris through jealous eyes. As their careers developed after leaving the protection of Denishawn, their positions reversed. Martha achieved a reputation and fame which always seemed to be the envy of Doris.

I have seen them in the same room at Juilliard and Connecticut College. Doris always averted her eyes from Martha's presence in an attempt to ignore her. Martha would finally rise, go over and greet Doris effusively. Her demeanor was blatantly patronizing. Each had their own particular means of attacking the ego of the other and they played the game of combat to the hilt.

It was no wonder that Doris was always a little bitter at what fate had given her. She felt that, because of her physical disabilities, she had been cheated of a full dance career, otherwise, she undoubtedly would have been destined for greater acclaim.

Her contribution to the field cannot be denied. Her dance structures are monuments left as a legacy behind her. Her theories on dance will provide stimulus for academicians for many years into the future. The angry demands that she placed on others, no matter how unpleasant, created a search for perfection which most of us would not have ever pushed ourselves to undertake on our own initiative.

José Limón was fortunate to have had a Doris Humphrey standing behind him. Maybe all of us need a Doris Humphrey, real or imaginary, in the back of our conscience, prodding us, inspiring us to strive constantly toward the best which each of us has to give.

ON JOSÉ LIMÓN

When José Limón first arrived at the Humphrey-Weidman Studio, he was advised by his mentor, Doris Humphrey, that it would be wise for him to return to his original vocation of painting and forget about becoming a dancer. Doris was of the opinion that José was too tight of body and awkward of mind to be molded into a successful performer. What Doris didn't take into account was José's complete obsession with the art of dance, and his passionate and unswerving determination to overcome any personal handicaps that might stand in his way.

José's body, structurally, was a typical example of the male dancer who begins his career only after he has entered his twentieth year. He was burdened with a tight pelvis, and legs which seemed firmly bound together. His extensions were basically nonexistent except through illusionary means. José's feet were flat and heavy, exhibiting little or no articulation.

José's most outstanding feature was a frightening objectivity about himself. He was able to evaluate his assets and liabilities with a clarity that seldom has been accomplished by any other individual dancer. Through sheer labor in analysis, he gained a meticulous knowledge of every muscle of his body. Because of constant, concentrated work, José discovered the boundaries within which he could move without forcing or locking his tendons, muscles, and ligaments. He observed that by dancing within these limitations, he could create the illusion of technical freedom whereas, in actuality, he was beset by vast limitations.

I used to watch José warming up backstage before a performance and wondered how he was able to transform his stiff body into the fluid and articulate medium for movement that he always presented to an audience. I would then watch him on stage, dancing through long phrases of movement giving no hint of the difficulties and limitations that lay within him.

I once questioned him concerning how he achieved this transformation. "In performance never push against your muscles, my boy, to the extent that you reveal that you are struggling. Always create the appearance that there exists within you a much greater range of possibilities for movement than you are using at the moment."

José's energy was enormous. It was matched only by his desire to dance. This and his continuous search for perfection helped him become one of the outstanding male dancers of his time. Certainly there were many more technically accomplished dancers. Certainly there were male dancers whose bodies more easily lent themselves to the facility of movement. Yet, few could match his beautiful and elegant carriage.

Usually, for dancers, the countenance of the performer is of secondary importance to the action of his body, but with José, the face was one of his most striking features. His gaunt, hollow cheeks, his prominent Mexican-Indian facial bone structure, and his smouldering eyes contributed vastly to his theatrical appearance. The charisma that he projected across the footlights was rare to behold. His loss of hair, as he grew older, gave him a much more distinguished appearance than he had possessed as a younger man. The one time that he tried to rectify this loss was in his dance, *Blue Roses* which was based on *The Glass Menagerie*, a play by Tennessee Williams. In the dance, José cast himself in the role of the gentleman caller, and in attempting to appear physically younger by wearing a hairpiece, he completely shattered his own personal image.

José and Pauline Lawrence, his wife, had an excellent working relationship. José's soft spoken manner was countered by Pauline's caustic and direct approach in dealing with other people. She was the only person that I ever knew who could treat Martha Graham as if she were an insignificant younger sister, and get away with it. Those people who thought José was an easy target because of his submissive manner did not count on contending with Pauline.

Pauline, herself, besides being a pianist and an excellent costume designer, had danced with Ruth St. Denis and Ted Shawn for a short time. Her rotund body, made the fact of her dancing a difficult one to imagine. Because of José being extremely unmaterialistic, Pauline took care of all career-management difficulties and business affairs. She paid the bills, solved difficult contractual problems, and kept all of the accounts. José's relationship with some of his male students and dancers must have created many difficult situations for her, but she seemed to manage to compensate for the problems that arose with a certain ease, at least superficially.

Artistically, Pauline never interfered while the process of rehearsing was underway. During the act of creating, José was left on his own to define and structure, but Pauline often paced the back aisles of the theater muttering comments to herself. Later, after the rehearsal had ended, Pauline's thoughts were heard to pour forth in vitriolic and caustic terms.

Like all major figures in dance who organize companies, José's duties expanded far beyond those which took place in the rehearsal halls and theaters where the sweaty reality of dance existed. Money had to be raised and patrons had to be courted and enticed into making major financial contributions. These were necessary endeavors that were used to sustain all companies. The resultant social situations in which these interactions took place were not necessarily unpleasant, but they were definitely time consuming and a drain on the limited energies of every choreographer/dancer/director.

During the short time that I worked with José, I was involved in a surprising number of these social relationships. The dinners which I had with José and Pauline while I was living with Peace and Carmen Alvarez, were familial but they did lead to an interesting situation, especially for one as inexperienced in the ways of the rich and the famous as was I.

José invited the three of us (Peace, Carmen and myself) to attend a dinner that was to be given by a potential sponsor. Why we were invited to the party, I have no idea to this day. Maybe it was to repay us for the many times that he and Pauline had dined at our apartment during the year.

The patron obviously had much to offer José if one was to judge by the sumptuousness of his Park Avenue triplex apartment. At the dinner there were a few other people present. None of them seemed to understand any better than the three of us did why they had been invited to this festive occasion. Only José and our lavish hosts seemed to have knowledge concerning the conspiracy that was taking place. The food was beautiful to behold and delicious to the palate. It was served in buffet style so that I could stuff myself to my heart's content without being the least bit embarrassed. The immediate consumption of whatever I could shovel onto my plate was of prime importance, so during the dinner hour the act of eating occupied my entire attention.

As the evening began to wind down my overindulgence in appetizing food and fruity wines took its effect and left me in a happy, but somewhat sleepy state of inertia. As I was lounging back on a richly decorative sofa, Peace secretly revealed to me that she had been told that this dinner was in fact a money raising event for José. All of the couples at the party were very wealthy and were being asked to contribute to the worthy cause of the José Limón Dance Company.

With this information in mind, I watched José from a new and different point of view. Because of the social situation, José appeared ebullient and most gracious. He was convincingly the most commanding figure in the room, moving from couple to couple with ease and alacrity. Certainly his endless energy which he always used to sustain himself on stage, led him through the evening without faltering for a moment. Peace telephoned José a few days later to thank him for including us in the invitation and out of curiosity inquired if the evening had been a success financially.

"What is money for my dear, except to help others?" responded José evasively but wisely.

In both New York and Connecticut, I had other opportunities to watch José in action while fulfilling different social commitments. Each time he proved himself to be as adept on the social scene as he was on the stage. Another time, a few years later, while I was still living at the exotic theatrical rooming house, the Morgue, I came home one evening to find José eating dinner in the basement kitchen as a guest of the two men who ran the house. Here the occasion was purely relaxed and without any financial ulterior motives. As a result, José let his hair down, what there was left of it, and in that friendly atmosphere he became a marvelously humorous teller of stories involving his early dancing career.

José's untimely death left a great deal of his work unfinished. He was at the end of his performing days, but still had much to accomplish choreographically and pedagogically. In the dressing room at Dance Players Studios after teaching one of his classes, José was holding forth about his great love of dancing.

"But don't get me wrong, my boy, I'm not worried about the future when I am no longer able to dance. When that moment comes, it will be time to direct all of my energy toward developing the dancers of the future".

It is those young dancers of the future who had to bear the brunt of José's early demise, for they missed the personal awareness of his magnetic and powerfully inspired presence.

ON HELEN TAMIRIS

Born a renegade under the legal name of Helen Becker, this unusual woman when she began her dancing career adopted the much more distinctive title of Tamiris. Later, when her performing days ended, she readopted the name of Helen and for the last few years of her life was known among her colleagues by the name of Helen Tamiris.

As a human being Tamiris was a paradox. Exoticism fit one side of her personality like a well-designed sequinned gown, bright and glittering. On the other side, Tamiris displayed a fighting stance for social justice and collaborative reforms. She fought for group action among dancers, feeling that these much beleaguered performers could only exist profitably if they banded together in communal efforts. Her attempts, in this regard, failed as her collaborators were much too individual in approach to give way to any group purpose.

It is strange that even with all of her actions toward unification with others, Tamiris always remained out of the main stream of modern dance. One thought first of the other great contemporary companies: Graham, Humphrey-Weidman, and Holm. One thought of the three matriarchs of modern dance: Martha, Doris, and Hanya. And always a little on the side, slightly to the left, was Tamiris. She was by far the most socially conscious and was certainly the most active in establishing the various reforms in which she believed. Long after the other three had left behind them their revolutionary dances of the 1930's which had been influenced by the loyalists of the Spanish Civil War and other worthy racial and economic causes, Tamiris was still choreographing from a social point of view.

None of the other three leading female creators spoke with enthusiasm about Tamiris. Perhaps she was too openly passionate for the cool stoicism of a Doris Humphrey. Perhaps she was too openly radical for the basic conservatism of a Martha Graham. Perhaps her outspoken, sometimes questioning Americanism was too revolutionary for a Hanya Holm who had a strongly developed sense of patriotism in relation to her newly adopted country. One always thought of the triumvirate, and then there was Tamiris.

She was a fiery woman who always spoke her mind. Often she was lacking in tact, but never spoke purposefully with the intent to hurt another. She had strong convictions and was determined to let nothing interfere with her beliefs. She used these beliefs in her choreographed works. Long before it was fashionable, Tamiris achieved success by combining Negro spirituals with movement. In later years, her spirituals were revived and performed by both black and white dancers. The color of skin of the performers made little difference to the power that they generated.

Tamiris, even as she grew older and ceased dancing, was a physically handsome woman, both facially and in body. She took great pride in her appearance so that when she became devastated by cancer she allowed only her closest friend to visit her.

I was not yet in New York when Tamiris was involved in her early concert years. My first awareness of her was after she had shifted into the world of Broadway musicals. I attended every audition for a Tamiris show that I could. I usually seemed to do better in her tryouts than at any of the others. Tamiris had a special liking for modern dancers and showed them a strong preference in the casting of her shows whenever it was possible. Unlike a good many of the modern concert choreographers, she had the benefit of a New York background and it helped her to exist in the hard-bitten world of Broadway. I almost always made the final line up for each of her musicals only to be eliminated in the last count.

I had never been introduced to Tamiris, but because of attending so many of her auditions, when we met on the street the two of us acted like we were old friends. There was always an openness and directness about her which I found to be refreshingly appealing. She seemed to have little or no pretense and expected none in return from those whom she knew.

Her last Broadway show, and my first, was *Plain and Fancy*, a musical that took place in the Amish countryside of Pennsylvania. It was a low budget sleeper and as Tamiris's fortunes on the Broadway musical scene were on the downgrade, the producers of the show found that they could hire her as the choreographer for a fairly reasonable sum of money. It was a marvelous feeling, after several years of tryouts, to be one of the few men selected from the hundreds who auditioned for the show. I think in my case I was selected because after so many years of auditioning Tamiris may have developed a curiosity concerning what I was actually like.

At the final audition for the musical, we were asked to dance anything that we desired so that Tamiris and the producers could see us perform using the movements with which we felt the most comfortable. I instructed the pianist to improvise seven's and gave him the tempo. I then danced the movement from the trio in Doris Humphrey's *Variations and Conclusions from New Dance*, adding on a little improvisation of my own at the end. I was in! The dance group that was finally chosen was an interesting mixture of modern, ballet, and show dancers. Danny Nagrin, Tamiris's husband, had already been hired as the lead solo dancer.

At the beginning of the rehearsals for *Plain and Fancy*, Tamiris appeared to be in complete control of the situation, but as time progressed tension and desperation became evident. Tamiris choreographed by means of suggestion and indication. Ballet dancers and show dancers who had always been given every little step either by familiar name or exact demonstration, were aghast at her method of choreography.

She was greatly belittled by most of the dancers and I am sure that she was well aware of what they were saying about her.

The worst happening occurred when, in a final dance rehearsal for a scene in which the men were tossed out of a bar door, Tamiris asked us to use more defined movement than the flailing that we had been giving her.

The response of the dancers was, "Show us the movement and we will be glad to do it."

Tamiris thought for a moment, and then in frustration screamed out, "Just give me a north, east, south, west movement."

Tamiris's intention was to have everyone flying in all directions as we came careening out of the bar. The only reaction that she got however, was quite different than her original aim, for all of the male dancers, in immediate response to her words, were sent rolling on the floor in uproarious laughter.

When at her most tense, Tamiris would start pulling at the ringlets that she wore tightly gathered on her forehead. After a long and arduous rehearsal, the ringlets turned into streamers that hung down and covered her eyes. By the end of a difficult rehearsal, the hair would be completely devoid of curl.

Tamiris worked with knowledge and sensitivity when dealing with musicians. Her close collaboration with Al Hague, the composer of *Plain and Fancy*, was fascinating to watch. Al accompanied all of our rehearsals on the piano. Tamiris would create the rhythms and the phrases as she choreographed, specifying clearly the spots in which she wanted the music to mickey-mouse the movement and the places where she definitely did not. Al improvised along with her, following Tamiris' every whim and giving suggestions here or there as he felt was necessary. He would then take home the finalized version of the day's work and return the next morning with all of the music completely written so that whatever changes needed to be made could be done in the working situation. This, of course, was only the piano reduction. The orchestrated version was to come later. This manner of working illuminated a close relationship between choreography and music that was only made possible by the collaborative efforts of two equally capable and adaptable artists.

The closely interwoven methods that Tamiris and Danny Nagrin used in working together was another point of interest. Tamiris's love and adoration of Danny was clearly evident. He, on the other hand, seemed to place tremendous demands upon her to fulfill his dance requirements. The two had worked together for such a long time that they often understood each other without needing to speak. When they did speak, it was in a language which only the two of them understood, totally indecipherable by anyone else.

Tamiris: "Danillo, give me a bah-bah-ta-dee movement."
Danny: "Helen, I don't think you want a bah-bah-ta-dee. A bah-
          bah-ta-dee-dum-ta-ta-dee-dee would work a lot better."
Tamiris: "No, Danillo, I don't really want that, but you might try
          bah-bah-ta-dee-dum-ta-ta-dee."
Danny: "Alright, I'll try it, but you won't like it."

With that Danny, while at the same time speaking the syllables, would
do a movement representing the rhythmic structure which was defined
by them. With a little more discussion and a bit more trial and error, they
arrived at a mutually acceptable phrase of movement, inventive and
rhythmically exciting. The syllables were always spoken in their rhythmic
pattern, but whether or not they represented something definite in movement, I never knew.

Often while trying to create something spectacular, Tamiris would ask
us to attempt physically impossible and dangerous movements. She
was much better at staging the musical numbers for the show than she
was choreographing the actual dance routines. Her favorite number
in *Plain and Fancy* was called, The Shunning Ballet. It was an actual
modern dance placed in the middle of a Broadway musical and was as
out of sync with the quality of the show as an authentic Amish horse and
buggy would seem if it were found being driven through the center of
New York City. In the dance, our screaming of sin and lust while
propelling ourselves across the stage chopping the air wildly with our
arms, didn't make the movement any more convincing.

The musical, not looking very successful, was put together just in
time, and with great anxiety, opened out of town in New Haven,
Connecticut. Here The Shunning Ballet was literally ripped out of the
entrails of the musical as the reworking of the entire show began in
earnest. In Boston a lovely Lantern-light Ballet was added. It was danced
to the lyric song of Young and Foolish and fit the mood of the moment
excellently.

By Philadelphia, everything was falling into place and the musical
received its first good reviews. There were a few more last minute cuts
and changes as the show gathered momentum on its way to the Mark
Hellinger Theatre in New York. After rehearsing a few days in the big
city, *Plain and Fancy* opened to excellent reviews and was performed
on Broadway successfully a number of years. Once the show began its
continuous run, for me, the excitement dimmed, and I remained with it
only a few months more.

Not too long before her death from cancer, Tamiris and Danny separated.
Why, I have no idea but it was devastating for Tamiris. Like the fighter
that she always was, she overcame the obvious external-hurt, but few
people ever knew what sorrow she carried within her.

I saw Tamiris often at The High School of Performing Arts following the separation. Rachael Yocom, the Director of Dance, knowing Helen's value and her emotional need, brought Tamiris into the school as much as she could to teach and to choreograph. She worked well with the students, having a real understanding of their energy and a close sympathy with their inherent wildness. They, in turn, responded well to her.

In spare moments at the school, I enjoyed the talks that we would have while sitting in the third floor dance office. We discussed everything from the students, to the New York dance scene, to the political unrest in Bulgaria, to the socio-economic factors of the drought in southwestern United States. Whatever the subject, Tamiris approached it with an enthusiasm, knowledge, and passion. She was a caring and involved human being as well as a marvelous conversationalist.

During one of our talks when I mentioned that I was thinking of asking for a grant that would help to start an intended project of mine, Tamiris's response was, "Don't do it at the beginning. Start the project. Put out your best first. Show them what you can do, and only then ask for the money to complete it. You will never be given anything for nothing."

Helen Tamiris's life was spent showing.us all what she could do in endless different projects. She battled equally for her own place in the dance world and for all of her colleagues as well. One can firmly believe that the battle was always fought cleanly and fairly and at her best.

ON LOUIS HORST

Dressed in my new royal-blue, sleek and shiny, two-piece dance uniform, I entered the make-do studio of the old Neighborhood Playhouse with a certain degree of trepidation. The nylon outfit that I wore not only clung to 'my body in strange places, but it rubbed against the edges of my mind as well, causing a surge of anxiety to pass over me. This was to be my first official dance class and as I sidled into the room, I was being cut in two by my first official dance belt which was the overly tight athletic supporter that I had been instructed to wear underneath my orchesis looking garb.

The subject matter of this initially scheduled session was choreography and it was to be taught by Louis Horst. Since I knew nothing about the art of dance, it didn't seem strange to me that I was to have a class in composition a few days before I had ever experienced a technique class. Both the dance belt and the choreography class fit my psyche a little awkwardly and uncomfortably.

Because most of us in the class felt a certain amount of nervousness, we arrived a good deal before the targeted time for the beginning of the class, and sat waiting for the instructor in anticipation. The only thing that any of us actually knew about Louis Horst was that he had been the early companion of Martha Graham, preceding Erick Hawkins by a few years. In our mind's eye we each pictured Louis Horst to be a rather romantic and dashing Lothario.

Finally the door opened and, to our surprise, in walked a heavy-set, elderly gentleman. His clothes which were the usual arrangement of a dark suit, shirt, and tie, hung loosely from his body and, although clean, looked badly crumpled from lengthy use. His strongest feature were jowls that equaled those of any bulldog. They hung down heavily from his face with such a weight that the red from underneath his eyeballs was constantly revealed, although sometimes it was hidden by the eye glasses that he almost always wore. With the glasses removed, his countenance took on the look of a very tired creature who might have come from some strange and alien planet. On the crown of this amazing face, lay a mass of creamy white hair that was untouched by any thinning. A Lothario Louis Horst was not, but he was an interesting and compelling figure who immediately commandeered attention.

Louis shuffled rather than walked into the room. He moved with his legs fairly far apart in order to gain a little better balance for his excessive weight. He progressed slowly across the room in a direct line toward the piano, and upon reaching it, he slumped down onto the piano bench with a sigh of relief.

Louis was accompanied by a youngish woman, whose name we later learned was Nina Fonaroff. She followed a few paces behind him which immediately defined their relationship. Nina was thin and small of stature, but possessed large, placating eyes. She purposefully worked at enlarging this facial feature by blinking both eyes constantly whenever she looked intently at any individual. Her hair, reddish in hue, gave the appearance of having been stuck in a curling iron for an overly long period of time. This wiry array was pulled back off of her face and tied behind her neck.

Louis Horst, on first meeting, displayed an evident humor, but seemed to most of us to be a bit ineffectual. His snorting and puffing as he spoke added to the strange picture of his total presence. I felt a distinct disappointment. Louis did not fit into any of my expectations of a dance teacher. It was a disappointment that was soon to be dispelled, for I quickly learned that I had to deal with Louis Horst with complete respect. He was capable of heaping ridicule on those of us who did not complete his assigned tasks successfully. All humor, wit, and satire during the class meetings were left to Louis and he had a wealth of it ready for use.

During the first year at the Playhouse, we studied Louis' Pre classic Dance Forms using dances such as the Pavane, Sarabande, Galliard,

Gigue, and Courante to help us elucidate the structuring of movement. Nina Fonaroff taught half of the students in the class the original dances as they had been performed in the French courts of Louis XIV, while the other half experimented with these same forms. We used their rhythmic structure and qualitative ideas to create a "free movement" or modern dance study. It seemed simple enough, but I was to find that it was a much more complex task than it appeared to be on the first try.

After two weeks had passed, I was ready to present my first assigned study, a Pavane. I began the composition on my knees, facing straight front toward the audience and then started to bend backward, slowing arching to the rear until my head touched the floor behind me. This I believed at the time to be a feat of technical brilliance.

With my crotch brazenly affronting the viewers, I drew the immediate sardonic comment from Louis, "I know you were trying to show us something, but I'm not sure that we were really interested in seeing it."

I was devastated. My new and exciting world of dance came crumbling down around my feet.

As all dances had to be shown twice, there could be no improvisation without it being detected. Every composition had to have a title when it was shown. Because of our emotional immaturity, we students created many "Revolt" and "Imminent Shadow" types of choreography. We all bared our souls before Louis and Nina and they, with great patience, dealt constructively with our evident ineptness.

For those of us who were chosen to return to the Playhouse for the second year, composition sessions with Louis consisted of his more advanced Modern Forms class. These studies began by dealing with the various different dynamic qualities of music and then progressed to the use of the already established forms of modern painting as points of departure.

In order to break the monotony of a continuous parade of compositions, we sometimes choreographed large group dances, working within the style that we were studying at the moment. Often these group works and our individual studies were performed on the Playhouse workshops. No matter how untalented we were both technically and choreographically, we all looked forward to having our creative efforts chosen for the showings.

Louis' approach to teaching dance choreography not only gave the actors at the Playhouse the chance to practice the craft of structuring movement, but it created for them an increased sensitivity in their relationship to the placement of other performers when on stage. Even more, Louis' teaching opened up to us a whole new awareness of the related art forms of music and painting.

It was no secret in the dance world that Louis loved pretty and charming women. I had gathered this information about him during the different times when he and Nina came to dinner at the apartment that I shared with Peace and Carmen Alvarez. Louis was always charming and openly solicitous toward all of the women who were present, and they, in turn, were obviously infatuated with him.

Pretty women without charm, brains, or talent certainly didn't attract his attention, but those fair souls who possessed a flair for working with Louis, definitely commanded his continuous interest. He dealt constructively also with the few men who were in his classes, but it was from a completely different point of view.

One not only learned composition from Louis Horst, one also learned how to survive in the demanding world of dance. Louis' criticisms were ruthless. Nothing was corrected by implication. He was often called sadistic by those who could not meet his high standards, but even Louis' supposed sadism was purposeful. It was aimed at developing a heightened awareness for movement within the individual, and as a result allowed the individual to develop an increased freedom of creativity.

Louis had a keen eye for talent and relished the challenge of bringing it forth, especially when it was lodged tightly in a delicate and pretty shape. Tears were constantly evident as Louis broke away the barriers that lay across the creative core of many a charming individual. For the students who could meet his challenges and answer his demands, Louis became a constant guide, and led the young choreographers through the rough obstacle course of dance composition.

As closely as Louis was related to Martha Graham professionally and personally, he also was the musical advisor for most of the other leading modern dancers of that day. His influence on all of them was major.

Louis Horst changed the approach toward the making of dances in two different but related, revolutionary ways. He developed a specific method for the teaching of choreography. Until the 1930's composition teaching in any guise had been almost entirely nonexistent. He also managed to free dance from the restrictive bonds that music had placed upon it.

Up to the early part of the twentieth century, choreography had been created only on a hit or miss basis. If the intended choreographer had talent, he displayed it by deftly putting various steps together in a manner which would clearly convey his intended meaning. If there was no obvious talent shown or difficulties arose in the process of choreographing, he gave up the craft and found other more productive outlets for his creative energy.

By relating dance composition to the various forms of music and painting, Louis discovered an effective means that opened up structural possibilities whereby dance choreography could be worked at and practiced as a craft. The choreographic abilities of the individual, whether evident or latent, could thus be developed. Louis' demanding and exacting method of teaching made potential choreographers probe and search deeper and deeper for new and better ways to construct their dances.

Dance composition at this time usually followed the chosen musical structure in its phrasing, often even to the extent of repeating verbatim actual note patterns and accents. The forms of music have been evident for a long period of time, and by following these forms dance found that they were excellent models for its own structural shape as well. In addition, Louis' procedure in freeing choreography from the facile pull of music was to make all choreographers count the music and choreograph in silence using only the predetermined counts, in order to allow no chance for the choreographer to follow the music's melodic line and dynamic energy. With this innovation, dance began its progression on a long and circuitous path, eventually establishing itself as an independent art form.

Louis not only taught composition and composed music for many of the dancer's creations, but he also edited a magazine, *The Dance Observer*. He had originated this periodical with the intention of giving the modern dance movement a special voice within the dance world; he often wrote articles and criticism for it. Strangely, his most noted review entailed no writing whatsoever.

At the beginning of his choreographic career, Paul Taylor had given a concert at the Lexington Avenue Y.M.-Y.W.H.A.'s Kaufman Auditorium. In this program Paul's movement progressed from zero to minimal and back to zero again. What little motion did exist within the dances was all of natural derivation. In the *Dance Observer* of the following month, Louis reviewed the concert in kind. He said nothing at all about it, but left the column allotted for the review completely blank.

A short time following the concert and its subsequent *Dance Observer* review, Paul and I stopped off at a Third Avenue bar on the way home after a particularly arduous class with Martha Graham. Our conversation turned to Paul's recent concert and I questioned him as to why he had choreographed it in such a manner. I had enjoyed its uniqueness, but the philosophy in back of the effort peaked my curiosity.

"Well", said Paul in his usual drawl, "It was just something I had to get out of my system, but I guess its going to be a long time before I get the audience to come back."

We were sitting on stools near the end of the bar. Slowly out of a puff of second-hand smoke that hovered above a stool on the other side of Paul, a strange, ephemeral figure began to materialize. With Paul's statement the figure quickly became delineated. Leaning forward toward us, he obviously, was trying to overhear our conversation.

"You just may never get them back, my boy, after that last concert you gave," the man chirped matter-of-factly. Immediately I recognized him. The figure was George Tacet, Paul's Jimeny Cricket who was always checking on Paul's conscience.

"Oh, be quiet Tacet. No one asked you to butt in", Paul answered him.

"It's about time somebody did butt in, or your career is going straight down the tubes, and won't be worth diddlyspit."

"I learned a lot by doing that concert, Pops."

"You learned that Louis Horst didn't think enough of it to even write a word about it."

"I really liked Louis' review. It was a little too short, but it had a – a certain unique charm about it."

"Well, you had best listen to him and change your ways – and soon."

The two became more and more involved in their argument. Being excluded, I slipped off the bar stool and left them engrossed in their heated discussion. Either Tacet or Louis must have had a tremendous influence upon Paul for he is still making dances, of a kind which, I am sure, both Dr. Tacet and Louis Horst would definitely appreciate.

Louis was always stubborn, and willful, but as he grew older, he became increasingly exacting and rigid in the manner in which he wanted studies created. There were often complaints that Louis had become too set in his ways, that there was no more room for creativity in his classes. Perhaps Louis had seen and experienced so much over the long period of his teaching that he became absolute in his ideas concerning what people needed to learn. Those students of choreography who because of these complaints, did not take advantage of his teachings were the obvious losers.

One hot summer's end at the Connecticut College American Dance Festival, Marni and I, and two of our daughters, Marina and Raegan (Ellis had not yet been born) were walking on the campus and met Louis by accident in front of the Crozier-Williams Gymnasium as he was coming out of the administrative offices. Louis studied our two small girls who were playing on the grass while we adults were exchanging a few pleasant words.

Still gazing at them, Louis wistfully but factually, stated "I guess I won't be around to teach them, will I?"

The inevitability of time. But it was true. They were never to be his students, for Louis Horst died January 27, 1964 while they were still children.

ON MARTHA GRAHAM

The only way to create an honest, comprehensive analysis of the personality of Martha Graham would be to have every person who had ever been affected by her write his or her own individual descriptive passage. One could then compile the various essays into a large volume, leaving for the reader the task of piecing into one cohesive whole a specific impression of her individuality. Martha was completely different to every person with whom she dealt during the process of a day. The company administrator, the grocer, a dancer in the group, the doctor, a new student at the school, the taxi driver, her sister Geordie, each drew from Martha a different temperamental reaction depending upon her immediate needs and her general mood of the moment. Also, to every individual with whom Martha was involved, she seemed a completely different person from one day to the next. None of us could ever feel secure in predicting Martha's reaction to the different traumatic or even everyday occasions that might arise.

Rather than conform to her surrounding environment such as do most creatures in nature, Martha had the power to make her environment conform to her. She arranged and rearranged people and situations to fit within the scheme of her plans.

All human relationships bear the weight of a certain degree of hypnotic power. One of Martha's greatest assets was her high degree of this power. Whether consciously or unconsciously used, it was the prime factor in most of her personal dealings. We all fell under her hypnotic spell and were drawn into her world as she beguilingly played the seductive siren, Circe, to each of our willing Ulysses.

Martha enjoyed the play of human relationships. The manipulation of people was a challenge which supplied her with vital energy. She loved to talk on the telephone. It allowed her to deal at a certain level of confrontation, but always in an abstracted manner.

One night I came back to my loft rather late in the evening to discover Martha had called in great anger. No matter what the hour was when I returned, she wanted me to answer her call. I was fully aware of the problem. Geordie, Martha's sister who ran the school, wanted me to teach the teenage demonstration classes at the end of the school term. Trying to rid myself of instructing children, I had not taught the little ones all year and so felt that I was really in no position to guide them through their paces. Geordie had dashed to Martha with the problem and Martha, in a fury, had called me.

There was no way out but to return Martha's call. By telephoning her, I knew that I would let loose an inevitable tidal wave of wrath and vengeance, but from experience, I was aware that her anger would soon spend itself; nevertheless, the process was never a pleasant one. I finally made the call. Once Martha's fury had run its course and our differences on the matter of teaching were settled, Martha shifted gears into her general late night telephone patter and we relaxed into a two hour phone conversation.

As Martha's personality covered the entire range of human behavior, so did most of her telephone conversations. No one can doubt that she was a philosopher/psychologist of great depth. She had a probing mind which passionately searched out any knowledge that would shed light on present day human personality by creating a direct link between it and the mythology and lore of the ancients. At the opposite side of her behavior, Martha displayed the character of a common fishwife who loved backyard gossip and personal conjecture. This allowed her an indulgence in sexual innuendo and at the same time kept her within the boundaries of her puritanical nature and upbringing.

That night Martha's conversation started with a discussion of her ex-husband, Erick Hawkins. She related to me for the nth time that he had deserted her cruelly. She then went into a lengthy description of her total devastation because of his leaving her while she lay badly injured in London during the first European tour. She ended the discussion of Erick with her usual rationale. The only reason that their marriage didn't work was that she, as a woman, had a much greater talent than he, which dug constantly into his ego. She was probably correct.

From there we progressed to finances, both professional and personal, and the difficulty of being a woman who was the director of a company and a school. According to Martha the struggle was continuous and because of its devious nature, was a constant strain. Martha was probably right on this matter also, but as I lacked any knowledge on the subject, I thought that her concept concerning women was rather silly and exaggerated.

Finally, as always, the conversation narrowed to Martha and my own personal working relationship. No matter how a conversation started, whenever we spoke on the phone it always ended up with the same comments.

"You won't play the game, David. You have to play a game with me. It's not that we are actually lovers, (I emitted an inaudible gasp) but we have to pretend that we are. Every relationship is a game, and one has to be willing to play it to get along in this world."

Bouncing off of my youthful sense of honesty, Martha's statement came as a shockingly dishonest declaration. Since that time, I have reconsidered greatly its validity and have come to various conclusions of my own. It is really not important whether I believe in the playing of games or not. I do think that Martha, herself, honestly believed in it.

Part of Martha's game playing came out of her need for protection. She was always beset by people who wanted a great many things of her. The playing of games allowed her to construct the practical barriers that she felt were necessary to keep everyone at a safe distance. The self-devised games that Martha played covered the whole spectrum of emotions from mock anger to a real sense of compassion. There were two emotional games that were the most evident. One consisted of an authentic but purposeful anger which often spurted out unexpectedly, erupting from her fiery Irish background. Another was an artificial coquetry used with all of the men with whom she was in contact. The least seen of all of Martha's emotional relationships or game playing was her honest expression of compassion without artifice.

In the twenty years of my association with Martha, there were very few occasions in which she reacted in a direct and simple manner. When she brought the books to my loft during my confinement for mumps, her action was extremely thoughtful, but upon confronting me at my door, she fell into her usual pattern of game-playing. When Marni experienced the still birth of our third child, Martha called the hospital to speak with her. Marni knew that she was going to call and dreaded it as this was a time when Martha's artifice was not needed. Following the conversation with Martha, Marni lay back in amazement. Martha had been very simple, very moving, and very helpful. With the aid of the telephone, the game of emotional relationships had come to a halt and reality, for a brief time, had taken effect.

The best example of a simple emotional reaction on Martha's part concerned Martha alone and was at a time when she thought no one was observing her actions. Pearl Lang was preparing to replace Martha for the first time as the Bride in *Appalachian Spring* and after much delay the rehearsal finally began. I was settled in a seat in the darkened theater waiting to see the run-through. Martha, not observing me, sat one row in front and a little to the right. She intently watched the stage as each character entered. When Pearl made her entrance, I could see Martha shiver a little and a few isolated tears roll down her cheeks. A part of her life was being severed and as it was extremely painful, she was hiding her sorrow in the shadows of the theater.

Reality in relationship leads to directness and that was one thing which Martha abhorred. She hated to be confronted by anyone. Her artifice provided her with a means of escape. This does not infer that Martha did not often do extraordinarily thoughtful things for people, but usually her theatricality became clearly interwoven with the deed.

At Marni's initial rehearsal in Israel, Martha brought down the front curtain and refused to let anyone watch while Marni was placed into *Clytemnestra* for the first time. When Bertram Ross danced the role of the

Minotaur in *Errand Into The Maze* in Rangoon, replacing the injured Stuart Hodes, Martha refused to allow anyone backstage to watch. In Israel Martha provided a mask for Glen Tetley without his asking when he was required to be a spear carrier in *Clytemnestra*. He, then, could retain his anonymity while performing this "menial" task. On the first Asian tour when one of the women attempted suicide, Martha remained alone with her while the rest of the company continued on to the next performance. Martha operated at the other extreme of human behavior as well, often becoming ruthless in the demands that she placed upon the members of her company. At times she removed dancers from the group just prior to departure for a tour. Passports and tickets were already in hand when for no known reason she would announce the designated changes. Martha certainly had a right to have whomever she wanted in her company, but her timing was disastrous. One never felt that Martha acted on whim, but it was often difficult to understand the convolutions of her mind. Nothing, in reality, was held sacred except her closely prescribed world of dance and the integrity of her performing company. Martha stood on the pinnacle of her career and those of us who worked for her rotated and whirled like sulfurous clouds beneath her, manipulated by her endless will and power.

Dancers, composers, designers, and choreography, all served Martha's avid and insatiable hunger for dance creation. No person was irreplaceable in her company. When she felt that it was necessary, she could eliminate any one. If a dancer placed too much pressure upon her for parts or other favors, they were soon removed. The same was true with phrases of movement. Any part of any choreography would be eliminated, no matter how beautiful it was, if it did not contribute to the total concept of the dance. Martha's studio was like the cutting room floor of an exacting film editor. Extraordinary passages of dance were continually left upon it to be forgotten with time.

Fittingly, Martha's imagination was always fired by the unusual and different. The "norms" of life and the so-called "normal" people did not interest her at all. One year while teaching the Saturday children's classes, I discovered two little girls, each approximately eleven years of age, who, I felt, posed major problems within the class. One child, when at the barre, would grab it and hang catatonically from it and refuse to let go. The other girl, every Saturday, stole one shoe from each of the other children in the class, and tried to take them home with her.

When I spoke to Martha of the problem, she interrupted me vehemently.

"It is not those two who worry me. They show a direct intent, and interest in what they are doing. It is those other complacent, supposed normal children that I worry about."

Martha truly did enjoy the odd and eccentric.

Martha's ability to speak was inspirational in every aspect of content and performance. Whether it was to a single person, a class or a lecture hall full of people, her discourse often lifted the individuals to levels of consciousness which they had never believed they could attain. One appreciated her speaking abilities not only because of her words, but also because the energy and belief that lay behind the words were used with equal conviction.

I doubt if Martha ever in her life planned a speech. Her manner of presentation was extemporaneous. She had a repertoire of anecdotes which she used over and over again when she could think of nothing new to say. She always hoped that something in the situation, something within the stream of consciousness of her thought, would spark an unusual idea. If it did, the lecture took flight, soaring on high with the use of her creative thinking. If nothing inspired Martha, she still provided a capable lecture, but without her usual magic.

One afternoon in Madras, India, we were taken to visit a school. Martha was guided separately through the institution and at the end of the tour she was shown its theater. Martha was led onto the stage only to find that an expectant audience was seated in the large auditorium awaiting her. She was introduced at once and it was announced to the audience that she would say a few words. Martha didn't blink an eye, but she immediately got her revenge. She spoke for approximately an hour and no one dared to interrupt her or leave the auditorium.

Some of Martha's best talks were not official lectures, but press conferences held during the first Asian tour. In Bombay, India, Martha was placed under accusation by a group of reporters from the local communist newspapers. They were openly hostile to anything American. Martha remained calm under a barrage of comments which attacked her personally and questioned her loyalty to the United States. Her answers to all of the questions came flowing back, charming, clear, and completely lacking in any irritation. Martha knew that her returned anger would do nothing more than provide the reporters with fuel for further attacks. She slowly spun her web and, without the reporters ever being made aware of what was happening, drew them into it. By the end of the two hour session, the men were all totally captivated. It took great guile and energy on Martha's part, but she was rewarded by the glowing reports that were written about her in the newspapers the following day.

Lecture demonstrations provided Martha with another excellent platform for speaking. The technique class was a framework on which she could hang all of her statements. Within the basic structure of the class, Martha's procedure was to improvise, expecting the company to answer each of her demands with ease. It was always nerve-wracking as we never quite knew what she was going to call for next. Once in a while she would get lost within the context of what she was saying, but it never stopped her flow of words. On one occasion, when introducing the men of the company at the beginning of a demonstration class, she began with Robert Cohan. Martha's mind then completely drew a blank when it came to naming the rest of the male contingent in the group. Nonplussed, she never faltered, but that day introduced all the rest of us as Robert Cohan as well.

If the activities of being a dancer, choreographer, or company director were balanced one against the other, there would be no question where the priorities of Martha Graham would be placed. In her own mind, she was always the dancer first, choreographer second, and last of all a director.

As Martha began aging, the energy that it took to satisfy her primary commitment to performance was increasingly draining. It became necessary for her to draw the needed energy from the other two of her equally demanding tasks. On the European tour of 1954, many pressures were placed upon Martha. Because of the fiasco of the previous London season her concentration was completely centered on being accepted by the British critics. There was such a strain on Martha in order to sustain her powers of performing that she neglected the choreography for *Ardent Song* which was to be given its first performance in England.

When it came time for the premier performance of the dance, the piece was in an unfinished and chaotic state. Unable and unwilling to rise to the occasion, Martha announced that the dance was to be canceled. Gert Macy, our company manager, upon hearing of the cancellation, rushed to Martha's dressing room and attempted to convince her that she could absolutely do no such thing. To cancel would create a disastrous situation with the English press. Fur flew. The company was dismissed for the rest of the day while Martha and Gert fought it out.

Early the next morning we each received a phone call. We were to come to the theater immediately as an attempt was to be made to salvage *Ardent Song*. Gert had won at least a partial victory. At the theater we were told by Martha that we would run through the dance to see if it was in any condition to be performed that evening. It was obvious that a compromise had been reached between the two women and Martha was sure that she would, in the long run, be the winner. *Ardent Song* would be canceled.

There were sections of the dance which were only slightly choreographed and other parts were not choreographed at all. The third section which was Pearl Lang's part of Dawn was the least finished of the three major divisions of the dance. There was a quartet of couples in which we agreed to follow visually whatever Bob Cohan decided to do. A trio of three women was given over totally to improvisation.

The company gathered together in unified effort and was determined to perform the dance that night. I have never known a group of dancers to move, breath and sweat together with such sensitive awareness and determination as we all did at that rehearsal. And it worked. The costumes had to be finished quickly, but *Ardent Song* had its premiere performance that night in London.

The season in which *Clytemnestra* and *Embattled Garden* were first performed proved to be another such time, Martha was depleted of so much physical energy that she could not complete the task that she had undertaken. Because of her self-involvement in *Clytemnestra* as a dancer, as well as the scope of that work, the full evening dance obviously held sway over the much less demanding, *Embattled Garden*.

The creation of *Garden* was started before that of *Clytemnestra*, but was put aside when Martha began the larger work. As time wore on, the four people involved in the dance became more and more desperate. When the first performance hovered on the horizon, they banded together and, using Martha's ideas, completed the work on their own. After *Clytemnestra* opened, Martha came in for the last few rehearsals to supervise.

Martha's energy had its limits and could only be spread so far. Her own performance was always of prime importance and her age was constantly taking its toll, making the act of dancing increasingly difficult for her. She always relied on the people with whom she worked to fill in the gaps that she was unable to complete.

When I first joined the Graham Company, Martha conducted every rehearsal except those in which the basic teaching of the movements took place. Once we learned our individual parts, Martha then took charge and began the work of whipping the dances into some sort of performance shape. Although I am sure that she was much more demanding with her original all women's company, she still, with us during the early 1950's, was an absolute taskmaster.

The first choreographic work of Martha's in which I participated was *Letter To The World* and as it had a slightly balletic quality in some sections such as the party scene, she was insistent on our dancing it as close to perfection as was possible. For hours we would repeat one little passage over and over again, never attaining a sufficiently accurate precision and correctness of movement in Martha's eyes.

Martha also rehearsed us diligently in *Diversion Of Angels*. Because *Angels* was the first successful work that she choreographed but in which she did not appear, Martha made good use of her unusual position as a nonperformer. She constantly altered and changed the timing of the piece and even reworked some of the movement. *Diversion Of Angels* was everyone's favorite dance, and we all fought to be cast in it.

As the pressure of needed energy fell upon Martha with an increasing demand, she began to rehearse the group works much less, until finally we were left on our own to try to bring the dances into a presentable condition. Sometimes out of absolute need, Martha came into the rehearsals at the last minute but only to stop the fighting that inevitably would occur because of the insistence of each of us on the correctness of our own interpretation of the work.

The last time that I remember Martha taking charge of a rehearsal was when she was preparing her three pieces for the Louis Horst Memorial in 1964. Martha was not performing in any of these works. She had returned from Israel shortly after the choreography had been reconstructed.

Sophie Maslow took charge of the rehearsals for *Primitive Mysteries*, but Martha also worked on the dance continuously. Sophie was amazed at how Martha's recent trip to Israel was now introducing a Jewish influence to the piece, slightly altering the work which had originally concerned the American Indians of the southwest.

Initially it was almost necessary to cancel the reconstruction of *El Penitente* as, for a time, I couldn't locate the set. No one seemed to treat this area of Martha's theater with any respect, including Martha herself. I found the apple which was vital to the choreography in the rear of the studio's basement by the furnace. In another section of the studio's cellar, I discovered the cart tangled in a pile of ropes and wood. It took me days to locate the hand-carved Noguchi cross. Finally I pulled apart a stack of wood in the basement that had long been scheduled for removal. At the bottom of the stack were the two sections of the cross, both broken.

Rehearsing with Martha for the Memorial performance was a pleasure. As in times past, she made demands for perfection which were unobtainable, but were stimulating to attempt.

At Connecticut, the night before the performance, Martha began to rip the dances to shreds, creating havoc with everything that had been accomplished during the earlier rehearsals. She basically had always opposed the reconstruction of the pieces and at the last minute was meticulously destroying them. I was furious and stormed out of the auditorium without answering Martha's calls, which followed me into the darkness of the night.

Early the next afternoon before the performance, Martha found me in the auditorium. She inquired about what had been wrong the previous evening. Still angry, I told her that I was tired of being treated like a child. I was a grown man and had children of my own. Martha was livid in return.

"I do treat you like a man", she screamed. "Here, I was going to give you these. Take them."

She reached into a bag that she was carrying, pulled out a small box and threw it at me. It hit me sharply on the chest and bounced off. Martha then stormed away.

The box was lying empty at my feet. I reached down and picked it up. Tiffany's! I looked around the floor. I spotted one solid gold, traditional, barbell, Tiffany cuff link. I knew there had to be two. On my hands and knees, I searched desperately through the rows of seats for fifteen minutes. Just as the audience began to enter the auditorium for the performance, I discovered the other cuff link lodged against one of the metal ventilators under a seat. I treasure the cuff links to this day.

The performance went well. Martha spoke beautifully about Louis as did José Limón. Everyone who had helped reconstruct the dances had been invited to the performance and they all came back to see Martha afterward. We male performers were all located in the green room with Martha so I saw and spoke with all of the dancers from the past. The last to enter was Erick Hawkins who, in a flood of tears, exclaimed over and over again that these were the truly great works of dance art.

When he finally left, Martha turned to us with a sigh of relief stating simply, "Erick always did cry too much."

Every type of emotional situation fed Martha. She sucked the energy from the circumstances that surrounded her. If there was nothing conducive in the environment, she often devised something at the expense of other people with whom she was involved. Even the act of leaving the designing and sewing of her costumes until the last minute created excitement that started her adrenal glands going and her energy level to rise. If Martha was able to work up a strong enough emotional state, she would develop a reservoir of energy which would last her the entire evening.

A few times, such as on the Asian tour of 1955–1956, the sheer exoticism of the countries in which we performed was enough to stimulate her without anything additional being needed. On that tour not only Martha but all of us were affected by the beauty of our surroundings, both in the external landscape and the theaters of each nation in which we performed.

The performance space that was built for us at the foot of the Schwedagon Pagoda in Rangoon, Burma, was typical. Because the theater was constructed in the open air, we could look out from the stage and see row after row of seats disappearing into the dark, ending with a bank of trees that delineated the back of the theater. In each tree, orange-robed Buddhist priests were sitting, giving the appearance of giant fruit ready to be picked. Because the rules of their religious order did not allow them to enter, they were watching the performances legally from outside the theater walls. Beyond the trees, shone the giant Pagoda, brilliantly lit as it rose gleaming into the darkness.

Martha needed roles to perform so it was necessary for her to continue to create dances even though she often said that she had no talent as a choreographer. She had no method. She only had instinct. Despite her words, many of her works have remained in the performing repertory for years. Dances such as *Appalachian Spring, Night Journey, Errand Into The Maze*, and *Diversion Of Angels* will probably continue to be performed by dance companies long into the future.

When danced by others, Martha's roles require a commensurate skill, both technically, and dramatically. Those roles that Martha drew for herself in her later years when she was unable to move fully are the most difficult to recreate. With them, Martha filled out what she could not accomplish physically with nuances of acting and a myriad of small mannerisms. These parts become nearly impossible for others to reproduce.

After Martha had finished choreographing a dance, she was hardly ever satisfied. The dances never lived up to her expectations and for two or three seasons following the premier, she would tamper and play with different sections of the works, trying to achieve some sort of satisfaction. After a few years she would lose interest in the older pieces. Martha's focus of attention basically lay in the immediate present and those past choreographed works had no value for her at all except as vehicles for her as a performer.

Martha speaks of herself as one of the world's greatest thieves. As a result, she is often accused of taking the credit for the choreography that some of her dancers had actually created. In reality, everyone involved with Martha contributed to the movement language of the various pieces, but there was much more to the choreography than just a series of steps. The original concept was Martha's. The structure was Martha's. The collaboration with the other artists was Martha's. The ideas and suggestions for movement were Martha's. The arrangement of the movement was Martha's. The actual steps that one may have contributed depended on the dancers' different choreographic abilities. Paul Taylor, Yuriko, Bertram Ross, and Ethel Winter made large inventive contributions toward each of their own roles. For those who found movement creativity a difficult task, Martha would work through indication or suggestion. There was seldom a time when Martha did not have the total controlling hand in her own choreography.

The season following the creation of *Clytemnestra*, I suggested to Martha that I be taken out of *Diversion Of Angels*. It was a difficult idea to propose as Martha geared everyone in the company to fight competitively for every part that we could. Once a role was gained no one ever gave it away and each of us fought to prevent anyone else from performing the part. *Angels* was a dance of young love and as I was headed toward my fourth decade, I felt that I should move on to more mature challenges. Withdrawing from the dance would not only give me more free time, but it would allow one of the new and younger men in the company to have a chance to perform this treasured work.

Martha didn't seem the least upset by the suggestion and told me that she would think about it. A short time later that same evening, Martha called me into the front hallway. Sitting on one of the long wooden benches, Martha came right to the point. She suggested that I become the rehearsal director for the company. I would be given the responsibility for putting together all of the dances in the repertory except for those that Martha was choreographing at the time. The creation of a weekly rehearsal schedule was also to be part of my responsibilities. As the company had never before had anything similar, the idea came as a complete surprise, but it was certainly an intriguing concept. Martha said that I should take time to consider the proposition carefully and then let her know my decision. I immediately told her that wouldn't be necessary, I definitely would do it.

With the decision made, Martha and I walked into the large studio where a rehearsal was taking place. Martha interrupted it and to everyone's dismay abruptly made the announcement of my appointment. She made it clear to everyone that my word was law and that I was responsible only to her.

In the beginning everyone was relieved to have an arrangement which created a certain amount of order out of chaos. The idea of having regularly scheduled weekly rehearsals was appealing to most of the company. Also, to have someone in authority to solve whatever disputes occurred made the rehearsals more productive. Nothing could possibly replace the inspirational input of Martha, but I could, at least, clean up the dances by clarifying the movement.

With the initiation of the position of rehearsal director, Martha and my working relationship improved. We had developed great difficulties during my tenure with *Plain And Fancy*. Martha hated the idea of my being in the show, accusing me of becoming brassy and vulgar as a result of my contact with the commercial world.

Bethsabee de Rothschild's last Festival of American Dance occurred during the spring that I was performing in *Plain And Fancy*. I was caught in a direct conflict between Martha's dances that were being done on the festival and my performances every evening with the Broadway musical. The producers of *Plain And Fancy* proved to be very cooperative and let me out of a part of the show each evening so that I could dance with Martha, but there were parts of the musical in which my presence was still required. Because I was needed to be in both the theaters, I had to time everything to the exact second.

Every evening I began *Plain And Fancy* at the Winter Garden Theater, leaving a pair of ready-to-wear khaki pants by the stage door. At exactly the proper moment, I dropped my Amish costume, put on my pants and raced up Broadway to the ANTA Theater where Bethsabee's festival was taking place. My costume for whatever dance I was doing that evening was waiting for me by the ANTA stage door. I performed the scheduled dance and after changing clothes once again, raced back down Broadway to finish the evening's work at The Winter Garden. None of this running back and forth made Martha terribly happy and I carried the tag of vulgarity around my neck until I agreed to leave the show that summer to teach for Martha at the American Dance Festival.

Martha and I also had difficulties during the creation of *Clytemnestra*. Originally I was to dance the role of the Watchman in that full evening's work. Martha had choreographed most of my part early in the rehearsal sessions. I came into the 63rd Street building for class one day and heard my music being played in the large studio. Even though the red cloth which meant stay out, was tied across the door, I could peek through the crack. I saw Martha and Gene McDonald working on a completely different version of the Watchman. Realizing the inevitable, I was totally crushed. I went into Martha's dressing room and waited for her. I knew that she would be angry because of my confronting her, but at that moment I didn't care. When Martha finally walked into her room, it was her turn to be surprised.

Martha at first hemmed and hawed and then excused her actions by saying that there were too many isolated characters in the work and she was condensing the roles into larger categories. The Agamemnon-Orestes role had been combined into one person already and now she was combining all of the figures that represented death or foreboding.

With the comment, "Maybe there will be some other part later in the piece, but I don't really know now." I was dismissed.

A few weeks later Martha approached me with the dances in which she wanted me to appear during the season. They were all pieces in which I had already performed many times. I was aware that time for rehearsing was of the essence, as *Clytemnestra* was eating up every second of Martha's rehearsals. Using that as my stake, I gambled and told Martha that if I could be in *Clytemnestra*, I would do the other pieces, but if I couldn't, I would do nothing. I usually was quite amenable to everything so Martha was taken aback, but said that she would consider it.

Martha called after a few days relating that she had found something for me in *Clytemnestra* she thought, but that she wasn't sure as yet. The role of The Messenger Of Death was the result.

I cannot adequately express the satisfaction that I felt on the occasion of the premier of *Clytemnestra*. As I stood in the down stage left wing nervously awaiting my entrance, I couldn't help but savor a sense of victory. The overture was played – a pause – and then on the crest of the sound of a huge crashing drum, I made my entrance and began Martha's epic work.

Being rehearsal director had some advantages and gave me a certain leverage to use every so often. One season I came down with 104 degree fever which physically totally knocked me out for a day. It was a Sunday and I wasn't in the matinee performance. In the evening, *Clytemnestra* was scheduled and I had no intention of missing it. A doctor came to the house and gave me a few pills to take which were supposed to bring down my temperature.

Marni called Martha and told her of my condition. As Martha loved emergencies, she quickly rose to the occasion. Nobody knew exactly what I did in *Clytemnestra* but Martha made up something for Dudley Williams to dance in my place. She gave him my costume, called my home, and left instructions for me not to come into the theater that evening. I came anyway.

As I passed Martha's dressing room in the theater, she spotted me in her mirror and called to me. There ensued a battle royal between Martha and myself.

"How dare you do this to me when I have a performance."

I was definitely providing Martha with enough energy for a marvelous performance that evening. After half an hour of heated interchange, I made my move.

"I think *Clytemnestra* is the work of a genius. We don't do it very often. I don't want to be cheated out of one performance."

I meant it, but I also knew that my comments would have an effect upon Martha. She stalled for a minute, giving me another opening.

"If I don't do *Clytemnestra* tonight, I won't dance next week at all", I threatened.

Martha screamed, "How can you. If you won't leave my room, I will."

With that she charged out of her dressing room. I went upstairs to my own room that I shared with Paul Taylor. In a few minutes we heard steps on the stairs outside of the door. Dr. Cobert opened it and presented me with my costume.

The next week Martha refused to speak to me. The last night of the season we closed with *Acrobats Of God*. Martha and I were standing in our opening positions waiting for the curtain to rise. At the last minute Martha whispered, "I hope you had a good time this week. I didn't."

My part of the taskmaster in *Acrobats Of God* was a direct result of being made the rehearsal director. The season in which both *Alcestis* and *Acrobats* were choreographed was probably the time when Martha reached the nadir of her drinking problem. Her parts in the two works of that season could not have been more disparate. *Alcestis*, who descended into hell to save her beloved husband, and the sly, tricky, creative plaything of *Acrobats Of God*. In her alcoholic state, Martha usually had little perception of which piece she was rehearsing. Day rehearsals were always a little better than those which were held at night, for in the evening Martha was often unintelligible.

The major part of Martha's attention was given to *Alcestis*. *Acrobats* became the secondary work. By the time that the season arrived, Martha had completed the group sections of *Acrobats*. My sections as the Taskmaster, when they related to the group, were also finished, but the parts of the piece that were reserved for the interplay between Martha and myself remained untouched. Either Martha didn't show for the scheduled rehearsals or if she did come, she was too inebriated to accomplish anything.

The day before *Acrobats* was to be premiered, Martha and I met with Robert Dunn, the rehearsal pianist for the season. We worked slowly through the dance until, because of Martha's exhaustion, we had to stop for the day. The morning of the first performance we met again and finished everything up to the flute solo that occurred at the end of the work.

"I'll have to stop", Martha said completely worn out. "We'll finish it tonight at the theater."

At the theater that night I met Martha while crossing the stage before the performance. In all innocence, I asked, "Have you thought about the end of the dance yet?"

"How can you ask me about that at this moment. I have other more important and immediately demanding problems to think about", she answered. Martha turned and strode off.

That was enough. I wasn't going to ask again.

Acrobats Of God was the closing work of the evening. As Martha and I stood in the curve of the stylized Noguchi barre before the piece began, Martha hissed out of the side of her mouth, "When we get to the end, just follow me and do the opposite of what I do."

The curtain rose.

When we arrived at the final flute solo, we were already at opposite ends of the barre. Martha began pacing from one end of it to the other. I did too. Martha nodded or threatened me as we passed each other. I retaliated. Martha turned front. I did too. Martha took three steps forward. I stepped forward too. Martha bowed. I bowed too. The curtain descended. The choreography never changed.

The job of rehearsal director only became difficult when the position shifted from company member to management representative. In the beginning, the task meant nothing more than devoting myself to extra hours of actual rehearsal. Besides the added sessions during the week, almost all of my weekends were given over to making up the complicated rehearsal schedules. As the company was not on salary, everyone had to have outside jobs, teaching or otherwise, in order to earn a living. These obligations had to be respected.

The members of the company were supposed to let me know when their hours of availability changed from week-to-week. At first they were careful to inform me, but as time progressed, they became less so. Often, after spending hours organizing everyone's times, one or two people would announce that their commitments had changed and it became necessary for me to completely revise the schedule.

In rehearsals, each person had to be dealt with individually. The members of the company all possessed strong personalities and the approach that worked for one could not be used for another. As rehearsal director, I received an "on the job" education in human psychology.

As the position was completely new, no one could figure out what I should be paid. The company management took advantage of the situation and paid me nothing. When the company was placed on rehearsal pay a few weeks preceding a season or a tour, I was given twenty-five dollars extra each week.

Martha actually was my greatest difficulty. As a season neared, every time that she saw me, she would mention that we needed to begin rehearsals. I told her that I couldn't start until I knew who was to perform the various roles. We would make many appointments to meet and settle the casting, but Martha would always fail to come. Martha hated to be pinned down. Up to this time she had always been able to toy with people, but now she was forced to be definitive. Finally I would give her an ultimatum and she, in fury, would come to the studio where we would go over the repertory, role by role.

The hardest dances to rehearse were the ones in which Martha was the central character. It was difficult to work around her empty space and she refused to come into the rehearsals until it was absolutely necessary, just before the performances were to begin.

Martha was fearful that the dances would become over rehearsed, stale, and static. For her, the energy that was created from the tensions of last minute chaos was as necessary for an excellent performance as any other part of the choreographic process. To be viable for her, life had to contain a certain amount of excitement. Excitement for Martha came from tension, often tension which was purposefully created. Emotionally, dance was a heightened mirror image of life and so it had to follow life's same patterns. The company all had to live and dance in the atmosphere which Martha created, an atmosphere which was bereft of security.

Martha, if she felt that the dances were becoming over rehearsed, would devise devious methods to counter it. Sometimes just before a season, she threw the company out of the studio, abruptly stopping all rehearsals. At other times she would call dancers out of practice sessions to design costumes, knowing that it would destroy the working situation. On one occasion, during the final run-through for *Diversion Of Angels* as the men made their last entrance, Martha "accidentally" let loose an assortment of dogs. They had been tied to a post in the studio and were patiently waiting for their masters to finish. Dogs, men, Ethel Winter and Martha all ended in a wild melee of unchoreographed movements, yells, and delighted barks.

When I was on tour, my responsibilities as rehearsal director greatly increased. I had the usual spacing and placement rehearsals that were called when needed and the constant checking on the dances in the repertory. Martha also had me make all arrangements for the lecture demonstrations that were held. Upon arrival at each new city, Craig Barton and I immediately had to go to the theater. We checked it to see if there were any special problems with the performing space. As rehearsal director, my time involvement on tour was much increased over that of our home seasons.

After some years, there arose difficulties and factions within the company. None of it was pleasant. For some dancers, I became a person to counter rather than a person with whom to work. During a cross-country tour, Martha had created an impossible situation in one of the dances and refused to solve it herself. No one else in the company was any help either. Everything came crashing down during a performance at U.C.L.A.'s Royce Hall.

After seven years, I said that I would direct the rehearsals no more. Because of the adverse situation, I was no longer productive, nor did I have the desire to put in extra hours for nothing. The idea of a rehearsal director for the Martha Graham Company had been firmly established and with that accomplishment, I felt that I had made a major contribution.

Every time one of the dancers left Martha's Company, it provoked a traumatic experience. One reason was that Martha's hypnotic power on all of us enlarged greatly as the amount of time spent with her increased. Also the more personally involved the interaction became between Martha and a company member, the more the bond between them grew in strength.

In order to create a closer relationship, Martha would often unveil intimate facts of her life and they were usually revealed under strange circumstances. One always felt that Martha was hoping for an even exchange of intimacies. Her love life with Erick was a common topic. She could have been made wealthy if she had accepted two lesbian relationships. She had a tipped uterus. She had never used contraceptives. She could not conceive. She would have given up her entire career if she could have borne a child. These supposed facts were related over the phone, in the studio while rehearsing, or even upon meeting accidentally at the front door of the school. In the exchange of personal matters there was an addictive excitement generated between Martha and certain of her dancers.

We company members became very attached to our way of life. The inspiration, magic, and even genius which Martha projected were difficult to find in other circumstances. When the trauma of departure of one of the company dancers was caused by Martha, the experience was devastating, but if the choice was that of the dancer himself, there was usually a fury released which none of us had ever before experienced.

Martha, despite her success, maintained a sense of rejection when a dancer, of his own volition, chose to leave her company. No matter how well it was done, no matter how logical the reason, no matter how carefully it was planned, Martha always took offense. It seemed actually to be a way of making the removal of the dancer complete, of entirely destroying the past relationship.

Unlike a newborn child that is given freedom from its mother when the umbilical cord is cut only to move up to the breast for further nurturing, Martha, whether out of malice or not, made sure that the rupture was complete. She wanted no clinging. Martha was interested only in that which was of the present. We used to say that after a dancer departed from the company, the first thing that Martha forgot was the name, then the face, and then the fact that the person had ever danced in her group.

Along with my abdicating the job of rehearsal director, I also intended to stop dancing and leave New York. I wanted to direct my interests in dance toward new areas of activity. The fact of Martha's continuing to dance despite her age, was admirable in concept to me, but not inspiring. Also, because of having worked for other people over a period of so many years, I wanted to see if the ideas taking shape in my mind were of any use or value.

I was determined that I would end my tenure with Martha amicably. I had too much respect and love for her to want to instigate the type of confrontation that I had witnessed other company members experiencing upon their departures. I planned each step carefully and for a time I thought that I had been successful.

Then one night Martha called. By the slur in her voice, I knew that she had been drinking heavily. Marni answered the phone and stayed on the other end of the line while Martha spoke.

I had never before heard Martha use language such as she did that night. She had created a totally fictitious allegation so that she was able to attack me. When I finally put down the phone, Marni and I both said that I had to do something about the situation right away. It was almost midnight, but I got into the car, as we were living in Yonkers, and drove into Manhattan, preparing for my last confrontation.

I went directly to Martha's apartment and rang the bell.

"Who is it?" Martha asked in a very slurred voice from behind the door.

"It's David, Martha."

"Just a minute."

It was a long five minutes before she opened the door.

Martha apologized profusely. Since she had spoken with me, she had discovered that the allegations that she had made were not true, and everything was now all right. She poured me a drink, a tumbler full of straight scotch whiskey. We began to talk. Martha sobered as the minutes passed. Her memory was amazing. Starting with the Neighborhood Playhouse, we slowly relived our relationship, through its twists and turns up to that evening. It was 3:00 A.M., and Martha and I had a total catharsis. It was done. It had taken a reliving of the past twenty years to cleanse our souls.

I still had parts and classes to teach. It all went smoothly without any further angry eruptions. I had a final teaching rehearsal for *Acrobats Of God* and during one section, Martha whispered in my ear, "This must be very painful for you."

In the end, Martha won. I finally played her game.

I answered, "Yes, it is."

I knew that was the response that she wanted to hear from me.

Actually it wasn't painful at all. The time had come to leave. By departing, I was merely carrying out what Martha had taught me so well: to live to the fullest every minute. I was beginning to feel drained in the studio and in the rehearsals. I was grateful for everything that Martha had offered me, every advantage that she had given me. But now I felt a release. There was life beyond Martha Graham.

That night I taught my last technique class and after fifteen years, with no one there to say "thank you", or even a simple "good-bye", but with a richness of experiences to take with me, I walked through yet another door and let it close firmly behind me.

10

ON MARRIAGE, BIRTHING AND AGING

Dance is a profession which demands total physical, intellectual, and spiritual participation. As a result, it is difficult for those involved in its performance to follow the usual path of human endeavor. Growth within oneself and competition with others provide the focus of attention. Freedom to experiment is essential to that growth. Some dancers choose to become "married" to their art. Dance, then, becomes a replacement for an idealized consort.

Endless hours of involvement are required; a transient existence is a necessity. Usually both preclude developing any personal relationships. Human interactions demand time. The dancer must be free and available, open to every possibility for furthering his career. The more complex he allows his life to become, the less he finds himself free to grasp each opportunity that arises.

There are certainly dancers who desire a relationship and are capable of fulfilling such a commitment. Some dancers mature more rapidly than do others. Some dancers have a much greater need for companionship.

Performing dance nevertheless, carries with it psychological demands which produce a large range of emotional highs and lows. It is often difficult for a person who is not involved in the art form to understand the tremendous emotional drain which performing creates. Rehearsals also can provide personal upheaval, and even dance classes can contribute to emotional turmoil.

To arrive at a solution it is possible for a couple to agree to an undemanding union, but the divergent experiences of each individual can pull them increasingly further apart. A certain amount of difference in experience can contribute to the enrichment of a couple's relationship, but when these differences become constant, the individual orbits intersect much less frequently. Finally the couple discovers that the alliance with each other has become more conceptual than real. The separate experiences create influences that pull them into different worlds. New acquaintances are made and these quite often replace, without great difficulty, the old attachments.

If only one member of the couple is involved in dance, the chances for establishing a permanent link are much greater. There then exists one stable person around whom the more transient dancer, can revolve. If the second occupation is related to the arts in some manner, there may be an increased empathy between the two people. While the requirements of each are different, they often are sympathetic in nature.

There does seem to exist a correlation between the intensity of the desire for a dance career and the success of a lasting relationship. Hanya Holm's alliance with a husband was of short duration when she was still living in Germany. As she moved further into the responsibilities of her career in the United States, the recreating of another such union seemed to recede from her mind. The marriage of Helen Tamiris and Daniel Nagrin, although of a long duration, ended in separation. Doris Humphrey married a sea captain whose profession often separated the two of them for great lengths of time, leaving Doris free from marital obligations. Doris's marriage, though, proved to be a lasting and rewarding one. Martha Graham lived for years first with Louis Horst and then with Erick Hawkins. She and Erick were married in the summer of 1948. Following the official ceremony, the union existed only for a short time before it explosively terminated.

In 1958 by the age of thirty-three, my life was beginning to alter its course. I felt less desperate about my ability to earn a living by dancing. I had paid off my debts, finally bought new clothing for myself, and had managed to obtain a decent place in which to live. I was open for new adventures, but I made no overt decisions about any rash changes in my life style. Having an offer from Mexico to teach and choreograph in Mexico City, I had made plans to leave Martha for a few months.

My plans didn't change. They were just enlarged upon. In a casual manner, Marni and I had gotten to know each other during the previous two years. Marni was to graduate from Sarah Lawrence College in June, 1958. I was to leave my monastic style of living in September of that same year. With Martha's approval, Marni became my demonstrator for the last three weeks of the 1958 summer session at the American Dance Festival. This provided me with the opportunity of seeing her many times each day. She began to look increasingly attractive and appealing.

Marni obviously had matured at a much faster rate than I did. In my high school year book an old girlfriend wrote, "It's too bad that you didn't grow up sooner." She had a point. Throughout my life I have always moved slowly and methodically. The emotional maturity that I had attained at thirty-three, Marni attained at twenty-two.

Following our wedding in Charleston, West Virginia, Marni and I flew to San Francisco. My mother sat directly behind us on the return trip and slipped notes of congratulations to us at hourly intervals. In San Francisco, Marni and I gassed up my car and began our leisurely drive south to Mexico City via the Mexican west coast highway.

The journey introduced us to new experiences, new sounds and new tastes. Around almost every curve in the road there seemed to exist something that was beautiful and different. The two of us were beginning to build an array of common experiences. We also used the trip to begin to establish priorities within our new relationship.

The roads of Mexico are not well cared for and we had many flat tires during our trip. On the first occasion, I was in the process of removing the punctured wheel when Marni suddenly appeared around the side of the car carrying our spare tire which she had taken out of the trunk. The sight of my small and fragile bride staggering triumphantly forward under the tremendous weight, appalled me.

"What are you doing?"

"Helping."

"Well, don't. Put it down now. You're going to hurt yourself."

I was very authoritative and strong.

Marni burst into tears. I had treated her cruelly and without consideration. Her position in our newly made alliance was being placed in jeopardy, but then so was mine. It was a stand-off. I finished changing the tire as the tears rolled down Marni's cheeks. We then continued our journey wrapped for a time in complete silence. It took me many years to learn to admit that women are much stronger than men in many different and varied ways. If they want to change a tire, for your own peace of mind, you had better let them do it.

The rest of the Mexican experience was full of shared events: automobile accidents, jail, trips to Aztec ruins, trips to the bull fights with Juanito our newly acquired eight year old amigo, drinking Mescal in Oaxaca, dashing out of Mexico City to the United States and back all in one weekend in order to legalize our car, even Marni's debilitating amoebas. We were developing a commonly shared bond of experience. We both felt that this was very important during the initial stages of our marriage. The stronger the shared experiences were, the stronger would be our evolving union.

The pattern that was established on that first trip to Mexico has been continued during the subsequent years of our marriage. We have participated in dance tours throughout the United States, Europe, the Near East, and Asia. Under our own aegis, we have taught in many institutions in a vast number of different countries. We have traveled to many new areas just for the pleasure of exploration or the gaining of a greater understanding of the different inhabitants. We have journeyed around the world together to investigate certain types of dance in their home territory. The experiences have given us a broad common denominator upon which we have built a strong and enduring union.

Marriage is not necessarily the only outlet for a serious combining of two people. In each pairing the individuals involved must discover for themselves what is the most fulfilling arrangement for their lives. For me, the formality of the ritual act of marriage helped to provide the reality of a relationship. It allowed for the easy actuality of sharing. It could be the physical sharing of oneself. It could be the sharing of time. It could be the sharing of one's private possessions. It could be the sharing of ideas and thoughts. It could be the sharing of experiences. It could be a sharing of the intangible, which cannot be defined by physical statement, but which bond two people together.

I doubt if many people would argue with the fact that the conceiving of a baby is a very simple and pleasurable process. I doubt if many people, at least among those who have had children, would disagree that it is from the point of conception that the real difficulties with parenthood begins. Few people who put themselves into the situation of being anticipating parents have any practical idea of what the on-coming event entails.

For dancers, the added responsibilities that accompany childbearing are vast. Their already demanding time-frame is now being extended to even greater limits. If they have not made allowance for this new demand prior to the event, the new parents are in for a rude shock when their baby arrives. If the mother is a dancer, there are many other major factors which come into play.

By physiological structure, it is the woman who must bear the long process of developing the fetus from conception to birth. The prospective father can sympathetically huff and puff with his wife as much as he wishes, but the actuality is that the total responsibility for giving birth to the child lies with the mother. The physical changes that take place within the woman's body make it necessary for her to interrupt her dance career, delaying or even preventing her from any sense of continuity.

In less informed times, the woman would lose the position that she held within a dance company because she had decided to use a natural function of her body. This is fortunately no longer true, and even in the competitive dance world, the right to maternity leave without penalty is a justly acquired benefit.

One of the marvelous things about dancing with Martha Graham was the automatic equation of human, "divine" rights. Along with racial, religious, and sexual acceptance of all people as being equal, so was there an easy acceptance of motherhood. There were within the company a continuing parade of pregnancies: Yuriko, two children; Linda and Stuart Hodes, two children, Miriam Cole, three children; Ethel Winter, one child; Mary Hinkson, one child; Matt Turney, one child; Marni and myself, three children. All of the mothers were forced to cease dancing during pregnancy, but were brought back into the company as soon as they felt that they could return to performance shape.

Today there are many more options open to the female dancer. Methods of birth control have been greatly refined. The legalization of abortion puts the choice of birthing fairly much into the hands of the women who must bear the burden. For dancers the choice of whether to opt for parenthood or not, now has becomes a rational choice. Today children of performers usually are a product of the planning of two mature individuals who have clearly thought about their actions and the subsequent results.

Five of the dance pioneers interrupted their careers in order to have children. Jane Sophie and Bill had one each. In Germany, Hanya Holm gave birth to a son, Klaus. Doris Humphrey bore a son, Charles Humphrey Woodford. According to Charles Weidman and José Limón, Doris was overdue to give birth and a performance at Lewisohn Stadium in New York was growing imminent. Charles and José found an old car and a bumpy road and spent the evening driving back and forth over it with Doris in the back seat. The next day Doris' baby arrived.

Once the child is born, arrangements for its care must be made. With both parents dancing, touring becomes nearly an impossibility. There have been a few occasions when an au pair has been employed to travel with the dance company, but the expense of such a luxury is enough to diminish greatly the earnings of the dancers. Also the divided attention between child and dancing can easily dilute the quality of both.

Marni and I found that it was impossible to tour with the children during one night stands or even one week stands. If there were residencies of longer duration or lengthy teaching situations, we usually brought the children along with us. Marni, in all honesty, bore the burden of the care of the children, but I was an able assistant. On our first teaching stint in Sweden, while Marni taught in the evenings, I fed and bathed the nine month old, Marina. As our oldest daughter was the messiest eater in Christendom, I would strip both of us down to complete nudity before I would even attempt the task of feeding her. By the time that we finished, each of us was covered from head to toe with the menu of the day. I then gathered Marina up in my arms and plopped both of us into the bathtub for a thorough cleansing. When Marni returned home from her teaching, at the academy, the two of us greeted her at the door well fed and shining brightly from a hard scrubbing.

During the time that we toured on one night stands in Europe or the United States, we were fortunate to have Marni's parents Andy and Marian Thomas who volunteered to take the children for us. Sometimes the tours were very lengthy, but the Thomas's always seemed happy to take care of their grandchildren and never complained. Every so often they would even join us on the tour so that we could have a brief visit with the children.

Time spent caring for offspring is now more clearly divided among most of the dancer/couples. Whether the male has finally received enlightenment or whether he has merely succumbed to the pressures that have been placed upon him, the result is the same. The hours now spent in child care are much more fairly shared between the father and the mother. This has the beneficial result of leaving both people more open to pursue their careers.

There are constant emergencies and needs which arise within the family configuration. The parents cannot plan for most of these events. School plays, dance recitals, gymnastic meets, and girl or boy scout jamborees, soaring temperatures, broken arms or legs, and a few concussions are occurrences which require the presence of the parents.

For me, family togetherness was always one of the central conditions under which I existed. I felt that the five of us should do everything as a unit.

Following our summer teaching sessions in Stockholm we always would rent or buy a car and take off in search of Jeanne d'Arc, the musical carrousels of Europe, the Swiss Alps, or once, enclosed in a tiny Karman Ghia which was smaller than a Volkswagen bug, we all traveled through England and Scotland to seek out my mother's family clan, the Scotch Kennedys. (Some people have said that our three daughters are all small and delicate because of being cooped up in that miniature vehicle.) I had a marvelous time sharing our new explorations with our young children. We discovered and learned everything together as a family unit.

Years later Marni confessed that she, in reality, had hated every minute of those excursions. The anxiety of the children's health, their spilled food in dining salons, their tantrums in hotel lobbies, and their screams when they couldn't have another ride in the playground; all made her life a nervous wreck. In order to make each of the trips work for everyone else, Marni never had a relaxed moment during any of them. It is strange that two people who existed so closely together could have such totally different remembrances of the same important events.

Our youngest daughter, Ellis, became an elite gymnast and competed at The United States Championships. We managed to make all of her meets. At about the same period of time, our second oldest daughter, Raegan, made the decision to begin to train seriously as a dancer. This was added to our already heavy schedule of transportation chores. There were many days when it seemed that Marni and I spent more time in the car driving the children from one event to the next, than we spent in any other vital activity.

Performances and competitions made us experts at weekend travels. We were jet-setting parents who raced from Albuquerque to Canada, from Seattle to Florida. One Thursday night in April 1986 while on our around the world jaunt, Marni and I finished our teaching and flew from Israel to Florida to see Ellis compete at the N.C.A.A. Gymnastic Championships. On the following Sunday afternoon in New York, after the athletic event had been completed, we caught a matinee of the Paul Taylor Dance Company in which Raegan was performing. By that Monday evening, we had returned to the Island of Crete to continue our trip. We tried to make believe that it had never been interrupted. Our sense of time was not even disturbed enough to allow for any jet lag. Marni and I found that most anything could be accomplished if we were to try hard enough.

Still, there was no way that we could continue our careers in dance at full scale while at the same time giving the amount of attention to our three children that they needed. If marriage for dancers requires special effort and time in order to achieve a successful relationship, the raising of children by dancers demands an even greater release of time and an even more purposefully directed effort.

Eventually freedom of activity for the parents becomes reestablished as the children arrive at the age of maturity. Usually for dancers this event happens too late for an actual performing career to be reinstated, but for careers in teaching and choreography, there is once again the freedom to take advantage of whatever new opportunities arise. Still, physical release from parenthood is not the same as emotional release. Although the newly matured adults are fully capable of taking care of themselves, the bonds which link parent and child together are maintained by a consummate primal instinct which no amount of sophistication can dispel. It is almost totally impossible for the parents to divorce themselves of their close attachment to their offspring no matter how much they may wish for it, and no matter how much the progeny themselves may desire it.

As the detachment between parent and child inevitably increases, the relationship of the parents with their offspring possibly grows even more nervous and frustrating than it has been. The father and mother now are no longer in charge of their children and must sit on the side with closed mouths and watch events take place. The emotional bonds have not been lessened, but the governing powers of the parents have to be placed aside.

When they were children I had promised Marina, Raegan, and Ellis to take the three of them to Venice, Italy, for a last family trip. The opportune moment to fulfill that promise arose in May, 1986, near the end of the around-the-world tour. Marina was twenty-four years old; Raegan, twenty-two; Ellis, twenty. The three daughters, making their own arrangements for flying into Rome where we were to gather, decided to arrive two days early in order to spend sometime sightseeing. Marina and Ellis came from California and Raegan flew in from New York. All Marni and I knew was that in their naiveté they had designated a nebulous, "somewhere in front of the Vatican", as their meeting place. We were never told if they actually met or not, for at that age, all of their activities had to be kept shrouded in deep mystery.

For us to all gather together in Rome seemed a simple enough task. Marni and I were to arrive at the airport from Athens two hours early. At least one hour ahead of time, we were all to meet at the gate from which the plane to Venice departed.

Marni and I got to the gate easily by the designated hour. Our daughters had not as yet arrived so I roamed around the passenger area while Marni read. At forty-five minutes to flight time, I sat and fidgeted. Marni stared into space. At thirty minutes to flight time, I started pacing rapidly. Marni gazed intensely at her book, but never turned another page. At fifteen minutes to flight time, desperation set in. Imagination took over my mind: maybe they had been abducted in Rome; maybe they had never even arrived there. I began muttering out loud. Marni's neck chords began to bulge. The plane to Venice began to board its passengers. At ten minutes to flight time, Marni's neck chords began to pulsate. I raced back to the metal detector from where I could look out over the concourse and see the various airline check-in counters.

Finally I spotted a strangely clothed young woman who sported an almost completely shaved head. She was frantically running around the concourse like a plucked chicken trying to escape from its executioner.

"Ellis, Hurry. Over here,"

It was our youngest daughter. In relief at seeing a familiar face, Ellis responded immediately.

"Where are your sisters?" I gulped, trying to appear nonchalant despite the obvious sweat that was dripping from my brow.

"Didn't Raegan come through the detector yet?"

"Oh, my God," I thought. "Raegan's lost." "Where's Marina?"

"I don't know."

I let out what I thought to be a subdued moan, but it must have been overly loud as everyone in the airport turned around to look at us.

At the same moment we both spotted Marina headed full speed down a corridor in completely the opposite direction. Ellis and I yelled at the top of our lungs. Marina suddenly stopped, listening intently as if she had just heard a primal call from the earth. She veered 180° and finally headed in our direction.

We raced to the gate where Marni and Raegan, who had actually gotten past me unnoticed, were waiting. Just as the officials were closing the gate, we slipped through it and onto the plane.

Marni and I were exhausted. Marina, Raegan, and Ellis were laughing uproariously. "If we told you what happened to us, you wouldn't believe it."

Marni and I, trying to appear calm and unconcerned, smiled weakly in agreement.

"You're absolutely right. We wouldn't so don't even try."

The plane moved full speed down the runway, and lifted easily from the tarmac. As we squeezed back into the cramped seats of the plane, our spirits with relief, easily took flight as well.

Parents often question themselves or are questioned by others, "Was the rearing of the children really worth it?" From each parent one receives different and personally related answers. For artists, the response is especially significant. The creation of the child, the birthing, its development, and its final release follows exactly the acts of creation by all artists be they writers, painters, musicians, or dancers.

My own feelings on the subject can be stated with easy clarity. Before the children were born, I wanted them. Before they were born, I loved them. After they were born, I cherished them. After they were born, I protected them. Since they have departed from home, I honor and respect them.

Usually the departure of the offspring from the home occurs at the same time that the parents begin to face the problem of growing older. The process of aging for most individuals is a difficult one to handle, and each person must solve it in his own individual manner. Some find that it is relatively easy to adjust to the added physical difficulties of age while others fight against each newly arising disability. In growing older, dancers as a sociological group are not uniquely removed from other human beings, but the painful effect that the ebbing of strength creates upon their psyches can be devastating. It strikes the dancer much earlier and much harder than it does most other individuals. Physical prowess is a prime factor in the occupation of dancers just as it is for competing athletes. As the power of the muscles diminishes, so does the ability to carry out the specific demands of the dance career.

A conflict eventually arises between the lessening physical capabilities of the artist and his increasing emotional maturity. This becomes immediately reflected in his performance. As the powers of projection achieve their greatest height, as the artist arrives at the point in his career when he can enrich and fulfill his personal performance far beyond anything that he has previously attained, his physical prowess begins to disintegrate and to fail him. The dancer, as he approaches the age of forty, begins to feel this inopportune timing, but there is little that can be done to combat the difficulty. It is an inherent element within the art form. The ability of the dancer to project to an audience is often the quality that keeps a performer dancing long after his physical body clearly tells him that he should stop.

If the artist's interests include teaching and choreography as well as performing, the problem of aging is less traumatic. Interest in one area can readily be displaced by another; however, if performing is the all-consuming activity, aging can become a terrifying experience. In such cases the passage of time is not considered by the dancer to be a maturing element, but rather an unwanted and premature ending to his career.

In contrast to their earlier years, when they injected an incomparable vitality and passion into their work, obviously all of the pioneering leaders of the modern movement eventually were affected by the pull of age. Each, however, had varying degrees of difficulty. For all of the innovators, dance was a totally involving obsession that continuously drained their energy and occupied their time. The art form became for them an intimate companion with whom they spent the major portion of their days and often a good part of their nights. The abrupt termination of performing was for some of these artists as emotionally disturbing as if an actual life-long friend had suddenly divorced himself from them. No matter how much their maturation provided an impervious honesty in performance, the awareness of the inevitable muscular insecurity was difficult for the dancer to handle.

The emptiness that they felt by the lack of physicality was hard for them to replenish. For some, there was anger and resentment in addition to the personal sorrow for the loss of movement ability. Of course, there were those few dancers who, upon the cessation of their performing careers, felt a tremendous release from the pressure of keeping themselves in a ready physical condition.

For Hanya Holm, the act of performing never was the intense passion which made it the central core of her artistic life. Discouragement by the critics about her performing could have been a factor, as she often received negative reviews. In the early 1940s before it became a necessity, by choice Hanya ceased her activities as a dancer. She allowed her strong powers of perception to lead her into new directions, soon becoming one of the outstanding creators of lyric theater in this country. When the drain of aging began to take its toll, she responded with ease and grace. Because of her diverse interests, Hanya avoided the trauma which most dancers feel with advancing age.

Alwin Nikolais had even less of a problem in ending his performing career. Although he had trained intensively over the years in dance technique, the act of creating movement, and its synthesis with music and design became the focus of his artistic attention at a relatively early age. His wide range of talents made the transition from dancer to choreographer an easy one.

Charles Weidman's world existed entirely within the boundaries of dance and dance creation. From the time that he was a young boy, performing dominated his life. He performed first as an amateur in Nebraska and then continued as a professional with the Denishawn Dancers. Dancing and breathing were the two elements that were essential for his existence. When age placed more and more limitations on his body, Charles became resentful, using alcohol as a means of solace. As with so many other things in his life, Charles could never come to terms with his advancing age.

Despite Doris Humphrey's obvious involvement with choreography, her exquisite dancing carried a great deal of the focus of her career. She was angered by the failure of her own body which forced her into a withdrawal from performance prematurely. She fought the painful calcification of her hip as long as it was possible, but she was finally overcome by the physical limitations that it placed upon her. She suffered the pain stoically, but her intense anger aroused by the condition was often times projected onto certain dancers with whom she worked.

Although Helen Tamiris never mentioned it openly, she seemed to take an easy pride in her physical appearance and the manner in which she was perceived by other people. It was evidently important to her to be viewed always from the best but most honest standpoint. When age became a designing force, Tamiris responded to it quickly with simplicity and truth.

"I am not a choreographer. I can only create dances by instinct. Basically they are vehicles which allow me to perform." Martha Graham's own words give an insight into her personal views on performing.

Dancing was her very reason for existence. The onset of age with its contributing arthritis was a horrifying reality in which she refused to believe. Martha had a tremendous will power. Her determination allowed her physically to accomplish movements which dancers of a much younger age could not technically master.

In frustration at one rehearsal during her last years of performing, she stated to her company, "Physically you all may be able to do things that I can no longer manage, but in performance, I have abilities that you will never be able to achieve."

Her determination allowed her to continue to dance well into her seventies, and even then, only under pressure from her company and her managers, did she acquiesce to their pleas for her to stop. Her magnetic presence on stage was a commanding revelation of power, but her increasing physical inadequacies because of age slowly destroyed her performances.

Because of her rare ability to deal only with the reality of the present, the all-important "now", Martha was able to turn totally to choreography in a desperate effort for further creative fulfillment but it never really answered her intense need for performing. It did, however, allow her to put to use her voracious reading and research. In her nineties, Martha came to the studio daily, choreographing new works, and up to the final year of her life, she traveled with her company on their national and international tours, guiding and directing them.

Even though I began to dance relatively late and thus continuously needed to press ahead with my career, age never became an obsession with me. I first became cognizant of developing physical difficulties in my early forties. Elevation in aerial work was always one of my strongest assets. In class one day, I realized that I could no longer jump to the height that I had previously attained. It became time for me to think about making some drastic decisions.

By 1967, Marni and I had produced our three children. The combined factors of my aging and the responsibility that I felt for our offspring led to a desire for developing some security for our future. Compromises had to be made.

This was not so difficult a task for me, as I had been surrounded for years by dancers who struggled against their diminishing muscular strength in order to continue performing. Although it was certainly valid for them, for me the struggle held no fascination. There were too many other things in dance that I wanted to accomplish. Teaching and choreography could still provide me with ample outlets for moving. The opportunity to establish a program in dance at the University of California, Berkeley, arose, and I took immediate advantage of it.

In the last few years, I have contracted a form of muscular dystrophy, which slowly but continuously lessens the power of the muscles in my extremities, as well as Parkinson's disease. As a result, all chance of actually dancing even while teaching has ceased. Still every day I am involved in moving. Internally, kinesthetically, I can still dance. I can jump, fall, run, and soar maybe further and better than ever before. I actually find that now I am a more capable teacher and choreographer. I no longer work within the limitations of my own body, but move beyond them into an area of kinesthetic imagination.

The physical disability has made me cognizant of the passage of time, the inevitable and the natural process through which all humans must pass. I am reminded of it because I become easily exhausted when I work. I am reminded of it every time that I observe my two grandsons, Benjamin and Joshua Sanders busily involved in playing their uninhibited games. The two opposites of energy-filled childhood and exhaustive work give rise to the developmental process that lies at the core of our very existence.

Although I envy today's dancers their active participation in the profession, I also sympathize with them because of the vast difficulties that have arisen within the field. Economics and physical problems beset the dancers constantly.

Even though some concert performers can presently earn a living solely by dancing, the competition for these paying positions has multiplied greatly. For those who are struggling to be employed, the economic problems are enormous. The financial demands of today make it next to impossible for hopeful beginners to train, audition, and at the same time earn enough money to sustain themselves.

Drugs also have become a major force in the world of dance. Experimentation with them may have taken place in earlier times, but now the pressures that present themselves because of the easy availability of drugs hang like shrouds over the active profession.

The onset of AIDS has also struck a devastating blow. The dancers of today in all areas: concert, film, television and musicals, are surrounded by the ominous presence of death. They are besieged constantly by fateful tidings of a friend or acquaintance who has been struck down by the illness. The strong desire to enter the present day profession is stretched far beyond what was necessary in the past. The words "personal strength" are not to be taken lightly.

A young graduate of our university program, Randy Wickstrom, headed for New York and a career in dance. After a few years he discovered that he had contracted AIDS. For Christmas 1988, knowing that he was to die, he wrote a poem as a gift for his parents which exemplifies the courage of so many of today's dancers.

> No burden rests
> on my shoulders
>
> No anger lingers
>
> I don't feel the icy cold
> of a snowy cap of fear
>
> My feet aren't rooted
>
> Instead I toss my bones
> freely, into the air,
> opening, a knowing heart
>
> I'm sharing love
> from you

Despite the difficulties, I was extremely pleased when all three of our daughters chose artistic professions. Marina developed her own direction, pursuing her initial love of drawing. She became a graphic designer with excellent technical ability and imagination. Raegan and Ellis successfully moved into the field of dance. Raegan performing with Paul Taylor, and Ellis performing with Dan Wagoner and Stephen Petronio.

When they were young, people often asked in supposed horror, "Would you really want your children to become dancers?"

Each time that they asked, I answered with easy assurance, "I can't think of anything that would please me more." There can only exist pleasure and pride in such a continuation from parent to child.

A couple of months ago, in November, 1992, when I was in New York, Raegan asked me if I would watch a class that she was teaching in a workshop at the Paul Taylor Studio. I readily accepted the invitation I was curious as to what pedagogical method she would use.

It was a cold, crisp morning, and the first snow of the season had just fallen. Paul's large studio was filled with reflected sunlight that flooded into the space through the large windows that ran the full length of the room. The students who were waiting for the class to begin, seemed no different from the students that one would find in studios the world over. Anxious, willing, and expectant, they waited quietly for Raegan to start to teach.

Raegan proved to be an excellent instructor: clear in explanations, solid in basics, and explicit but sensitive with corrections. She slowly built the dynamics, evolving constantly toward a beautifully devised lyrical phrase of movement at the end. I sat watching the class intently, not realizing how involved I was becoming in its progression.

"Expand your movement more," Raegan kept repeating. "You need to lengthen yourselves."

In watching, I observed that the dancers were able to follow her instruction only when the movement was one which stretched completely in all directions. At those moments, the students developed beautifully extended lines, but when the given movement was broken or angular, the dancers pulled their energy inward. It became locked within themselves, creating a harsh, dense quality rather than the flowing lyrical feel that was required.

My analytical mind began rapidly to work. "In order to create lyricism in broken angular movement, each segment of the arm, leg, or body needs to be lengthened and elasticized as an entity in itself. The dancer must fight against his instincts and maintain the outward flow of energy instead of allowing it to become introverted because of the natural inward pull of the muscles."

Despite all of my years of teaching, this concept had never occurred to me before. Observing the class I became more and more excited by my discovery. Why had I not realized this previously?

Forty years earlier while watching Alwin Nikolais teach a class for Hanya Holm, I had become so excited that, without any awareness of what I was doing, I jumped up onto the bench on which I had been sitting in order to watch more closely. At that time, I must admit, there was a definite naiveté in my enthusiasm. The addition of forty years to my age disallowed my jumping onto my chair that morning, but the excitement that I felt, although hopefully more knowledgeable, was equal in every other way. I was not only enthusiastic because of the newly discovered physical realization, I was enthusiastic because after forty years of teaching, I could still be compelled by what I saw, by the innate awareness that there are always new things to learn and new discoveries to be made. Raegan little realized that she had just given me a valuable gift. A cycle of age in time had now been completed. For years I had taught Raegan, and now it was her turn to teach me.

The usual appreciative applause ended the class. Raegan came over to where I was sitting.

"Well?"

"It was excellent, Raegan. A very good class."

Suspiciously, she stated, "You can tell me what you really think about it later."

Raegan's reactions are sometimes very similar to mine. We both have difficulty believing compliments that are easily given. She disappeared into the dressing room to change her clothes, and returned in a couple of minutes divested of her dance attire, and looking like a civilian.

She quickly offered, "We can catch a cab. I'll drop you off at your apartment and then I'll take my subway home to Brooklyn."

"Would you like to get a bite to eat?" I asked hopefully.

"I'd love to Dad, but Benjamin and Josh are home waiting for me. You understand."

After three children, I did. Only too well. One more cycle of age in time was now completed.

Downstairs we hailed a cab. Sitting in the rear seat, we both spoke rapidly and at the same time. I was overflowing with the enthusiasm that I felt from the discoveries that I had made while watching her class. Raegan's conversation was a mixture of her feelings about teaching the class and her plans that afternoon for her two boys.

The cab slowed to a stop in front of my apartment house on Fifth Avenue.

"You sure you won't change your mind about lunch?"

"I can't Dad. We'll do it another time. Maybe next week."

She gave me a kiss on the cheek. After I exited from the back seat, she handed me my cane. Then with a good-bye wave, closed the cab's door behind me. The taxi edged into the heavy traffic, moving cautiously down Fifth Avenue toward Washington Square Arch. I stood on the curb immobilized by the demands of time. I could see Raegan's head through the rear window bobbing up and down. Then the cab turned right from Fifth Avenue into Waverly Place, and carrying Raegan further forward on her desired journey, it slowly disappeared from view.

INDEX

Other titles in the Choreography and Dance Studies series: